- for essay Q on Teb Carp use e.g. ch 5 "Continuity for Crisis"

p. 192 + p. 196
check w/ my figures for ministers (in Teb. Carp.

+ p 197

After Hitler, Before Stalin

PITT SERIES IN RUSSIAN AND EAST EUROPEAN STUDIES

Jonathan Harris, *Editor*

AFTER HITLER, BEFORE STALIN

CATHOLICS, COMMUNISTS, AND DEMOCRATS IN SLOVAKIA, 1945–1948

JAMES RAMON FELAK

UNIVERSITY OF PITTSBURGH PRESS

Published by the University of Pittsburgh Press,
Pittsburgh, Pa., 15260

Manufactured in the United States of America
Printed on acid-free paper

10 9 8 7 6 5 4 3 2 1

Library of Congress Cataloging-in-Publication Data

Felak, James Ramon, 1957–
After Hitler, before Stalin : Catholics, communists, and democrats in Slovakia, 1945–1948 / James Ramon Felak.
p. cm. — (Pitt series in Russian and East European studies)
Includes bibliographical references and index.
ISBN-13: 978-0-8229-4374-7 (cloth : acid-free paper)
ISBN-10: 0-8229-4374-3 (cloth : acid-free paper)
1. Slovakia—Politics and government—1945–1992. 2. Slovakia—History—1945–1992. I. Title.
DB2828.7.F45 2009
943.73'042—dc22

2009002526

To my mother,
Barbara Janosik Felak
and
In memory of my father,
Ramon Charles Felak
(1930–2000)

CONTENTS

PREFACE

This book is the result of an attempt to combine a number of my interests—Catholicism, Communism, East Central Europe, political parties, and the fateful times immediately after the Second World War. It is the most thorough study to date in the English language on Slovakia during the three crucial years from the end of the Second World War to the Communist takeover. Moreover, it treats a historically neglected but profoundly significant dimension of the period—the role of religion, in this case Catholicism, in public life.

The period from spring 1945 to February 1948 was a particularly critical one in the history of Czechoslovakia and of Slovakia. Spring 1945 brought liberation. The war ended, and along with it the period of Nazi Germany's influence and occupation. Deportation of Jews to death camps came to a halt. The Czechoslovak Republic was reestablished, with relations between Slovaks and Czechs put on a new footing. It was a time of reconstruction, and of retribution. Courts prosecuted wartime leaders and lesser collaborators. Most Germans and many Hungarians were expelled from the country. It was a time when the resurrected Czechoslovak Republic tried to find its place in a Europe growing increasingly polarized between the Soviet Union and the West. And it was a time when the Communist Party was on the ascendancy, culminating in its seizure of power during a political crisis in late February 1948.

Most studies of this period deal with events in a Czechoslovak-wide context and examine the period mainly as background to the Communist takeover or as a part of the growing cold war between West and East.[1] With few exceptions, Prague takes center stage. Another issue that is central in studies of this period, as indeed in many studies of Czechoslovakia, is Czech-Slovak relations.[2] While I appreciate the importance of the Communist takeover, Czech-Slovak relations, developments in Prague, and larger issues of East-

West relations, I have chosen to approach this period in a somewhat different manner. Rather than proceeding from the vantage point of Prague, dealing with Slovakia chiefly as developments there impinge on the Czechoslovak Republic as a whole, the center of gravity of this work is clearly in Slovakia. Though I do not ignore Prague or relations between Czechs and Slovaks, I view developments in Slovakia first and foremost as products of Slovakia's political landscape, and only secondarily as part of the broader Czechoslovak context. I also want to avoid a primary focus on Slovak grievances against Czech rule. This is in accord with my belief that an overemphasis on the Czech versus Slovak dimension of Slovakia's history, important as that may be, gives a distorted view of developments there. I offer my study of the 1945 to 1948 period in part as a corrective to these approaches. Though it ends with the Communist takeover of Czechoslovakia in February 1948, the narrative focuses above all on the Catholic Church, the Communist Party, and the Democratic Party as they interacted in Slovakia, in accordance with issues of importance to Slovakia's inhabitants. Though my research contributes to our understanding of the Communist takeover, it is more than that and should not be read simply as background to the February 1948 coup.

Even more important, I want to address in my work the relative neglect of the religious dimension of East Central European history. Questions of religion have long been marginalized, if addressed at all, in works on the region in the twentieth century.[3] But in fact, religious questions and conflicts have lain at or close to the heart of a number of key developments in the region's history. Interwar Czechoslovakia, for example, was plagued by troubled relations between Czechs and Slovaks, the latter disaffected in part on religious grounds and rallying in large numbers around a Catholic party led by a Catholic priest, Andrej Hlinka. Whether it was the papal nuncio leaving Prague in 1925 in protest against a state holiday honoring Jan Hus, Archbishop Adam Sapieha of Kraków objecting to government attempts to have Poland's great leader Piłsudski buried in Wawel Cathedral, or the crisis in interwar Yugoslavia over a concordat with the Vatican in 1937, across the region one finds a religious dimension to social, cultural, and political conflicts. As Communism swept across the region after the Second World War, religious questions became even more acute, and the communist parties and the churches engaged in evolving and complicated relationships with each other throughout the entire communist period, the details of which we are only today gaining a deeper knowledge of and appreciation for. This study of immediate postwar Slovakia presents and analyzes these early years of Communist-Catholic relationship.

Not only does religion connect with key developments in the region, it also provides a means of deepening our understanding of particular times and places, revealing additional layers of complexity. For example, we can learn much about how a state or a political party operates by examining its relationship to religious institutions and issues. The Communists, for instance, despite an atheistic outlook and a desire to cripple the influence of the churches, were not unequivocally hostile to Catholics in this period; rather, their attempts to weaken the Catholic Church ran simultaneously with efforts to build positive relations with Catholics and woo them into their camp. This was the case in Slovakia, for example, with Communist support for catechism classes in the public schools or Communist sympathy for the founding of a Catholic political party. Of course, these were decisions based on tactics, not conviction, as Communists often believed that their ends could sometimes be achieved more readily by accommodating rather than assaulting Catholics.

Few European venues are more propitious for examining the interaction between Catholics and Communists than Slovakia. First, Catholicism was by far the major religious confession in Slovakia, and Catholicism and the Catholic Church were extremely closely connected with the major developments that marked Slovakia's history in the mid-twentieth century.[4] Slovakia's leading political party in the 1920s and 1930s, Hlinka's Slovak People's Party (HSĽS), was Catholic and led by a priest.[5] It spearheaded the Slovak national movement and ultimately reaped the benefits of Adolf Hitler's push into East Central Europe by gaining first autonomy and then independence for Slovakia. The independent wartime Slovak Republic, a close ally of Nazi Germany, was led by a Catholic priest and Catholic political party, and the Catholic Church in Slovakia received a large boost in its role and influence under this new regime. The close connection of Catholicism to a pro-Axis regime meant trouble for the church after the war ended and the Third Reich went down in defeat.[6]

From 1945 to 1948, Catholics were a focal point of a number of key developments. They were often targets of retribution against collaborators, most famously in the trial and execution of the leader of the Slovak Republic, Father Jozef Tiso. They were engaged in issues connected with the postwar reconstruction of state and society and battled the state over crucial social-cultural issues such as education and land reform. They were the chief electoral prize as Slovakia's two main political parties, the Communists and the Democrats, vied with each other to woo Catholics into their respective camps or at least keep them out of their rival's grasp. Their votes decisively determined the outcome of the May 1946 parliamentary elections, the first in Czechoslovakia since 1935 and the last democratically contested ones until 1990. They were the main target of an alleged antistate conspiracy, which helped pave the road for the ultimate Communist takeover of Czechoslovakia. Catholicism also figured in policies toward the Hungarian minority in southern Slovakia, where the state was intolerant of Hungarian clergy and Hungarian language worship. Religion also influenced the debate over the degree of autonomy permitted for Slovaks, as the central government in Prague tended to look with suspicion on Catholic Slovak nationalism. Moreover, real and imagined underground resistance in Slovakia after the war was closely associated with Slovak Catholics loyal to the Tiso regime. Nearly everywhere one turns in postwar Slovakia, one runs into issues and conflicts that heavily involved Catholicism in some way, including the efforts to promote, protect, suppress, channel, manipulate, or harness it.

Other factors also contribute to making Slovakia an ideal laboratory for examining Catholic-Communist relations. Czechoslovakia was the only East Central European country with a legal and functioning Communist party throughout the interwar period. Although Communists in Slovakia during this period never achieved the political support enjoyed by Hlinka's Slovak People's Party,[7] they were able to capitalize on their key role in the wartime resistance in Slovakia as well as the Soviet Red Army's victory over Nazi Germany to assume a decisive place in determining Slovakia's political future at war's end. Hence, postwar Slovakia presents us with a venue where a rising and emboldened Communism ran up against a weakened but still strong Catholicism. Moreover, Czechoslovakia, including Slovakia, enjoyed a degree of political and cultural freedom achieved nowhere else in East Central Europe, largely owing to the fact that Soviet military forces left the country, along with American forces, by late 1945.

By comparison with the other successor states of the former Habsburg Empire, no country besides Yugoslavia had a stronger native Communist resistance movement than Slovakia during the war. Nor was Catholicism traditionally such a major political force elsewhere in the region. Only Austria and Slovenia had Catholic parties that figured as prominently in their respective lands as did the HSĽS in Slovakia. Furthermore, nowhere in the region, including Austria, was there such freedom from foreign military occupation in the postwar period, making Czechoslovakia the one place where externally induced distortions of the political landscape were less acute. Finally, unlike Yugoslavia, where the Communist takeover was accomplished by the war's end, or the other states of East Central Europe, where it was pursued aggressively right from the start and largely complete by 1947, Czechoslovakia remained a functioning multiparty state until nearly two months into 1948.[8]

This book is not a history of postwar, pre-February Slovakia.[9] Nor is it a history of Catholicism during this period.[10] Rather, it focuses on relationships between Catholics and the two key political parties in Slovakia at this time, the Communists and the Democrats. These relationships, complex and dynamic, were at the heart of developments in Slovakia during the period under consideration. By tracing them through the period leading up to the Communist February coup, when Czechoslovakia still had a significant if limited degree of political pluralism, we can get a fuller, richer, and deeper picture of how Catholics, Communists, and others sought to navigate this significant period of transition from Hitler's world to Stalin's.

On one level, this work is a study of Catholic adaptation to a new environment. We see a whole spectrum of Catholic responses to the new political situation. Some Catholics sought blatant collaboration with the Communists, others eagerly embraced the Democrats, some reluctantly allied with the Democrats, and still others sought a Catholic "third way." On another level, this book deals with the tragedy of the rise and fall of the Democratic Party—winner of an electoral landslide that it was unable to translate into proportionate political influence, and a party that met its demise by early 1948. Nothing illustrates the Democrats' quandary better than the vain hopes, dazzling successes, genuine dangers, and pitiable failures that a policy of outreach to Catholics brought it. On yet another level, this study examines a key facet of the Communist attempt to gain control of Czechoslovakia—the party's policy toward religion. It demonstrates how Communists in Slovakia tried to avoid alienating Catholics while at the same time attempting to weaken the church and attack the Democratic Party for its own outreach to Catholics. Indeed, one of the most striking aspects of this period is how far Communist rhetoric went in its attempt to appeal to Catholics.

I have based this book very heavily on sources, mainly primary ones in the Slovak language. I employed documents from the Slovak National Archive in Bratislava, mostly from the collections of the Democratic Party and the Central Committee of the Communist Party of Slovakia. I also utilized collections from the Office of the Presidium of the Slovak National Council, the Central Action Committee of the Slovak National Front, the Central Presidium of the Board of Commissioners, as well as the collection of the National Court at the State Regional Archive in Bratislava. Another very significant source is the periodical literature of the time. I drew heavily from *Čas* and *Pravda*, the daily newspapers of the Democratic and Communist parties, respectively, and from the weekly of the Catholic bishops of Slovakia, *Katolícke noviny*. I also used *Nové slovo* and *Nové prúdy*, weekly current affairs journals catering to Communist and Democratic oriented intellectuals, respectively. Additionally, I referenced a number of memoirs of important figures of the time, especially those of Democratic leader Ján Ursíny and prominent lay Catholic leader Pavol Čarnogurský.[11] I found some published documentary collections especially helpful, above all Karel Kaplan's collection of documents pertaining to retribution trials and František Vnuk's collection of documents pertaining to the Catholic Church in 1945–48.[12] Among the secondary sources employed for this book, I found six works to be especially useful—the surveys of Slovak historians Barnovský and Letz; Petranský's study of church and state from 1945 to 1946; the study of Czech-Slovak relations by Rychlík; and monographs on the retribution trials in Slovakia and on the Magyar question by Jozef Jablonický and Štefan Šutaj, respectively.[13]

I would like to thank all those without whose assistance I would not have been able to complete this project. First of all, I express my gratitude to the International Research and Exchanges Board for funding my primary research trip to Slovakia. I would like to thank professors Michal Barnovský and Róbert Letz for their help and hospitality during my stay in Slovakia. I would also like to thank the archivists and librarians who assisted me, especially those at the Slovak National Archive and the Comenius University Library in Bratislava. Most deserving of thanks is Peter Magura, whose kindness and expertise are among the highlights of a trip to Slovakia. I would like to thank the following people for reading and commenting on portions of my manuscript or conference papers based on it, or for other types of scholarly assistance related to this project: Bradley Abrams, John Connelly, David Doellinger, Dennis Dunn, Herbert Ellison, Carol Leff, Norman Naimark, Sabrina Ramet, Jaroslava Soldanova, M. Mark Stolarik, František Vnuk, James Ward, Edward Wynot, and Jennifer Wynot. Furthermore, I thank the participants in the Christianity in Eastern Europe Project sponsored by Calvin College, especially Bruce Berglund and Brian Porter, for especially helpful and stimulating commentary on parts of this research and on religion in Eastern Europe generally. Finally, I would like to thank my wife, Cheryl, and my children, Stephen, Susanna, Thomas, and John Paul, for keeping my home life exciting, challenging, enjoyable, and rewarding during the gestation of this project.

After Hitler, Before Stalin

1

SETTING THE STAGE

From Liberation to the April Agreement

THE spring of 1945 brought significant changes to Slovakia. The Slovak Republic, the wartime regime that represented history's first Slovak state ever, collapsed along with its patron and ally, Nazi Germany. The Soviet Red Army drove the German military out of Slovak territory and ultimately, with the help of American forces, out of the Czech lands as well, leaving Czechoslovakia jointly occupied by American and Soviet troops until December 1945, when foreign armies left altogether. The Czechoslovak Republic, destroyed by the events of 1938 and 1939, was reconstituted under its former president, Edvard Beneš.[1] But while Czechoslovakia was back, it came back under very different circumstances and with quite different features. Gone was the situation of the interwar period, when as many as twenty-nine parties, and never fewer than sixteen, competed for parliamentary office, and never fewer than fourteen parties were represented at one given time in parliament.[2] Now, only a handful of parties would be allowed to operate—the Czechoslovak Communist Party (KSČ),[3] the Czechoslovak Social Democratic Party, the National Socialist Party, the Czechoslovak People's Party in the Czech lands; and in Slovakia the Democratic Party (DS)[4] and the Communist Party of Slovakia (KSS).[5] Together they made up the new Czechoslovak government, formally established on April 4 in the newly liberated eastern Slovak city of Košice. Some of interwar Czechoslovakia's most important political parties were banned, namely the Czechoslovak Agrarians, who were (unjustly) accused of collaboration with Nazi Germany in the 1930s, and the HSĽS, which was likewise accused of collaboration with the Nazis, having run Slovakia during the Second World War under Nazi German auspices. This was particularly significant for Slovakia, as the Agrarians and HSĽS jointly accounted for nearly half of all votes cast in Slovakia's last two interwar parliamentary elections, and for the great majority of the votes cast by Slovaks.[6]

The decisive institution for this markedly limited political spectrum, with the interwar right and even right-center largely eliminated, was the Czechoslovak National Front. The National Front functioned as an umbrella organization for all political parties. Its decisions were binding on the central government, on parliament, and on all organs of local government.[7] The National Front alone had the right to authorize the existence of new parties. Because the Front insisted that all new parties agree upfront to the government's program, a legal opposition in effect was prohibited. In Slovakia, the Communist Party and Democratic Party established their own Slovak National Front, through which leaders of Slovakia's two political parties maintained regular contact and sought consensus on policy questions.

Another feature of the new Czechoslovak system was the greatly enhanced role of special interest pressure groups, in particular the trade unions, which were unified into the Central Council of Trade Unions, and the various organizations connected with the wartime resistance—partisan organizations, veterans clubs, organizations of former prisoners of war. Overwhelmingly dominated by Communists and pro-Communist left-wing Social Democrats, these groups were mobilized to press for Communist policies and interests at key times during 1945–48. This was especially the case in Slovakia, where the Democrats had very little presence in the trade union movement, and where partisan organizations played a significant role both in Slovak consciousness and society owing to Slovakia's large-scale uprising against the Nazis in August 1944.

Postwar Czechoslovakia also represented a new expression of relations between Slovaks and Czechs. The constitution of the First Republic regarded Czechs and Slovaks as a single Czechoslovak nation, speaking a common Czechoslovak language. Prague was the country's administrative center, and, despite a few nods to local autonomy, the state was essentially centralist, something that caused a considerable degree of discontent in Slovakia across most of the political spectrum. Now the Republic officially recognized the existence of separate Czech and Slovak nations, each with its own separate language, and promised sweeping autonomy to Slovakia. The Košice Program, the blueprint for the new Czechoslovakia promulgated in April 1945 by the new Czechoslovak government, promised that Slovaks would be "masters in their Slovak land" and that their relations with the Czechs would be "equal with equal."[8] Klement Gottwald, the leader of the Czechoslovak Communist Party, later called the Košice Program the "Magna Carta of the Slovak nation."[9] Institutions that were developed by the Slovak Resistance during the war, the Slovak National Council and Board of Commissioners, became an integral part of Slovak government and administration.

As the new Czechoslovak authorities took over in spring 1945, a series of policies were carried out that made the postwar Czechoslovakia even more different from its predecessor, establishing a new type of state known as a "people's democracy." First, nearly all of the ethnic German population was expelled from the country, and many from the Hungarian minority were either deported to Hungary or relocated to the Czech lands. Bohemia and Moravia, which together had once been nearly 40 percent German, became almost completely Czech, while the proportion of Hungarians in Slovakia dropped from approximately 17.6 percent in the 1930 census to 10.3 percent by 1950.[10] Second, left-wing dominance in Czechoslovak politics, combined with a public mood increasingly open to socialization, led to the construction of a system in which a large proportion of the economy was nationalized, mainly through the state takeover of large industrial and commercial enterprises. Along the same lines, the state established an expanded social welfare network and instituted a land reform aimed at dispossessing large landholders. Third, Czechoslovakia's foreign policy orientation underwent an important shift. In the 1920s and 1930s, the Republic was oriented to the West, especially toward France, though from 1935 on, the Czechoslovak government cultivated good relations with the Soviet Union as well. Now, situated in a part of Europe largely occupied by the Soviet Red Army, disappointed by the Western Allies for abandoning it in the Munich Agreement in 1938, fearing German revanchism, led by a government in which Communists and left-wing Social Democrats played a decisive role, and desirous of distinguishing itself in postwar Europe as a bridge between East and West, Czechoslovakia has positioned itself as a solid ally of the Soviet Union, and in some respects leaned more to the East than to the West.

From 1945 to 1948 there was increasing conflict between Communists and their non-Communist rivals in the struggle for political power in the state. The elections of May 1946 were an important milestone in Czechoslovakia's political development at this time. In the Czech lands, the left won a resounding victory, with the KSČ taking 40.1 percent of the vote and the Social Democrats 15.6 percent.[11] The Czechoslovak National Socialist Party and Czechoslovak People's Party, themselves rather leftish with respect to issues like nationalization of large industry and state support for social welfare, took the remaining 23.5 percent and 20.2 percent of the vote, respectively, and together constituted what could be called the "Czech Right" in a system that technically did not allow a right wing to exist. This was a remarkably strong showing for the left, though it was not replicated in Slovakia. There, the DS clobbered the KSS by 62 percent to 30 percent (two recently established smaller parties gathered in the remaining 8 percent of the vote). This electoral discrepancy between the Czech lands and Slovakia had a number of significant consequences. It made Slovak Communists far less sympathetic to autonomy for Slovakia and prompted Czech Communists to come out decisively for a reassertion of Prague's control over the area. This played out in the promulgation of the so-called Third Prague Agreement of June 28, 1946, the final in a series of modifications of relations between Slovakia's organs and the central government that diminished Slovakia's powers of self-government.[12] The discrepancy also convinced the Communists that the DS was their most dangerous enemy, and from May 1946 onward, the Communists aimed every weapon in their arsenal at the Democrats. It also made Catholic cooperation with the DS the biggest issue in Slovak politics, as Communists sought to use the very situation that brought the DS victory in order to destroy that party.

When the resurrected and reformed Czechoslovak Republic was established in early spring 1945, Slovakia had two, and only two, political parties—the Communists (or, more specifically, the Communist Party of Slovakia, separate but closely connected with and ultimately subordinate to the Communist Party of Czechoslovakia) and the Democrats. Both parties trace their origins to the events connected with Czechoslovakia's demise and incorporation into the Nazi empire. When Czechoslovakia was destroyed in March 1939, Slovakia's Communists were cut off from the Communist Party of Czechoslovakia and, on the orders of the Comintern, founded a separate Communist Party of Slovakia in May 1939.[13] By 1943 the KSS was heavily involved in resistance to the Slovak regime. The Democratic Party emerged during the war, representing those Slovaks who opposed the regime but who did not identify with the Communists. The most important element in the

DS was former Slovak Agrarians, and its two most important leaders, Jozef Lettrich and Ján Ursíny, had both been Agrarians in the interwar period. The DS also attracted Lutherans, a group that historically tended to have friendly relations with the Czechs and which found a Catholic dictatorship particularly distasteful and alienating.[14] Beginning in late 1943, Democrats and Communists worked together in the Slovak resistance, forming a legislative body called the Slovak National Council (Slovenská Národná Rada), and jointly taking part in the Slovak National Uprising in late August and September 1944, where they managed to liberate a portion of central Slovakia for nearly eight weeks. During the uprising they jointly administered the liberated territories through a board of commissioners (Zbor Povereníkov). After the war, Communists and Democrats continued their cooperation, supporting autonomy for Slovakia in the new Republic and successfully arguing for the institutional continuation of the organs they had established during the resistance. These organs were affirmed in the Košice Program as integral to the new Slovakia. Since only two political parties were permitted in Slovakia, positions were distributed evenly between Communists and Democrats in the staffing of these organs.

Though they represented very different political ideologies—atheistic Marxism looking to the Soviet Union for inspiration on the one side; democratic, largely Protestant Christian values on the other—Communists and Democrats cooperated closely on a number of issues. Both were hostile to the wartime regime; both drew their legitimacy above all from their role in the uprising and looked back on it as a fundamental part of their heritage; both favored the reconstitution of Czechoslovakia, but with considerable autonomy left to Slovakia; both favored extensive social programs and nationalization of the economy, though the Communists went farther along these lines than the Democrats; and both favored the nationalization of education.

While substantial numbers of Slovaks identified with either of these two political camps, probably an even larger number identified with neither. These were chiefly Catholic Slovaks—hostile toward the atheistic Communists, leery of the Lutheran dominated Democrats, sympathetic toward or at the very least ambivalent about the wartime regime. With the banning of their party, the HSĽS, which had attracted the votes of nearly 50 percent of Slovaks during the interwar period, they were in a sense political orphans. However, they had the right to vote, and if they voted as a bloc they could decide elections in Slovakia. This meant that the two Slovak parties that defined themselves in part by their hostility toward the wartime regime had to vie for the votes of a large segment of the population that felt quite differently about the Slovak Republic. This fact, more than anything else, set the stage for the dramatic events that transpired in Slovakia over the next three years—events laden with promise, with danger, and with irony for both sides.

That the Catholic Church, Catholicism, and the issues connected with them figured prominently in Slovakia's political affairs after the fall of the Tiso regime was nothing new. Right from the founding of the First Czechoslovak Republic, religion was a central issue in Slovakia's place in the political order. Already beginning in 1918, relations between the Catholic Church and the First Czechoslovak Republic were troubled in a number of ways, a fact that had significant influence on Slovakia.[15] First off, Czechs were far more likely to take a critical stance toward Catholicism than were Slovaks. Opposition to Catholicism had an important place in the Czech self-understanding. Jan Hus, burned as a heretic in 1415, was a national hero to the Czechs. The Battle of White Mountain of 1620, where a Protestant led rebellion by Bohemian elites was crushed by the Catholic Habsburgs, was remembered as the end of autonomy for the Czech lands. Nationalist Czech radicals in the late nineteenth and early twentieth centuries, like their German counterparts, shared the anti-Catholic motto "*Pryč od Říma*" ("*Los von Rom*" or "Away from Rome"). Slovaks, conversely, brought far less baggage regarding the Catholic Church into the twentieth century and generally saw the church as a positive force in their historical development.[16]

In the early months of Czechoslovakia's existence, the Catholic Church was attacked on many sides—radicals tore crucifixes off walls of schools and other public buildings and destroyed religious statues, most notoriously the Marian column on Prague's Old Town Square. The new regime instituted policies inimical to Catholic interests, including the seizure of church lands and the takeover of Catholic gymnasia and other educational institutions.[17] Attempts, albeit ultimately unsuccessful, were made to incorporate the strict separation of church and state into the constitution. The administration of Slovakia was placed in the hands of Vavro Šrobár, a lapsed Catholic unfriendly to the Catholic Church. Slovak Protestants (mainly Lutherans) were favored over Catholics in the apportionment of state jobs and other coveted positions.[18] In the Czech lands, some renegade priests founded a "Czechoslovak Catholic Church," which 750,000 Czechs, including President Tomáš G. Masaryk, joined. Thousands of Czech government officials, teachers, and other professionals moved to Slovakia, many of whom brought with them a hostility to Catholicism and a contemptuous view of the Slovaks as a backward, priest-ridden people.

It was opposition to such attacks on their Catholic faith that prompted Andrej Hlinka and a group of fellow Slovak priests in late 1918 to found a Council of Priests and soon thereafter to resurrect the prewar Catholic, nationalist Slovak People's Party.[19] This party went on to become the leading champion of autonomy for Slovakia during the interwar period. Because Czechoslovakia's new regime denied the separate existence of a Slovak nation, opting instead for a "Czechoslovak" nation with a Czech and a Slovak branch, ruled the state in a centralistic manner from Prague, favored Slovak Lutherans over Catholics in the distribution of political and administrative positions, and implemented measures against the interests of the Catholic Church, many Slovaks rallied around the HSĽS and its Catholic, nationalist program. Thus, almost from the birth of Czechoslovakia, a close connection existed between Slovak nationalism and Catholicism.

Interwar Czechoslovakia saw plenty of tensions between church and state. For example, in 1925, the papal nuncio even left Prague in protest against a national holiday in honor of the heretic Hus. Nevertheless, the Czechoslovak regime pursued normalized relations with the Vatican, and in March 1927 the Holy See and the Czechoslovak government reached an agreement, known as the Modus Vivendi.[20] This pact realigned diocesan borders of the prewar period, making sure that no neighboring bishop or leader of a religious order had jurisdiction over clergy and members of religious orders in Czechoslovakia. Furthermore, the Vatican agreed to have candidates for vacant bishoprics vetted by the government and required candidates for bishop to take an oath of loyalty to the state. Property questions proved thornier, and commissions set up to deal with them had not yet completed their work by 1938, when the First Republic came to an end.

The foray of Adolf Hitler and Nazi Germany into central Europe in 1938 brought the Anschluss in March, the detachment of the Sudetenland from Czechoslovakia in September, and the establishment of an autonomous Slovakia within a reconstituted Second Czecho-Slovak Republic in October. Less than six months later, Germany occupied the rest of the Czech lands, thereby wiping Czecho-Slovakia off the map and replacing it with a Nazi occupied "Protectorate of Bohemia and Moravia" in the west and an independent Slovak state in the east. These momentous changes in the region brought with them, among other things, equally momentous changes in the place of the Catholic Church within Slovakia's political life.

Jozef Tiso, who succeeded Hlinka as head of the HSL'S in summer of 1938, became president of the new republic. This meant that a Catholic priest was both head of state and leader of the state's dominant party. Catholic clergy were heavily involved in governmental, administrative, and political life.[21] In the early years of the republic, around 20 percent of the ministers of parliament were priests, as were three members of the eighteen-member state council, including the Bishop Ján Vojtaššák. The mayor of the capital city, Bratislava, was a priest. Dozens of Catholic priests were active functionaries of the HSL'S at all levels. Two of its six county organizations and sixteen of its sixty district organizations were headed by priests, and clergy were well represented at the local level. Since the HSL'S was the only party allowed to represent Slovaks, the role of Catholic clergy in managing Slovakia was considerable.

The influence of the Catholic Church was particularly strong in education.[22] Priests served in teaching functions from the university level on down, and nearly all education at the lower levels was parochial, either Catholic or Lutheran. The Slovak state restored crucifixes to the walls and religious education to the curriculum in all the schools, undoing two of the educational policies of the Czechoslovak Republic. Students were obliged to attend Sunday worship, and teachers were not permitted to belong to any antireligious organizations or even marry outside a church.

Church influence increased in a number of other areas as well.[23] Catholic publishing experienced an upswing, church influence in the military was augmented by the requirement that all soldiers attend religious services, and the state considered itself, at least on paper, to be inspired by papal social teachings. Slovakia experienced a boom in church construction and renovation, and priests frequently served on the boards of trustees of private firms.[24]

Given the favorable position that Catholicism had attained within the wartime state, the collapse of the Tiso regime in conjunction with the defeat of Nazi Germany in the spring of 1945 brought a dramatic change in fortune for the Catholic Church in Slovakia. With the reestablishment of a Czechoslovak Republic, the church now had to face a state that was suspicious of Slovak Catholicism, both because of its ties with separatist Slovak nationalism and its opposition to what most Czechs and leftist Slovaks regarded as progress.[25] The

Catholic Church was immediately put on the defensive. All of Slovakia and most of the Czech lands were occupied, until the end of 1945, by the armies of the Soviet Union. Slovakia's Communists were more confident and well placed politically than ever before. Wartime supporters of Tiso's regime faced arrest and detention, including some clergy and even bishops. Every one of the six political parties permitted to exist was suspicious of Slovakia's Catholicism. Right from the start, the new regime tried to reestablish the republic on grounds less favorable to the church than even those of the First Czechoslovak Republic. These included the secularization of education, a ban on Catholic organizations and periodicals, and other progressive/repressive measures. It is in this dramatically new context that we will begin our investigation into relations between Slovakia's Catholics and the two dominant political forces of postwar Slovakia, the Communists and the Democrats.

From the end of World War II through the spring of 1946, Slovakia's two political parties engaged in a pair of closely related yet mutually contradictory undertakings. The Communists and the Democrats worked both to weaken Catholic influence in Slovakia and to woo Catholic voters. The first of these undertakings brought the two parties together; the second fed the rivalry between them. Through the summer of 1945, Communists and Democrats waged a veritable *Kulturkampf* against the Catholic Church in Slovakia, on top of which were superimposed attempts to attract Catholics into their respective camps. Through the fall and winter, pressure on the Catholic Church eased somewhat, while political intrigues from one side or the other grew more intense. Catholics, for their part, sought by an assortment of ways to navigate the postwar situation. Communist efforts to exploit Catholic disaffection both within and outside the DS were foiled when that party's leaders cut a deal with leading Catholics on March 31, 1946. This so-called April Agreement brought the great majority of Slovakia's Catholics into the Democratic camp and constituted a profound alteration of the political constellation in Slovakia.

In the first months after liberation, Slovakia's new authorities instituted a series of decrees and policies aimed at weakening the position of the Catholic Church. The educational system was nationalized, with parochial schools becoming the property of the state. Shortly thereafter, dormitories were likewise nationalized. Catholic clubs, in particular youth organizations, and charitable institutions were dissolved and their property appropriated by the state. A number of priests and even some bishops were interned, and Catholic periodicals were completely disallowed.[26] These and other similar measures provoked a response from the Catholic Church at several levels.

There was no issue where the church felt its rights more violated or where the authorities acted more unyieldingly than that of education. It stood at the center of conflicts over the relationship of church and state, and of conflicts between Communists and Catholics. The takeover of Slovakia's educational system by the state dates to September 6, 1944, when the Slovak National Council issued, during the Slovak National Uprising, a decree nationalizing schools at all levels. In April 1945, the Slovak authorities began assuming control of private and parochial schools along with their moveable and unmoveable property. This prompted a Catholic response. On May 23, Archbishop Karol Kmet'ko, as chairman of the Slovak Bishops' Council, sent a memorandum of protest to the Slovak National Council (SNR), in which the bishops made their case against the nationalization decree.[27] To begin with, Kmet'ko argued that in depriving the church of its right to establish and maintain schools, the authorities were violating their pledge that the freedom of the church would be respected and defended. Citing the church's belief that it had the right and obligation to found schools, Kmet'ko expressed the church's feeling of "a very heavy and painful intervention into its life." The memorandum pointed out that parochial schools were allowed in those countries which guaranteed the church's freedom, and noted that France, with its long tradition of secular education, was again reinstituting parochial schools.

In the bishops' view, it was not just the rights of the church that were being violated by the nationalization decree, but those of society as well. Kmet'ko asserted that parents "have a natural and indisputable right to educate their child and to determine the direction along which this education takes place when they entrust their children to the schools for the long-term." He also pointed out the undemocratic nature of the decision to nationalize schools. It was simply decreed by the SNR, which itself was not an elected body. Since such a matter was not so urgent that it needed to be dealt with immediately (in contrast to questions involving transportation, military defense, or food supplies), yet important enough to warrant discussion by the elected representatives of Slovakia's citizens, there was no reason why it could not wait until after forthcoming elections were held. Claiming a tradition of popular support for parochial schools in Slovakia, the memorandum held that the state's attempt to monopolize education would never have passed an elected

Slovak representative body. In circumventing such democratic procedure, the government was calling into question its commitment to its own rhetoric about being a "people's democracy" responsive to the "will of the people." In defending parochial schools, Kmet'ko also made recourse to the "historic right" of the church in Slovakia to found schools, earned through centuries of commitment to education. "Parochial schools should be preserved and supported out of gratitude," for, thanks to the church, Slovaks were able to become a "cultured and civilized nation." Responding to the contention that parochial schools were potentially harmful to state or society, the memorandum pointed out the extensive regulation under which these schools had to operate (e.g., the state approved textbooks, certified teachers, set curricular standards, etc.). Regarding the claim that parochial schools caused division within the nation along religious lines, Kmet'ko argued that it was rather the refusal of the state to respect religious differences, manifested in policies such as the nationalization of schools, that was the real cause of division in society. In conclusion, the memorandum accused the state of starting, by its unilateral and rash actions, a *Kulturkampf* against a church that was eager to cooperate with it in rebuilding Slovakia. Kmet'ko urged that the nationalization decree not be implemented.

The Catholic response to the nationalization of schools did not end with Kmet'ko's memorandum. The bishop of Banská Bystrica, Andrej Škrábik, wrote to Kmet'ko on May 29, recommending that the church organize a petition drive against the nationalization. Škrábik argued that the memorandum "was sure to remain only an academic matter," while "among the 'people's democratic' government only the will of the people, manifested in hundreds of thousands of signatures, would carry weight."[28] The bishops were aware that the assault on parochial schools had agitated Slovak Catholics. Both Škrábik's letter and Kmet'ko's memorandum mentioned localized demonstrations by Catholic parents and students against such matters as the mixing of Catholic and Protestant students in classes, the tactless assignment of teachers of a religion different from their pupils, and the removal of religious symbols from the schools.[29]

Although Škrábik urged that the petition action be presented as something instigated by lay Catholics,[30] the campaign was launched in churches across Slovakia on July 8 with the reading of a pastoral letter issued jointly by Slovakia's bishops.[31] The state's response was swift and forceful. The police searched Kmet'ko's office as well as those of several other bishops and a number of priests, and they arrested a number of clergy.[32] Among other things, the police confiscated some allegedly incriminating material, including the draft of a pastoral letter (never issued), and the text of a prayer asking Jesus Christ to "not allow Your enemies, through godless schools and faithless education to deprive [children] of faith and innocence and so tear them away from You."[33] Communist dominated professional organizations, such as the Union of Educational and Cultural Workers, as well as more localized bodies of school inspectors and teachers, condemned the petition drive and expressed themselves strongly for state schools.[34] Local administrative bodies and factory councils did likewise. On July 16, the Slovak National Front (SNF) held an extraordinary session,[35] where the top leaders of the KSS and DS issued a "Proclamation on the Misuse of Religion for Politically Subversive Actions."[36]

The proclamation said in fact very little in defense of the nationalization of schools. Rather, it concentrated on attacking the church's involvement in politics that it saw the petition campaign as representing. It stressed the state's commitment to equal rights for religious believers and freedom of religion and argued that, because catechism classes were allowed in the state schools, the policy violated neither principle. The proclamation addressed the petition campaign not as an attempt to defend parochial schools per se, but as the thin wedge of an effort by reactionary Catholics to restore and rehabilitate the HSL'S. To this end, the documents confiscated at Archbishop Kmet'ko's office came in quite handy. Particularly useful to the state authorities was the draft of a pastoral letter that spoke not about education but rather issues connected with postwar justice in Slovakia.[37] The draft spoke favorably of those Slovaks who worked for the good of the Slovak nation in the past, including those who were imprisoned simply for serving the wartime Tiso regime. Their imprisonment was likened to punishing a ship's captain for attaching his boat to another ship in order to keep it from sinking. Condemning hurried trials and convictions without sufficient proof as characteristic of postwar Slovakia, the draft asserted that many people were being held in prison unjustly, needlessly causing harm to their families. Arguing that the Slovak nation was too small to afford a bloodletting, the draft condemned the practice of making denunciations of one's enemies for personal reasons as a terrible sin for which one would have to answer to God. While admitting that some people were indeed guilty (i.e., of enriching themselves from the war, of injustice and violence), it portrayed the system of people's courts set up to deal with war criminals and collaborators as animated more by personal revenge than by justice. The draft concluded by calling on Catholics to stand united in the present crisis situation and to be proud, not ashamed, of being Catholic.

In commenting on this draft, the SNF proclamation stated that "these words make it clear that several highly positioned church dignitaries do not hesitate to misuse their position to try to justify fascist criminals . . . they do not hesitate to misuse their position to justify a politics of fascist Populist separatism . . . they do not hesitate to misuse their position to try to terrorize the courts of the people, who have their mandate from the orphans and widows and sacrifices of the martyrs of our national struggle."[38] Thus, the confiscated draft gave the Communists and Democrats the opportunity to shift the discussion from the justice of the state monopoly of education to the question of the punishment of collaborators and clerical intervention on their behalf. By combining the contents of the draft with those of another document found in Kmet'ko's office, an unsigned letter in Latin containing the sentence "It is necessary to work with all means in order that a third political party be established,"[39] Slovakia's political leaders were able to depict the petition drive as the opening salvo in a campaign aimed at reviving and restoring the HSL'S. As the proclamation states regarding the HSL'S, "all attempts at its political renewal, or political actions undertaken in its spirit, are illegal and directed against the living interests of the Slovak nation and the Czechoslovak Republic."[40] On July 20, the chief daily newspapers of both Slovak parties published the proclamation, along with favorable commentary on it.[41]

Three days later, Kmet'ko penned his public reply, as chairman of the Slovak Bishops' Council.[42] His statement began by expressing the church's disappointment over the SNR's nationalization of education, and in particular over the SNR's refusal to consult the church before implementing the decree, despite alleged earlier assurances that it would. He pointed out that by early July he still had not received a reply from the SNR to his memorandum of May 23. He also reiterated the church's responsibility to defend parochial education, citing both canon law (no. 1372f) and Pope Pius XI's encyclical of December 31, 1929, on the Christian education of youth. Kmet'ko denied that parochial education was opposed to national unity and pointed to a number of places where it was permitted, including Belgium, Holland, China, India, and even France, and mentioned that the Catholic University in Soviet occupied Lublin, Poland, was reopened immediately after the war.

Kmet'ko also defended the petition campaign, denying that it was political or antistate, but rather the exercise "of the most elementary right of every person, the right of petition and appeal." For exercising this legal right, the church was subjected to searches of episcopal and pastoral offices, confiscations of written material and typewriters, and a hostile press campaign. With regard to the allegedly incriminating documents, Kmet'ko pointed out that the confiscated draft of a pastoral letter was among a number of proposals, complaints, etc., normally sent to church leaders by local Catholics and that the draft in question was in fact rejected by the bishops, who prepared instead a very moderate pastoral letter. As far as a third party was concerned, he denied that the church had given any directive to organize such a party and pointed out that leading Slovak and Czechoslovak statesmen themselves had called for a third party in Slovakia. Kmet'ko's statement concluded with a reminder that the Catholic Church in Slovakia had already expressed its "sincere joy" over the renewal of the Czechoslovak Republic and its desire to cooperate with Slovakia's new rulers, along with the expectation that its rights and freedoms would be respected.

The conflict over education lay at the heart of the conflict between the church and state authorities. Unlike some other issues of conflict—for example, whether criminal proceedings should be initiated against collaborationist clergy or whether church lands should be confiscated and redistributed in a land reform—education meant far too much to both church and state to be settled satisfactorily to both sides in the given context. There was an insurmountable conflict between the way the political leaders and church leaders viewed education and its place in society. At the same time, both sides held significantly different understandings of relevant terms and concepts.

First, church and state had very different ideas of what religious freedom ought to entail. For the church, the freedom to establish schools was an essential element of religious freedom, as was the freedom for parents to send their children to schools operated in accordance with their religious beliefs. The state defined religious freedom far more narrowly. It meant merely the freedom to affiliate oneself with whatever religious confession one wished and the freedom to worship and engage in other purely religious activity. Similarly, both sides differed sharply in their understanding of just what the social role of the church should be. The state favored a narrow construction—the churches were to be concerned about the spiritual needs of their flocks while everything else lay in the domain of the state. Thus, churches were expected to refrain from political activity, follow the lead of the state in social, economic, and cultural matters, and serve as cheerleaders for and cooperators in reconstruction work initiated and directed by the state.

Catholic social teaching, on the other hand, saw the church's role as something quite different. The church had the right, and indeed the obligation, to address matters of political, economic, social, and cultural import. The seminal documents of modern Catholic social teaching, such as Leo XIII's 1891 encyclical *Rerum novarum* and Pius XI's 1931 encyclical *Quadragesimo anno*, established and affirmed this teaching. Moreover, a series of popes, including Pope Pius XII, specifically asserted the church's right to educate Catholics in her own schools.

"Democracy" was another term that was understood quite differently by church and state, most tellingly as it pertained to education. According to the church, if Slovakia was indeed a democratic country, then the will of the people should decide the matter of parochial schools. To the state authorities, particularly the Communists among them, democracy meant that the state was to be governed according to democratic principles, which allegedly included separation of church and state. For the Communists, democracy meant rule by the elites, who dominated organizations purportedly representing the people, such as the KSS and Communist dominated veterans organizations, trade unions, and other social organizations. Thus, if these groups opposed parochial education, they were being "democratic," even if the large majority of the population wanted them.

"Antistate" was another term that church and state viewed quite differently. For the state, it was defined very broadly, meaning anything that opposed the basic program of Czechoslovakia's postwar government. Thus, if one opposed the nationalization of education or of certain industries or enterprises, one was antistate. The church regarded antistate activity much more narrowly—that to oppose and work to change government policies was not identical to opposing the state. To be antistate, one really had to be working against Czechoslovakia's new regime. Of course, because Slovakia's new rulers defined nationalization of education as an essential component of a people's democratic regime, from their perspective, to challenge the state in this matter was to attack it at its very roots and was tantamount to treason.

Hanging over the entire debate on education was Slovakia's recent past. Because the church had a privileged position under the Tiso regime, where it dominated an educational system that was essentially parochial, its present embracing of the principles of pluralism and freedom in education was branded as "opportunistic." The church, of course, could not disagree. It was simply adapting itself to changing circumstances, as it had done for nearly two millennia, in pursuit of its interests and religious and social vision.

When Slovakia seceded from Czechoslovakia in 1939, the Catholic Church assumed an influence in education that it had not known for decades. The postwar regime, reacting against the church dominated education of the Tiso regime, which was itself a reaction against the aggressive secularizing of the First Republic, banned parochial education altogether. When the Catholic Church contested this, it was seen by the authorities as harboring sympathy for the Tiso regime and could thus by implication be associated with all the other aspects of the wartime years that looked bad in 1945—the destruction of the Czechoslovak Republic, the wartime alliance with Nazi Germany, the privileged position of Germans in Slovakia, the Hungarian occupation of southern Slovakia, the internments of opponents of the regime, discrimination against Protestants, military defeat, and the inhumane deportation of Jews to Nazi death camps. In the eyes of the postwar regime's propagandists, parochial education carried with it all these negative associations.

Catholic defenders of parochial education sought to limit discussion strictly to the issue of education itself. They complained that the state was imposing on Slovakia a foreign model that negated Slovakia's traditional educational patterns.[43] They complained that the Catholic Church was not consulted regarding the reform but simply handed a fait accompli, and that the leading positions in education were entrusted to non-Catholics.[44] They argued that moral-religious education was a critical social need, especially in the wake of the war, and one that the state simply could not do effectively on its own. In trying to fulfill this role, the state was overstepping its bounds and aggrandizing itself via an "educational totalitarianism."[45]

Alongside the major issue of the nationalization of education, Catholic leaders complained about a number of policies that, though not essential to a nationalized school system, likewise damaged Catholic interests and offended Catholic sensibilities. These included the ban on crucifixes, prayer, and Catholic greetings from classrooms; the transfer of teachers belonging to religious orders to places where they would be unable to live in common life with their coreligionists; and the assignment of non-Catholic teachers to schools where the student body was completely Catholic.[46] Such measures, variously aimed at secularization, social engineering, and efficiency, provoked angry opposition among Catholics at all levels. One such issue was the fate of teachers in religious orders, of whom Slovakia had 272 at war's end.[47] They ran forty-six schools and taught in an additional sixty-three. In 1945, 102 teachers from religious orders were reassigned by the state, with little consideration given for locating them in places where they could live the community life, or even where there was a Catholic church. In response to popular protest in various parts of Slovakia, including Nitra and Topol'čany, and complaints from the bishops, the Commission of Education, led by the Communist Ladislav Novomeský, took some steps to address Catholic concerns. Though this resulted in greater attention to the religious needs of the teachers in religious orders, the situation remained unsatisfactory as a number of such teachers remained at considerable distance from their religious houses.[48]

Another area where state policy encroached on church interests and independence was in the seizure of various Catholic institutions, including dormitories, orphanages, social service organizations, and clubs. These included, significantly, Catholic youth and women's organizations. Similar to the nationalization of education, these measures served both to weaken the church's social influence and to aggrandize the state by giving it an advantage over its main competition in the battle for the hearts and minds of Slovaks, and by increasing the scope of its social functions. The nationalization of dormitories was a particularly touchy issue, as Catholic and Protestant churches in Slovakia had long been used to having their own dormitories, whose importance would be all the greater in fostering a religious identity in students now that schools were nationalized. In fact, nearly two-thirds of Slovakia's one hundred college and high school dormitories were under church administration.[49] Novomeský made the case for nationalization to the SNR on July 2 and 25, 1945. State-run dormitories would eliminate the problem of the interwar period, where dormitories like the Catholic Svoradov in Bratislava became "hotbeds of reaction" and produced the younger generation of Populists.[50] It was also, according to Novomeský, the logical corollary to the nationalization of schools, a step toward overcoming religious differences and thereby fostering national unity.[51] Finally, it was more efficient, giving the state greater flexibility in locating dormitories where they were needed and allowing for a maximum utilization of available space. Novomeský's policy passed the SNR and was implemented, but not without a debate in which Protestant representatives argued that only formerly "fascist" dormitories should be nationalized, not formerly democratic ones.[52] L'udovít Šenšel, for example, pointed out that the Štefánik House in Bratislava, a Lutheran dormitory, nurtured students in a democratic, tolerant spirit and produced a number of members of the Slovak wartime resistance to the Nazis and the Tiso regime. Indeed, Novomeský himself had lectured there during the war.[53]

Another issue that posed a constant irritant between the regime and the Catholic Church, though not as intensely and overtly as education, was the so-called minority question. This meant above all what to do with the relatively large Magyar population remaining in Slovakia at war's end, as well as the smaller numbers of ethnic Germans.[54] Slovakia at the war's end had well over half a million Magyars, most of whom lived in the southern regions bordering Hungary.[55] While a significant minority of Magyars were Calvinist, most belonged to the Roman Catholic Church. In mid-1946, Slovakia had 305 Roman Catholic priests and 125 members of religious orders of Magyar ethnicity.[56] The Košice government program decreed that all German and Hungarian citizens of the Czechoslovak Republic would have their state citizenship rights abrogated, except for those who had actively struggled in the past against "the Henleinists and the Hungarian irredentist parties."[57]

In dealing with Magyar clergy, Magyar parishes and other religious institutions, and Magyar believers, the state pursued a number of policies. It sought to confiscate the property of Magyar religious institutions, ban worship in any language but Slovak, end or severely curtail state financial support for Magyar clergy, deprive them of the right to teach, and ban intrachurch correspondence in the Hungarian language.[58] These repressive measures constituted part of a much broader minority policy, which initially entailed placing large numbers of Magyars in internment camps in hopes of their eventual deportation abroad. As these hopes faded when the Great Powers refused to allow a wholesale expulsion of Slovakia's Magyars, as they did with the Germans in the Czech lands and Poland, the authorities in Slovakia pursued alternative solutions—the deportation of Magyars to the Czech lands to be settled in territories left vacant by the expulsion of the Sudeten Germans; a population exchange with Hungary, according to which ethnic Slovaks in Hungary would be resettled in Slovakia, while a comparable number of Magyars from Slovakia moved to Hungary; and a "re-Slovakization" campaign, whereby Magyars in Slovakia could officially claim Slovak ancestry and identity, thereby regaining citizenship rights in exchange for national reidentification. Communists and Democrats often quibbled over minority policy, for example, over whether to privilege the worker and peasant classes in re-

Slovakization, or whether policy toward the Magyars should be in the hands of experts or the police.[59] Each party also sought to woo Magyars into its camp while accusing their rival of doing the same.[60] Nevertheless, on the most fundamental aspects of minority policy, all parties were in general agreement as to the proper approach. It was the Catholic Church, rather, that came into conflict with the regime over its policies on a number of levels.

An immediate concern for the church in Slovakia was the pastoral impact of imprisoning minority clergy or otherwise stripping them of their clerical functions. Already on March 11, 1945, Bishop Jozef Čársky sent a complaint to Slovakia's commissioner of the interior that twenty-nine minority priests had been removed from their functions, including thirteen who had served at predominately Slovak parishes.[61] As the postwar regime continued to implement its harsh policies toward the Magyar minority, Slovakia's bishops began to raise humanitarian concerns. Kmeťko sent a letter to the Slovak National Council's presidium on September 5.[62] He asked that the Magyars and Germans interned in camps be treated humanely and that those who had not transgressed against the interests of the nation and state be promptly released. He also urged that any "transfer" of the minority population be done in accordance with international agreements with the affected governments. Finally, Kmeťko asked that religious services be allowed in the internment camps and that Catholic charities be permitted to minister to the internees. In a pastoral letter published in *Katolícke noviny*'s November 4 issue, Slovakia's bishops condemned the notion of collective guilt, writing that "every person should be judged according to his actions, not his racial or national affiliation. For this reason . . . the bishops appeal to the authorities to deal with Catholics in a humane and Christian manner, without regard to nationality."[63] In mid-November, bishops from Slovakia and the Czech lands met jointly in Olomouc and sent to the Czechoslovak government a letter of their concerns. Regarding the minority situation, the letter pointed out that "how the Germans and Magyars are sometimes being treated is not in accordance with Christian sentiment and with the good name of our nation."[64] The pastoral letter issued by the bishops at this same conference also made some reference to the minority situation.[65] Though the bishops did not condemn population transfers per se, they asked that any transfers of population be carried out peacefully and humanely. Remarkably, the letter stated, "We cannot allow even a shadow of the cruelty of the former concentration camps to stain us, because history has penetrating sight and in future years every blunder could be placed on the pillory the way today we are pillorying the cruelty of the camps at Dachau, Auschwitz, and elsewhere."[66] Citing the specific request of Pope Pius XII that minorities be treated justly, the bishops asked that the innocent not be punished along with the guilty, and that those deprived of their freedom have access to Christian clergy.

Catholic leaders kept up their protests and appeals on behalf of persecuted Magyar Catholics, especially clergy, through the immediate postwar years. A central focus of Catholic concern was the language of worship.[67] Though by law Magyar worship was permitted in those churches that had it before November 1938, in practice local authorities often tried to restrict or shut it down completely, not infrequently aided by anti-Magyar lay Slovak Catholics.[68] This issue was particularly acute in the regions of Slovakia inhabited by Magyars, for with the elimination of Hungarian political parties, national organizations, and schools, the churches were one of the few places where Magyars could give public expression to their language and culture. The church came to the Magyars' defense, based on its principle that worship should be in a language that the believers understood.[69] In Kmet'ko's view, it was the right and duty of the church to proclaim God's word in a language intelligible to the people. To fail to do so also undermined the goals of the preacher, whose success was dependent upon his being understood by his hearers.[70] Slovak bishops in the affected regions again and again tried to counter attempts to ban or severely restrict Magyar worship, not without success. For example, Bishop Pavol Jantausch protested sharply to the commissioner of the interior, Július Viktory, when police officials ordered some local Magyar clergy to preach and sing in Slovak.[71] Viktory accommodated Jantausch by instructing the police to stop mixing into purely religious affairs. When local authorities tried to restrict Magyar language worship in Košice to a single small church and forbid singing in Magyar, Bishop Čársky refused their request, correctly citing both Czechoslovak and canon law on his behalf.[72] When local Magyars and Slovaks got into conflict over the language of worship, the bishops usually settled the issue through compromise, either by providing two masses, one in each language, or using Slovak and Magyar alternatively in a single Mass.[73]

Closely connected to the language issue was the status of Magyar clergy. Here there were two central issues—the state's halting of financial support for Magyar clergy (the so-called Congrua) and the state's attempts to deport Magyar clergy to Hungary as part of a population transfer or exchange.

Given that their loss of salary or pension put many Hungarian clergy in dire economic straits, the church repeatedly lobbied the authorities for its restoration, or at least that government loans be made available to them.[74] Failing to address the issue or even to implement stopgap measures that had been passed, the state dragged its feet right up to February 1948. The church also repeatedly expressed its concerns that Magyar priests not be categorically deported, which would leave many Hungarian Catholics without pastors who spoke their language.

A final issue that took a long time to settle was the question of the church property that was in Magyar hands at war's end. The state regarded such property as belonging to enemies of the Czechoslovak Republic, and hence to be confiscated. The church regarded it not as Magyar property but as church property and sought merely to transfer it from the control of Hungarian bishops or religious orders to Slovak ones. The state, for instance, assumed control of the property of Hungarian religious orders, took over their schools and other social organizations, and, despite protests, generally kept the former Magyar controlled property from passing to the church in Slovakia.[75]

The press was another domain in which the state sought to restrict Catholic influence. Permission from the commissioner of the interior was needed for any periodical to operate in postwar Slovakia, and the Slovak authorities refused to grant that permission until September 1945, when permission came to issue *Katolícke noviny*, a weekly newspaper. (In the Czech lands, Catholic periodicals were allowed from June 1945.) By the end of 1945, a number of other Catholic periodicals were permitted, nearly all of which dealt exclusively with themes such as faith, family, and devotion. *Katolícke noviny*, by contrast, distinguished itself in its coverage of and commentary on current political developments of concern to Catholics. Though the SNR had resolved in June to allow a Catholic weekly only if a group of "progressive Catholic priests" could be found to run it, the newspaper that emerged in September 1945 was in the hands of men committed to defending Catholic interests in the face of inimical policies by the regime. Henceforth, *Katolícke noviny*, and in particular its brash columnist Jur Koza-Matejov, would repeatedly come into conflict with Slovak authorities, and in particular with the KSS.[76] Despite the concessions in the form of Catholic periodicals in the fall of 1945, Church leaders complained that they had been allowed far fewer periodicals than during the interwar period, and that *Katolícke noviny*, unlike a number of other Slovak newspapers, was allowed to come out only weekly and was limited to four pages.[77] Moreover, *Katolícke noviny*'s editors were regularly called to the office of the KSS's press division, to be criticized and threatened for publishing material that the Communists regarded as offensive or inappropriate.[78]

Another pressing conflict between the church and the authorities was over the internment of Catholic clergy after the collapse of the Tiso regime. Dozens of clergy were interned, including two bishops, Ján Vojtaššák and Michal Buzalka. While Buzalka was released on June 27, 1945, Vojtaššák remained in detention until the fall of 1945, and Catholic complaints focused on his case. Vojtaššák was interned "for reason of state security and the consolidation of the situation" in Slovakia.[79] Specifically, he was deemed particularly unreliable for a number of reasons. During the war, he was decorated by the Tiso regime and a member of its state council. Furthermore, Vavro Šrobár, acting as Minister of Education for the Czechoslovak government in exile, reported to the SNR that he had met with Vojtaššák while on a visit to Spišská Kapitula in the winter of 1945, and that Vojtaššák had expressly refused to recognize the new Czechoslovak government, professing instead his allegiance to the crumbling Slovak Republic.[80] Through the summer of 1945, the Communist press attacked Vojtaššák, pointing out his membership on the state council,[81] citing letters he wrote in 1944 which referred to the Partisans as "bandits" and which closed with the words "Na stráž!"[82] and alleging that he was an enemy of the children of workers and peasants.[83] Lacking a press of their own, Catholics could not respond to these charges publicly. In September, however, the SNR resolved to release Vojtaššák from internment, and by November he was able to return to his episcopal see and functions in Spiš.[84]

Despite the release of Vojtaššák and the allowance of some Catholic periodicals, a number of irritants remained in relations between Catholics and the new regime. In January 1946, Slovakia's bishops met with Czechoslovakia's President Edvard Beneš in Prague and presented him with a list of their complaints regarding the situation of the church and Catholics in Slovakia. Alongside the already mentioned issues involving education, Catholic organizations and institutions, and the press, the bishops had a number of other complaints—that the land reform was threatening to confiscate and parcel out the so-called *patronáty* (i.e., lands owned by the church and used to finance various Catholic spiritual and social undertakings); that the state salaries for clergy, the so-called Congrua, were raised in the Czech lands, but not in Slovakia, where clergy received exceedingly low salaries and pensions; that many Catholics had been sitting in prison since the end of the war without proof of wrongdoing or for relatively minor transgressions, without access to religious services or sacraments, and with family members who were being denied jobs, housing, and access to food on account of them.[85] The bishops also protested that the social, sanitary, and religious conditions of the 20,800 Magyars, Germans, and Slovaks still in internment camps in Slovakia were "very unpleasant and unbearable," a violation of "basic notions of humanity," and they called for a fundamental improvement. The bishops also asked that any exchange of population with Hungary be carried out "in accordance with mutual agreements of the interested states and the precepts of humanity."

The ebb and flow of tensions between the church hierarchy and the state authorities ran simultaneous with, and was much affected by, the vying of Slovakia's political parties for the Catholic vote. Both Communists and Democrats sought to attract Catholics into their respective camps, or at the very least keep them from helping their rival. This led to a tug-of-war over Catholics between a party that was run by Lutherans whose relations to many politically involved Catholics had been quite strained over the past two and a half decades, and a party imbued with an atheistic ideology historically hostile to Christianity, especially Roman Catholicism. This situation, strange as it may seem, is quite understandable in the context of postwar Slovak politics.

The KSS followed a three-pronged policy with regard to the religious question in Slovakia. The Communists' goals were simultaneously to weaken the Catholic Church, to sow dissension and division within the Democratic Party, and to attract the support of Catholics, clerical and lay. Wooing Catholics would entail some sort of outreach both to Catholic clergy and to former Populists. In December 1944, as the front raged across Slovakia, Communist leader Václav Kopecký reproached the Slovak Communists for having no representatives of the moderate wing of the HSĽS in the SNR, which he labeled as the council's greatest weakness.[86] In February, Gustav Husák, one of Slovakia's leading Communists during the wartime resistance, reported for the Communist leadership on the religious situation in Slovakia.[87] While arguing for the need for a radical purge of Catholic institutions, Husák believed that the church would, for tactical reasons, profess its loyalty to the new regime and not mix into politics. He believed that Catholicism could be won for the new regime and argued that tensions between Catholics and Protestants could be used to the KSS's advantage given Catholic suspicions about Lutheran domination of the DS. At the March 13, 1945, meeting of the Central Committee of the KSS, Edo Friš confirmed this view in a report on "the inclination of the Catholic priesthood to the KSS for confessional reasons."[88] The KSS was clearly examining the potential for attracting Catholic priests alienated by the Lutheran dominance in the DS.

As Slovakia's liberation proceeded and Košice fell into the hands of the Soviet Red Army, Husák developed ties with Pavol Čarnogurský, who became his liaison with Catholic circles, including the church hierarchy.[89] Čarnogurský was an appropriate person for the task. He had personal relationships with Communists dating to the prewar period, and knew Husák and Novomeský well; he also had the ear of a number of Slovakia's bishops. Though a parliamentarian for the HSĽS during the war, he was among the most moderate Populists. Moreover, he was interested in reconciling Catholics to the changing political environment and getting them positively engaged in the new situation. Husák and Čarnogurský kept in regular contact, and Čarnogurský sent him weekly reports on matters pertinent to relations with the church. As an indication of KSS interest in the Catholic Church, top-level Slovak Communists met on April 25, 1945, in Košice with Čarnogurský, the Croat priest and resistance veteran Tomislav Kolakovič, and two representatives of Bishop Jantausch.[90]

It is clear from Communist documents that the KSS, with some qualms, was attracting former members of the now-banned HSĽS into its fold. In the summer of 1945, the Communist Gustav Husák stressed that even a religious believer can be a KSS member, and that "the little people . . . who have not committed any crimes can be good patriots and they have a place in our ranks, if they agree with our program."[91] In July 1945, at a joint meeting of the Central Committees of the KSČ and KSS, Friš mentioned that "a not inconsiderable portion" of the members of the KSS "were former HSĽS members or under the influence of that party for a whole six years. . . . Thus we run into remnants of the Populist ideology not only in the local communist organizations but even at the district and regional conferences."[92] It was not uncommon, in Slovakia as elsewhere in Eastern Europe, for collaborators in the crimes of the wartime regime to seek refuge in the Communist Party. Democratic Party officials from Bánovce nad Bebravou noted, in situation reports of October and November 1945, that war criminals were joining the KSS out of fear of the Communists, who were accepting them as a means to win the support of former Populists.[93]

An important aspect of the KSS's approach toward Catholics was its efforts to find sympathetic priests and laymen who could be co-opted by the party. Toward this end, the Slavic Catholic Committee (SKV) was set up in Košice in late March 1945.[94] The SKV exhorted Catholics to support the Communist Party line with respect to "the eternal brotherhood of all Slavic nations," and the Czechoslovak-Soviet alliance that resulted from and manifested that brotherhood.[95] Composed mainly of unknowns, the Communists hoped to use the SKV to attract, concentrate, and coordinate "progressive" Slovak Catholic clergy (i.e., priests who had Communist sympathies).[96] The most prominent such priest was Jozef Straka. Born in 1903, Straka was a priest in the Banská Bystrica diocese and an activist in the Slovak branch of the Czechoslovak People's Party during the interwar period.[97] He clandestinely joined the Communists in 1941 and fought in a Partisan unit during the Slovak National Uprising.[98] After the war, he was active in the SKV, served as the head of the religious affairs department of the Commission of Education, and was the chief commentator on religious affairs in the Communist press. He also took part in the arrest of Vojtaššák in March. In the summer of 1945, Straka tried to interest the KSS in expanding its cooperation with progressive Catholic clergy. In two meetings with a party official, he stressed "the sincerely democratic thinking" of part of the Catholic priesthood and their desire to engage themselves in building up the new people's democracy within the framework of the KSS. Straka argued that if the party was supportive of these progressive priests and provided them with opportunities for educational work among the Catholic clergy and population, it could enlist many of the younger generation of priests to its cause. He also proposed, in the name of the SKV, that he be granted permission to revive the weekly newspaper *Katolícke noviny*, in order to educate the Catholic masses in the spirit of people's democracy and Slavic reciprocity. He proposed several priests for its editorial board, all cofounders of the SKV.[99]

Reporting on his conversations with Straka, a Communist official stressed the urgency of the party taking action regarding cooperation with priests, given their great influence in Slovakia and given the fact that the DS had already taken some priests into its leadership at its recent party congress.[100] He urged the Central Committee to consider whether to appoint at least one Catholic priest as a KSS representative to the SNR and whether to direct local and district KSS bodies to name priests to the national committees in their locales. While these latter suggestions were apparently not accepted, the party did resolve on July 13 to group all progressive Catholic priests around the SKV and increase its activity, to put the St. Vojtech Society in progressive hands, and to arrange that a Catholic weekly be set up as soon as possible, exclusively run by progressive Catholics.[101] This latter resolution, in fact, had been approved already on June 25 by the presidium of the bipartisan SNR.[102]

Alongside the SKV, the KSS sought other ways to attract Catholics through the officially sponsored Pan-Slavism. Each year, All-Slavic Day celebrations were held in early July, which included a rally near the ruins of Devín Castle outside Bratislava. Communist intentions with respect to Catholics are clear in a report on the preparation for the first celebration of 1945, given by Novomeský at the June 13 meeting of the KSS's Central Committee. According to Novomeský, the event was to stress the Slavic Cyrilo-Methodian tradition,[103] and "these celebrations must be placed on ideological foundations which are very close to the Catholic folk (*l'udová*) base of society, thus giving us ideological access to the wide Catholic masses."[104]

An important aspect of the Communist effort to woo Catholics was the way Catholicism and the church were treated in Communist periodicals. *Pravda* and *Nové slovo* dealt with church related questions rather frequently, and alongside the expected defenses of nationalized education and attacks on collaborationist clergy, one can find dozens of articles aimed at winning Catholics over to the Communist camp. The Communist relationship to Catholicism was developed along at least four lines in the Communist press—(1) neither the KSS, nor the Soviet Union, nor Communism in general, are enemies of Christianity, but rather defenders of its freedom; (2) Christianity was a positive historical force, both for Slovakia and for Europe and the world; (3) most Slovak Catholics were good people, with nothing in common with the Tiso regime and its abuses; and (4) Tiso and his supporters were actually bad Catholics, harming the church and pursuing policies condemned by church leaders, including the pope, in the service of anti-Catholic Nazism.

In asserting the Christian friendly nature of Communism, the Communist press carried articles on religious freedom in the Soviet Union. *Pravda*, on November 11, 1945, praised the Soviet constitution for its recognition of the freedom to perform religious rites, which led religious believers to rally in appreciation behind the Soviet state in the war against Hitler. As evidence of the current positive situation for religious believers in the Soviet Union, the article cited remarks by the Moscow Patriarch on his recent visit to Prague, where he praised the freedom of confession current in the Soviet Union and the Soviet regime's willingness to give the church whatever help it needed.[105] On May 31, 1945, *Pravda* published an article by a Slovak Catholic priest entitled "Red Army Returns Religious Freedom to Poland," which argued that the Soviets saved Polish churches and cultural monuments from the vandalism of "neopagan" Nazism, and pointed out how Catholic organizations, seminaries, press, and the Catholic University in Lublin were all reactivated under Soviet occupation.[106] But Slovak Communists did not need to look abroad to find Christianity benefiting from the Red Army. In Slovakia herself, as KSS Secretary-General Štefan Bašťovanský argued in a lead article in *Nové slovo*, the Red Army and Communists exposed the lie of fascist propaganda. Despite predictions that a Soviet occupation would mean the murder of priests, persecution of believers, desecration of religious symbols, and destruction of churches, Bašťovanský argued that "after ten months there has not been a single case of antireligious violence in Slovakia."[107]

Communist writers also depicted Christianity in a rather positive light. Both Bašťovanský and Straka made reference to the Cyrilo-Methodian tradition in Slovakia in an effort to orient Catholics to the Orthodox Slavic East rather than to their German-Hungarian neighbors.[108] Straka also praised the great work of "national construction" by prominent Slovak Catholics in the nineteenth century.[109] Husák, a former Catholic, not uncommonly made religious references in his speeches and articles. In his Christmas message of 1945 in *Nové slovo*, he quoted St. Luke, the Old Testament, St. Francis of Assisi, and Dante. In line with the Communist interpretation of the past, he praised the progressive character of early Christianity, with its concepts of love and justice, attacked "pagan values," called for cooperation between Communists and Catholics, and branded opponents of progress as "false prophets."[110]

In appealing to Catholics, Communist propaganda was careful not to identify the Tiso regime with Catholics or Catholicism. In fact, in a series of articles in December 1945, the Communist press went to pains to dissociate Tiso from Catholicism. Front-page lead headlines, with titles such as "The Protest of the Vatican Against Tiso's Policy," "The Vatican Against Tiso," and "Tiso Betrayed Even Catholicism," drove home the point. These articles, responding to the publication in *Katolícke noviny* of a Vatican protest on May 5, 1943, against Tiso's deportation of the Jews, asserted that Tiso disregarded Vatican protests against his racist policies and the persecution and deportation of Jews because, for Tiso, "the authority of Hitler was higher than the authority of the head of the Catholic Church. His own reactionary aims took precedence over the principles of Catholicism.[111] "Tiso sinned not only against the interests and future of the Slovak nation, but also against the teachings of the Catholic Church," despite warnings from the pope.[112] Slovakia's bishops, some of whom were being branded by the Communists individually as collaborators, were collectively set in opposition to Tiso for their pastoral letter of March 21, 1943, which condemned the policy of the Slovak regime toward the Jews as a violation of general legal civil norms and the moral and religious law.[113]

In seeking to discredit Tiso in the eyes of Slovakia's Catholics, Communist rhetoric also stressed the anti-Catholic and anti-Christian character of Nazism, which was labeled as "neopagan," or even "satanic," and pilloried as a persecutor of Catholics and Christians in general.[114] In contrast to Tiso and his supporters were the good clergy, those who were imprisoned by the Germans for their ties to the Czechoslovak London government in exile, for helping the Slovak National Uprising and for being loyal to "Czech-Slovak reciprocity."[115] These priests, according to Straka, wanted a purge of the collaborationist clergy who supported the Tiso state.

While Communists sought ways to woo Catholics, they nevertheless were strongly committed to crippling Catholic social, political, and cultural influence. At the Central Committee meeting of July 13, 1945, KSS leaders debated party policy toward the Catholic Church. Coming in the wake of the church's petition campaign in defense of parochial education and a controversy over the All-Slavic Days at Devín, the meeting dealt with "our standpoint toward the Catholic Church and its clergy in view of recent events."[116] Both Husák and Novomeský claimed the church was taking advantage of Communist goodwill in attempting to mobilize Slovakia's Catholic population in defense of its political interests, which the Communists equated with those of the HSĽS and the Tiso regime.

Husák presented a program for dealing with the church, leading to a series of proposals being accepted by the committee. Among other things, the KSS resolved that police measures be taken against priests who zealously championed the Tiso regime, and that "politically compromised" Catholic clubs be dissolved. At the same time, efforts to nationalize and laicize the education system were to be carried out through to completion, with compromised clergy and members of religious orders removed from their posts if they did not pass the verification procedures implemented by the Communist led Commission of Education. The party and its press were authorized to launch a large-scale campaign calling for church lands to be parceled out as part of the land reform, and the possibility of seizing other church property, such as Salesian athletic halls and fields, was to be examined.

The KSS was careful to couple its antichurch measures with increased efforts to unite progressive Catholics in the SKV, and to found a progressive Catholic weekly and get the St. Vojtech Society into the hands of Catholic clergy willing to collaborate with the Communists. At the same time, Communist efforts to both weaken the church and court Slovak Catholics were bound closely to and complicated by KSS relations with the DS. The KSS line in relations with the DS called for close cooperation.[117] The KSS perceived that the DS was undergoing a "differentiation process," with an intensifying conflict between a "progressive" wing open to cooperation with the KSS on the basis of the Košice Government Program and a "reactionary" wing that sought to harbor Tiso supporters and appeal to HSL'S veterans.[118] Communist policy was to foster this division in the DS. At a meeting of the KSS Central Committee on July 14, 1945, Husák urged that "the KSS must concentrate on supporting the progressive wing of the DS, also from below."[119] He stressed the need to engage the Democrats, via the Slovak National Front, in a struggle against reaction in Slovakia, arguing that the campaign against reactionary clergy was a good opportunity for implementing this policy. A day earlier, Bašt'ovanský told a meeting of the KSS's Broad Presidium that "it is necessary to enlist the DS and National Front to the full degree in a campaign against the Catholic clergy, in order that this must not be an action of the KSS alone."[120] One result of this Communist policy was the proclamation of the Slovak National Front against the alleged misuse of religion issued in July. By making sure the DS got some of the credit, and blame, for public attacks against clerical activism, the Communists tried both to deepen rifts within the DS over the issue and to alienate Catholic voters from that party.

Communists also at this time put pressure on Father Augustín Pozdech, who as an opponent of the Tiso regime was named a dean for the church in Bratislava and was active in the DS. At a meeting of the SNR's presidium on June 18, Husák complained that Pozdech was too slow in fulfilling his promise to purge Slovakia's monasteries of dubious characters.[121] Communists also expressed their displeasure when Pozdech, in advance of the All-Slavic Days in early July, sent a circular to Bratislava's Catholic parishes, urging them not to attend the state sponsored celebrations and proposing a Catholic alternative instead. Pozdech was pressured into rescinding his plan and coming out publicly in support of the All-Slavic Days.[122] The KSS interpreted Pozdech's initial action as a Catholic attempt to use the festive days as an occasion for a political demonstration.[123]

On July 8, the same day that the Catholic petition action against the nationalization of schools forced the religious question to the top of the Communist agenda, the DS was holding its party congress. Gauging the place religion played at the congress depends upon where one looks. A list of resolutions passed by the congress makes no mention of any church related issues and even omits religious freedom from the list of civil rights.[124] Likewise, a DS report entitled "Our First Congress" ignores religious policy questions altogether.[125] The document outlining the party's programmatic principles, however, lays out the important components of DS policy as it stood in the summer of 1945.[126] The party opposed discrimination on the basis of church or religious affiliation and hailed religious conviction as "one of the fundamental rights of a free man." It regarded religion's task as being to cultivate among the people "love and truth, a sense of moral excellence, and universal and eternal values." Religion thus understood was to be a component of national education. The educational system itself, however, was to be state-run, and the DS's programmatic principles contained a strong affirmation of the necessity of nationalizing education at all levels. Religious institutions were to have a claim to the state's protection and support, but "only to the degree that they actually carried out functions in accordance with genuine religion." The use of religious institutions for nonreligious, mainly political goals was to be prevented. Regarding the role of Christianity within the DS itself, the party stated the rather tepid and vague principle that "Western Christian culture was and remains the basis of our whole national awareness and development. We desire to and must maintain these bonds in the interest of the further development of our whole civilization."

More extensive and assertive was the speech given at the party congress by Ján Ursíny, DS chairman from its founding during the war and a deputy chairman of the Czechoslovak government, thus, along with newly elected chairman Jozef Lettrich, the highest ranking member of the DS. In a speech published by the DS as a brochure entitled "The Way of the DS," Ursíny commented, among other things, on the religious question.[127] Alongside the typical affirmations of freedom of confession and religious equality and homage to "Christian values," Ursíny called for the cooperation of all churches and the end to religious hostilities. He asserted that the DS "is not a party of a single confession, but a Christian party, including adherents of all Christian churches, and not excluding non-Christians either." Since the DS was predominately in the hands of Lutherans, this comment was surely aimed at Catholic voters. It was Ursíny's comments on religion as it related to patriotism, politics, and education, however, that displayed his most serious outreach to Catholics. He stated, "We do not place religious interests into conflict with national interests, because they are not in opposition. As [nineteenth century Czechoslovak poet and national awakener Ján] Kollár wrote, nationality and religion are sisters. One cannot impede the other." But, Ursíny went on to warn, "never can they be allowed to come into conflict with the interests of the state." He praised clergy who, with but a few exceptions, supported and aided the Partisans during the Slovak National Uprising. Regarding the role of clergy in politics, Ursíny said that

> We do not consider it as correct or proper that clergy be excluded from political life. This would lower them to a second-rate position. At the same time, political life cannot be directed by them alone. Nor in the future can it happen again that the Church becomes an instrument of politics and thereby damages itself. The recent past has shown us how the Church and nation can get on the wrong path.

Here we see Ursíny once again combining an olive branch to the churches with a warning that there are lines that must not be crossed.

Nowhere did Ursíny woo Catholics more forcefully than in his commentary on education. While the DS's programmatic principles strongly affirmed the nationalization of education and spoke vaguely about the need for Christian values in schools, Ursíny framed his views within the context of a broader understanding of religious freedom. He wrote the following:

> Religious freedom is not supposed to mean simply that a religious spirit is cultivated only in churches. It is supposed to mean that a religious spirit is maintained at school and everywhere a Christian demands it. While we do not want anyone to have a religious conviction forced upon them by someone via whatever sort of means, at the same time we do not want to deprive anyone of that which they consider as necessary for their soul. We have already seen such a religious freedom—it was like that at the beginning of our republic, after the First

World War: although we had religious freedom, many people made a mockery of high Christian values.

This jab at the religious policy of the First Republic, which had caused much bad blood among Slovaks and helped to fuel the rise of the HSĽS back in the early 1920s, was certainly designed to woo Catholic voters to the DS.

The coincidence of Ursíny's remarks with the Catholic petition campaign (they occurred on the same day), however, put the DS in a position whereby it had to pull back the hand it was offering to Catholics for a time and clasp hands with the KSS, who insisted on a joint proclamation against clerical abuse of politics. Nevertheless, it was becoming increasingly clear that the DS was serious about making a pitch to Catholics.

The DS's party congress elected Lettrich as the new party chairman. Like Ursíny, Lettrich recognized the vital importance of reaching out to Slovakia's as yet largely uncommitted population of Slovak Catholics. At a DS rally in mid-June, Lettrich addressed the question of relations between Catholics and Protestants. According to him, the important thing was not whether someone was a Catholic or Protestant, but whether they were a good person or a bad one. He expressed his party's desire that the churches help to consolidate, not divide, the nation and avoid superfluous conflicts.[128] At the meeting of the SNR's presidium on June 27, Lettrich mentioned Catholic opposition to the nationalization of dormitories and expressed a desire to discuss with Novomeský the implementation of that policy with the aim of carrying it out "more benevolently." What Lettrich had in mind was allowing the nationalized dormitories to remain denominationally specific in their student composition as a way to satisfy church circles.[129]

Despite the hullabaloo over the Catholic petition action in July and the subsequent SNF proclamation against the misuse of religion, the DS took some significant steps in the summer of 1945 aimed at improving its relations with the Catholic Church and winning over Catholic voters. In July, Lettrich met with the lawyer of interned bishop Vojtaššák, Ľudovít Obtulovič, to discuss Vojtaššák's release.[130] In August, the DS proposed as representatives to the Provisional National Assembly in Prague two prominent Slovak Catholics, Canon Andrej Cvinček, a former functionary of the Czechoslovak People's Party in Slovakia, and Jozef Kempný, a representative of the young Slovak intelligentsia.[131]

The Communists had their own ideas about what to do about the large mass of Slovaks who were not sympathetic to Communism but at the same time leery of the Protestant dominated DS. Everyone in Slovak politics was aware that in the hands of these noncommitted Catholic voters, who Husák estimated at roughly 33 percent of Slovakia's voters and some placed as high as 55 percent, hung the balance of the first parliamentary elections.[132] The KSS took pains to prevent the DS from presenting itself as more Catholic friendly. We have already mentioned Communist pressure to get the DS to join with it in the SNF proclamation in July. In August, when the DS presented its nominations for Slovakia's representatives to the Provisional National Assembly, the Communists objected to a number of the proposed names but not to the Catholics Cvinček and Kempný.[133] They also agreed to the release of Vojtaššák from internment, which led to his eventual return to his diocese in Spiš on November 30.[134] Finally, the Communists agreed to the reissuing of *Katolícke noviny* as a weekly, the first issue of which appeared on September 9, 1945.

The case of *Katolícke noviny* is quite telling. On June 25, the SNR authorized the Commission of the Interior to give permission for the establishment of a Catholic weekly, if a group of "progressive Catholic priests" is found and requests such a periodical.[135] The Communists reiterated the same policy at their party presidium meeting of July 13.[136] Nevertheless, the Catholic weekly that was allowed to emerge in September 1945 was not run by clergy the Communists would regard as "progressive." Prominent among the editors of *Katolícke noviny* were Pavol Čarnogurský, Rudolf Čavojský, and Jur Koza-Matejov, men who, while hardly reactionary were quite unlike Straka in that they were willing to defend what they regarded as Catholic interests in the face of political and administrative pressure. Already by early October the KSS secretariat complained that these men, "collaborators who belong before the National Court," should be replaced by Straka and other "democratic priests," and that the newspaper should be published by the Slavic Catholic Committee.[137] Communists, though they would threaten and harass *Katolícke noviny* regularly, never achieved these objectives until they seized power in Czechoslovakia in February 1948 and were free to alter all publishing in accordance with their wishes. The fact that the KSS allowed a Catholic periodical to emerge outside its control is most likely explicable as a way to keep Catholics from being drawn into the Democratic camp. A similar concession, dating from approximately the same time, was the establishment of the Central Catholic Chancellery (ÚKK),[138] a church body founded to coordinate Catholic activity throughout Slovakia.[139] Though these concessions to the Catholic Church were connected with the rivalry between the DS and the KSS for the support of noncommitted Catholics, the bishops helped pave the way when, on August 22, they issued a ban on political activity by priests and proclaimed their positive attitude toward the Czechoslovak Republic.[140]

The fall of 1945 saw a continuation of the rivalry between Slovakia's two political parties for the Catholic vote. Catholics themselves, for the most part, remained aloof. Some, like Pozdech, were active in the DS, and others, like Straka, collaborated with the KSS. Most, however, took a "wait-and-see" attitude.[141] Despite the recent relaxation of tensions, the regime and the Catholic Church remained in fundamental conflict over issues such as education. Many Catholics continued to regard themselves as people without representation, forced to choose between an atheistic and a Lutheran party.

Among those Catholics who were not taking sides, some other options existed. First, there was the Slovak underground. Rather than a coordinated, centralized movement, the Slovak underground consisted of a hash of individuals and small groups who began displaying their hostility to Czechoslovakia's people's democratic regime and sympathy for Slovak independence and the Tiso regime through various illegal or semilegal means—publishing and distributing leaflets and broadsheets, posting provocative slogans in public view, occasionally engaging in petition actions, demonstrations, and acts of violence and vandalism.[142] Generally, localized and acting on their own without directives, these individuals and groups were mainly composed of young Catholics, in particular college students or recent graduates.[143] A typical example was the group led by Jozef Bačkor, a college student and soccer star in Bratislava. In the summer of 1945, he and some friends formed a secret group aimed at infiltrating the state administration in preparation for the renewal of an independent Slovakia. The group was exposed in November 1945 and its members arrested.[144] While underground activists often took part in Catholic initiatives such as the petition drive in defense of parochial education, and sometimes had ties with local priests, they did not receive the backing of the Catholic bishops or the church as a whole, which was careful after the war to stress its loyalty to the new regime.[145]

One aspect of the underground that greatly concerned Czechoslovakia's authorities were the links, real or imagined, that some members of the underground had with the Slovak political emigration, in particular with the circle around Ferdinand Ďurčanský in Rome.[146] Regarding the London-based

Slovak émigrés as too cautious, Ďurčanský in January 1946 founded a rival center in Rome, the Slovak Action Committee (SAV).[147] Based in a Roman monastery, he placed his hopes in a future war between the United States and the Soviet Union that he believed could lead to a resurrection of the Slovak Republic. The SAV issued a number of memoranda arguing for the legal continuity of the Slovak state, including three sent to the peace conference in Paris. Ďurčanský also transmitted illegal radio broadcasts and sent agents to Slovakia, with meager success, with the aim of establishing ties with Slovakia's homegrown resistance. Though his influence in Slovakia was marginal, he was for the authorities, as well as for the Communists, the *bête noire* whom members of the underground were suspected of serving.[148]

While the underground was virulently anti-Communist and anti-Soviet, there also existed an option for those Catholics who were not averse to cooperation with Communists and the Soviet Union. This was the group around the Croat émigré priest, Tomislav Kolakovič. Kolakovič left Croatia in 1943 at age thirty-seven on account of his pro-Russian and antifascist views. He soon developed a following in Slovakia, among clergy, intellectuals, and especially university students. His core disciples were known collectively as the "Family." Kolakovič combined Russophilism with a strong desire for social justice. During the war he participated in the Slovak National Uprising and hid in the forests with Partisans. After the war, he visited the Soviet Union, hoping to meet with Stalin and get permission to evangelize Russia. Not permitted access to Stalin, he did meet with some Soviet officials and claims to have baptized several Soviet security officers that he encountered during his travels.[149] Internationally, Kolakovič favored a rapprochement between the Vatican and the Soviet Union, advocated a Czechoslovak foreign policy that was equally aloof from East and West and harbored hopes that Russia would experience a Christian revival thanks to what he perceived, incorrectly, as a greater openness on the part of the Soviets after World War II. Kolakovič combined Pan-Slavism, admiration for the Eastern Orthodox Church, and social justice to form a worldview that placed great hopes in Russia while not ignoring its past brutality and shortcomings. In the tradition of papal social teaching and the teachings of Catholic philosophers such as Jacques Maritain, he saw the need for Catholics to engage more zealously in social justice issues, both because of the demands of the Gospel and as a way to block Communist inroads among the lower classes.[150] At the same time, he was open to cooperation with Communists on social questions. In terms of Slovakia's domestic politics, Kolakovič and his followers kept aloof from both political parties but were more leery of the DS than of the KSS. They regarded the DS as a party of Protestant sectarians, following anti-Catholic policies, especially in the realm of education. They also saw the DS as characterized by "bourgeois capitalism," which ran counter to Catholic social reformist goals, and as politically reliant on the United States, which would only serve to antagonize the Soviet Union and Czechoslovakia's Communists. While Catholic cooperation with the DS could scare the Soviet Union and have dire consequences for the church should Czechoslovakia fall into the Soviet sphere, cooperation with the KSS would help the church find a modus vivendi should Slovakia become Communist dominated.

Thus, Kolakovič's vision consisted of a paradoxical mix of pessimistic pragmatism (i.e., the need for Catholics to prepare for a future in a Communist dominated bloc) and fantastical hopes (of converting Russia to Christianity). Its appeal was to Catholics who were leery of the West and of capitalism, who wanted to more energetically match the Communists in work for social reform, and whose Russophilia outweighed any reservations about the Soviet Union and its sinister past. Unlike Straka, however, Kolakovič never equated Catholic interests with those of the KSS. In early 1946, several students with ties to him were arrested as members of underground networks, which led to Kolakovič's arrest, several months of being investigated while in detention, and eventual release in July 1946, after which he emigrated to Belgium.[151]

Another option for Catholics was legal passive resistance. Simply waiting for their bishops to convey to the authorities Catholic dissatisfaction with the new regime and desire for redress of their grievances was not enough for many Catholics. In December 1945, large numbers of them, especially students, began wearing small metal crosses, generally affixed to their lapels.[152] While far less dangerous than involvement in the underground, the so-called Cross Action drew immediate attacks from the Communists. The KSS took the Cross Action very seriously, regarding it as a blatant political provocation. The Communist press attacked the action as the work of antistate elements, namely supporters of the wartime regime trying to hide behind Christian symbols.[153] From its very beginning, the party tried to find out who was wearing the crosses, where they came from, and how they got them.[154] By January, Communist run commissions were taking administrative measures against the action. The Commission of Education, for example, sent a circular to the directors of every school in Slovakia, asking them to identify wearers of crosses, investigate how they got them and why they were wearing them, and take measures to ban their display.[155] Communist rhetoric encouraged violence. For example, after a rally of Partisan organizations in late January in Banská Bystrica, cross-wearing Catholics were harassed and assaulted on the street, their crosses forcibly removed.[156] *Hlas oslobodených*, the organ of the Communist dominated Union of Anti-fascist Political Prisoners in Slovakia, urged in early March that it was time to put the cross-wearers in their place.[157] *Katolícke noviny* rallied to the defense of the cross-wearers. While acknowledging that there may be cases of people wearing crosses for antistate reasons, the newspaper interpreted the action as a popular expression of people's Catholic faith and their disapproval of the anti-Catholic measures taken by the state since it came to power in spring 1945.[158] It also pointed out that these were the same crosses worn in conjunction with the Statewide Congress of Catholics of the Czechoslovak Republic held in Prague in 1935. On February 12, the Commission of Education issued a ban on the wearing of any sort of insignia at high schools, trade schools, and teachers training schools, except for the symbol of the Czechoslovak Republic and ribbons in the national colors.[159]

Besides the cross, another rallying point for Slovak Catholics was the person of Jozef Tiso. Catholic actions on Tiso's behalf ran the gamut from peaceful interventions by the bishops with the state authorities to acts of vandalism. The KSS was extremely concerned about Tiso, and at the meeting of its Central Committee on November 26, 1945, party leaders discussed Tiso and his upcoming trial in great detail.[160] Friš gave the main report, laying out the party's goals and the means toward achieving them. The trial was to be used not only against Tiso, but also against the Populist movement, Slovak separatism, and clericalism. It was to be combined with a purge of Slovak public life. The KSS was to make an effort to isolate Tiso from Catholicism by stressing his betrayal of Catholic Poland and his alliance with Nazis, racists, and neopagans, all condemned by the Vatican, and by engaging Catholic clergy in the anti-Tiso campaigns.[161]

The party planned and began implementing a multifaceted and multilayered propaganda campaign, involving newspapers, radio broadcasts, film presentations, photographic exhibits, posters, and leaflets. Communist controlled organizations, including Partisan and wartime resistance organizations, were to organize rallies across Slovakia, at which participants would call for Tiso's execution. Collections for the widows and orphans of fallen Partisans were linked with the anti-Tiso campaign. Friš recognized that the trial had far-reaching political significance, especially with respect to Slovak Catholicism, and proposed that the SNR appeal to the Slovak bishops to take a clear position regarding Tiso and other priests suspected of war crimes. He also stressed the importance of getting the DS involved in the anti-Tiso campaign, though he recognized some serious obstacles to this—the DS's desire to attract the former Populist vote and the fact that some of the DS's functionaries, as Agrarians, had cooperated with Tiso when Slovakia got autonomy in October 1938.[162]

At the time the Communists were formalizing and launching their anti-Tiso propaganda campaign there were sporadic manifestations of pro-Tiso sympathy among the Slovak population. These included the distribution of illegal leaflets protesting Tiso's arrest and imprisonment, local petitions calling for his release and a referendum on his guilt or innocence, applause when Tiso appeared on newsreel footage before movies, the smashing of windows at the Czechoslovak Foreign Information Office where a photograph of Tiso in chains was displayed, and pro-Tiso shouts at rallies.[163] The KSS and the Slovak police looked upon these localized, sporadic incidents with great concern.

Tiso also found some support in more official places. On January 8, 1946, Kmeťko and five other Slovak bishops wrote a letter on Tiso's behalf to the presidium of the SNR.[164] The bishops justified their intervention both on the grounds that Tiso was a priest and that his case would have "far-reaching influence on the opinion and behavior of parts of the Slovak nation towards the ČSR and its representatives."[165] They went on to make the following case. First, they contended that Tiso was known as a zealous priest who lived a blameless life, never personally enriching himself from his career. Second, they argued that in public life he strove for the good of the whole and that the majority of Slovaks are convinced that his intentions were the best. Third, they criticized the one-sided judging of Tiso in the Slovak media at the time. Rather, his accomplishments needed to be taken into account along with his mistakes, and it was the bishops' belief that the former outweighed the latter. Furthermore, Tiso had to be evaluated in accordance with the context within which he operated. The bishops pointed out that the events connected with the Žilina Agreement, where Slovaks demanded and received autonomy on October 6, 1938, from a Prague leadership reeling from the trauma of the Munich Agreement, was not the work of Tiso and the Populists alone, but "of almost all Slovak political parties." (The bishops left unsaid, but it is clear from the context, that this included some DS leaders now in the postwar leadership of Slovakia.) They also pointed out that Slovakia's declaration of independence of March 14, 1939, which was seen as Tiso's ultimate act of betrayal of the republic, was, as documents released after the war showed, a result of an impending threat from Hungary. Regarding the notorious anti-Semitic decrees of the Slovak state, the bishops argued that Tiso nearly resigned in protest against them and worked to moderate them and to prevent a greater evil. Finally, the bishops asserted that efforts to evoke hatred of Tiso were socially divisive, precisely at a time when national unity was needed for the daunting task of postwar reconstruction facing Slovaks. In conclusion, they urged that Tiso's case be solved "in a tactful way and not with ruthless rigidity."

Thus, Slovak Catholics, in the fall and winter of 1945–46, pursued a number of options that were independent of or went beyond the circumscribed party politics of postwar Slovakia. Some Catholic intellectuals and activists, however, began to seek a place for Catholics in those politics by supporting the creation of a Catholic party. They were joined, in October 1945, by a number of disgruntled Catholics from the DS. During that month, sixteen Catholic parliamentary representatives from the DS met at Kempný's office to discuss secession from the DS and the formation of a new party.[166] They were disaffected because they held disproportionately fewer seats among the DS contingent in Parliament than they felt they deserved, because they had relatively little influence in the DS and because they did not get along with the Protestant parliamentarians in their party.[167] Of the sixteen representatives in attendance, all but two voted to create a new Christian Republican Party (KRS).[168]

When it came to determining the character of that party, however, its founders were divided. While most could agree that it should be a progressive party in its view of political and socioeconomic life, there were differences regarding the party's relations to the question of Slovak nationalism and autonomy.[169] Some wanted to unite the party with the efforts of Vavro Šrobár to found a party in Slovakia, efforts which had the backing of President Beneš.[170] Most, however, realized that Šrobár, a lapsed Catholic with a well-justified reputation as a staunch supporter of a centralized Czechoslovakia and opponent of a distinct Slovak national identity, would be unable to generate more than a minimal following in Slovakia. Others, namely Kornel Filo and Ján Ševčík, wanted a party that stressed the connection with the Czechs but which was manifestly Catholic and not connected with Šrobár. Kempný, and Miloš Bugár, a former secretary of the Czechoslovak People's Party in Slovakia, favored a party that stressed Slovak nationalism and had a modern character similar to the Christian Democratic parties then emerging in Western Europe. This view resonated with that of many members of the young Slovak Catholic intelligentsia outside the DS, whose leader, Čarnogurský, had been pursing the idea of a Catholic party already since at least July.[171] In early December, the circle of activists around Čarnogurský held a joint meeting at the offices of *Katolícke noviny* with the Catholic secessionist group from the DS and other Catholic intellectuals, where they came to agreement on key questions regarding programmatic and personnel concerns of the new party.[172]

The Communists and Democrats responded very differently to Catholic attempts to establish a new political party. For the Communists, this new development was seen as an opportunity to lure voters away from the DS and divide the large non-Communist vote in Slovakia. A second non-Communist party could thereby enable the KSS to win a plurality. The idea of using a third political party as a means to split the DS was on the minds of some Communists already in the springtime, and they broached it at a joint meeting of the central committees of the KSČ and KSS on July 17–18, 1945.[173] New KSS chairman Viliam Široký became the prime advocate of this tactic, arguing that a third party "will ease the situation in the National Front; discussion will not be between two, but between three parties; at times, we can rely on the right, at other times on the left party."[174] This, of course, presupposed that the third party would indeed be more leftist than the DS. Some Communist leaders feared, rather, that a Catholic party in Slovakia would be clerical and reactionary, concentrating and energizing those forces who formerly supported the HSĽS.[175] Nevertheless, the KSS not only took steps in late summer of 1945 to improve its relations with the church and with certain Catholic intellectuals, but it began to encourage Catholics in the DS to form their own party. According to Kempný, Široký even visited him at his office to encourage him to submit a proposal for a new party to the Slovak National Front.[176] Čarnogurský likewise notes that, around the same time, a group of Communists from Nitra visited Bishop Kmeťko's residence in order to convey their approval of a Catholic party.[177]

The DS had even greater reason to fear a Catholic party than the Communists had for placing hopes in it. First, it would entail a rift in the DS and mean the secession of the Catholic faction, effectively undermining Democratic attempts to draw Catholics into their fold. Second, it would present a formidable new rival for the DS in the upcoming election. Catholics who may have voted for the DS as the lesser evil, out of fear of Communism, would now have a potentially more attractive alternative. Nor was the possible reinvigorating of the Populist current in Slovak political life something many Democrats would welcome.

The DS had its work cut out for it in the winter of 1945–46. The party needed to thwart the establishment of a Catholic party and thereby prevent a split in its own ranks. But simply forestalling the establishment of a Catholic party would not be enough. At the time, there were indications that many Catholics might vote for neither Communists nor Democrats in the upcoming parliamentary elections, but rather turn in blank ballots (so-called *biele lístky*). A DS activist in the region around Topoľčany reported that former Populists were urging this move, which was supported by the local Catholic clergy. Democrats needed to counter this campaign, as it would serve to strengthen the KSS by keeping the non-Communist forces in Slovakia disunited. With elections slated for spring 1946, the DS urgently needed to woo Catholic voters.[178]

During the winter of 1945–46, the DS energetically sought to reach out to Catholics through articles in its periodical press. Democratic writers placed increasing stress on the party's Christian worldview,[179] and *Čas* and *Nové prúdy* went to pains to deny that the DS was anti-Catholic. Past Catholic contributions to the Slovak national cause, and past cooperation between Catholics and Protestants in Slovakia, were praised.[180] DS speakers and writers, such as the Catholic priest Jozef Lukačovič, denied Communist accusations that the DS was a Lutheran party.[181] Like the KSS, the Democrats made a rhetorical distinction between those Populists who betrayed Czechoslovakia, and the Catholic and even HSĽS rank and file. Lukačovič warned against confusing political Catholicism with religious Catholicism.[182] An article in *Nové prúdy* in February denied that the Catholic people and clergy were to blame for problems in relations between Czechs and Slovaks in the interwar period. It went on to argue that Slovak Catholics were against Slovak independence and wanted a resurrection of the Czechoslovak Republic. It pointed out that many Catholics fought in the Slovak National Uprising, including predominately Catholic Slovak units which helped liberate parts of the Czech lands. The author asserted that it was individuals seeking personal glory and profit, not Slovak Catholicism, that betrayed Czechoslovakia.[183]

While denying Catholic charges of repression of Catholicism and persecution of the Catholic Church, Democratic writers acknowledged and condemned certain excesses in government policy against Catholics. These included an overreaction to the petition action of the summer of 1945 (an overreaction that DS leaders at the time themselves took part in), the removal of crosses from schools, and the codes against clerical dress by teachers, which served to exclude from the teaching profession teachers from religious orders.[184] DS periodicals were sure to point out all the party had allegedly done, and was planning to do, to further the interests of Slovak Catholics. DS representatives in the SNR were given credit for championing church-run dormitories, schools run by religious orders, and higher state salaries for clergy.[185] An article in *Nové prúdy* stated, "The leadership of the DS is not only ready, but considers it as its obligation to satisfy the claims of the Slovak Catholic majority for seats in the SNR and National Assembly, which would finally stop the gossip about it being a Lutheran party. It has decided to respect the religious divisions in drawing up its candidate lists and give to each what belongs to him."[186]

Evidence of a reinvigorated DS committed to attracting Catholics was seen in the party's internal publications and correspondence. *Zápisník*, the newsletter of the DS secretariat, wrote in its February 25, 1946, issue that "finding peace between Catholics and Lutherans is one of our primary goals. . . . To a genuine Democrat it is all the same whether a Catholic or a Lutheran stands at the head of his district or local organization; we want and require only that he be capable and morally, politically, and nationally spotless."[187] Democratic Party officials were instructed to encourage good relations between Lutherans and Catholics, and not to blame Catholics for the destruction of the First Czechoslovak Republic. *Zápisník* also urged local party secretaries to be sensitive to the local context in which they were operating, including its religious composition.[188] The regional secretary in Nitra, for example, on February 14 instructed party secretaries in his district to make sure that party functionaries were chosen above all from the ranks of Catholics.[189] The DS also took care not to condemn the wearing of crosses that swept Slovakia at the turn of 1946.[190]

Another way the DS sought to attract Catholics was by distinguishing itself from the Communists on the crucial question of religious education. Both the KSS and the DS came out officially against parochial schools right from the beginning. Yet neither party advocated the sort of radical secularization of public education to which, for example, many Americans have been accustomed in the latter part of the twentieth century. The KSS, so as not to alienate religious believers who made up the vast majority of Slovaks, favored students taking religious instruction classes at school, with specific teachers for each confession. In their pitch to Catholics in early 1946, some Democrats went much farther, proposing religious education across the curriculum—that is, education permeated by a Christian worldview.[191]

The tug-of-war between Democrats and Communists over the issue of a Catholic party can be seen in several developments from late winter of 1946. On January 9, *Pravda* reported that the KSS's Broad Presidium at its recent meeting in Košice had announced that it had no objection to a change in the party political structure in Slovakia that would contribute "to a consolidation of the progressive and democratic forces."[192] In the wake of this apparent Communist endorsement of a Catholic party, Lettrich met with high church officials to discuss the possibility of meeting Catholic demands within the framework of the DS.[193] At the same time, Rudolf Fraštacký, a leading Democrat and commissioner of Food and Supply, met with Čarnogurský and other Catholic intellectuals and urged them to seek their goals within the DS and negotiate with Lettrich and Ursíny.[194] In mid-February, Lettrich, at a working conference of the DS in Žilina, gave a report in which he rejected the idea of a Catholic party on the grounds that sooner or later such a party would be taken over by reactionary and antistate forces, "the heirs of fascisized clericalism," as he put it.[195] *Pravda* responded by defending those Catholic circles in the DS that supported a Catholic party, arguing that the Catholic opposition in the DS "originated out of dissatisfaction with the reactionary policy of the leadership of the DS."[196] Then, on March 11, the DS's executive committee resolved to replace its two commissioners who were involved in organizing the new party, Filo and Ševčík. The KSS came to the defense of these dissident Democrats, and by blocking acceptance of the DS move in the SNF and attaching unacceptable conditions to it, enabled Filo and Ševčík to remain in their posts.[197]

Meanwhile, plans to establish a Catholic party were proceeding apace. In early January, its organizers met with a delegation of church dignitaries, led by Archbishop Kmet'ko, where they discussed issues of interest to the church, especially education.[198] The bishops had no objection to the formation of a Catholic party. Other obstacles, however, presented themselves. Any changes in the political party structure in Slovakia needed the approval of the Slovak National Front, which was composed of representatives from the DS and KSS.[199] While the DS was hostile to the idea of a Catholic party, even the

KSS had certain qualms. As Barnovský writes, the Communists "wanted the new party to emerge at the expense of the DS and be 'more democratic' than the DS, to rouse Catholics but not be a new Catholic, confessional form of the HSĽS, to be a mass party of influence but not more influential than the KSS, to be an independent party, but at the same time obedient."[200] Beneš, at first favorably inclined to a Catholic party in Slovakia, became cool to the idea after it became clear that the party was unlikely to end up in the hands of Šrobár and his supporters. On March 5, the KRS submitted its request to the SNR for recognition. As justification for the new party, the KRS's organizers pointed to the fact that there were four parties in the Czech lands but only two in Slovakia, and that a party was needed for those citizens of Christian, democratic, and republican sentiments who had not found a place in the existing parties.[201] The party's program stressed that it was for Slovak justice, Christian justice, and social justice.[202] Its rather vague program made no mention of Catholicism specifically, nor of any particular policies that the party advocated. Basically, the KRS shared the support for land reform and nationalization of big industry and finance common to all of Czechoslovakia's postwar parties. It stressed cooperation of all Christian churches and condemned confessional intolerance. It stressed Christian education and wanted schools to educate in a Slovak and Christian spirit.[203] On March 9, the Central Committee of the KSS resolved to meet with the organizers of the new party to discuss Communist objections to its name and to clarify its programmatic points.[204] On March 13, the presidium of the Slovak National Front met and resolved to accept the party, provided that it met two conditions. The first was that the party change its name, dropping the words "Christian" (too divisive) and "Republican" (too reminiscent of the banned Agrarian party, whose official name was the Republican Party of Agriculturalists and Small Peasants). The second was that the new party sign the proclamation of the Slovak National Front, in which the KSS and DS committed themselves to the main principles of the Košice government program. Significantly, these included the condemnation of Tiso and those active in his regime, and the nationalization of schools and dormitories. The KRS had surely hoped to remain silent or ambiguous about these issues, which, if successful, would have distanced them from positions of the DS that were unpopular with many Slovak Catholics. The National Front, however, thwarted this possibility by its insistence that the new party sign on to its proclamation.[205]

On March 20, Cvinček wrote to the Slovak National Front on behalf of the new party.[206] He defended the original and proposed name, arguing that the term "Christian" reflected the party's commitment to Christian principles, was nonconfessional, and conflicted in no way with any SNF resolutions. He defended the term "republican" as in no way an attempt to claim the legacy of the Republican Party, but rather as a way to affirm his party's commitment to the democratic republican form of the state. Cvinček hoped that the SNF would now accept the KRS, but if not, he proposed the alternate name of Party of Freedom (*Strana slobody*). He concluded by agreeing to sign on to the SNF proclamation.

Despite Cvinček's assurances, the organizers of the new party were in fact divided over whether to accept the conditions for permission to operate. A number of them had qualms about the conditions and doubts about the potential success of the new party,[207] and, while willing to go to Prague for the SNF meeting scheduled for March 27 to discuss the matter, still kept the option of a deal with the DS on the table. When this SNF meeting was put off until early April owing to a scheduling conflict with the Czechoslovak Communist Party Congress, several leading Catholics perceived a delaying tactic aimed at depriving the new party of sufficient time to prepare for the spring parliamentary elections. Consequently, Cvinček authorized Kempný and Bugár to draft an agreement between the Catholics and the DS, which they did at the Slavia Café in Prague on March 27. That evening, the draft was presented to Ursíny, and the next day DS and Catholic representatives met to finalize the agreement, which was signed on March 31 at Lettrich's apartment in Bratislava as an inner-party document. Because it was not ratified until the DS's presidium met on April 5, and the public informed of it only on April 7, it became known as the April Agreement.[208]

The April Agreement read like a Catholic wish list. The DS's presidium was reconstructed to include Cvinček, Kempný, Bugár, Filo, and another Catholic activist, Emanuel Böhm. Cvinček became a deputy chairman of the party, and two new top administrative posts were created for Kempný and Bugár—general secretary for economic affairs and general secretary for organizational affairs, respectively. It was agreed that Catholics would be represented in all party organs as well as economic and financial enterprises connected with the party at a 7:3 ratio with Protestants. Representation on ballots for parliament and the SNR was to be allotted at a 2:1 Catholic to Protestant ratio, and the newspaper *Demokratické hlasy* was to be transformed into a daily catering to Catholics. Potentially having the most far-reaching electoral appeal was one of the few stipulations that dealt not with personnel but with policy. Article I-3 stated, "As far as education, both in school and out, is concerned, the party leadership holds the view that the party's line should agree with the views of the Christian churches, above all the Catholic Church, and that the DS should pursue this position, if necessary, with regard to the present political situation."[209] Thus, the DS appeared to be committing itself to making the Catholic Church's views on education its own, albeit within the constraints of the current political situation.

The April Agreement marked the culmination of the opening period of Slovakia's postwar political realignment. The Communists saw their efforts to court Catholics pay few dividends, and now had to face the fact that Slovakia's largest potential voting bloc was allying with their sole political rival. If Democrats could convince Slovakia's Catholics to vote for them, a smashing electoral victory was on the horizon. However, the April Agreement threatened to bring disadvantages and dangers to the DS along with benefits. The Catholic Church, for its part, now had a major Slovak political party taking up its cause, but under circumstances that would expose it to some of the same dangers and disadvantages that would plague the DS.

2

BRINGING HOME THE LION

The Democratic Party's Electoral Victory

THE April Agreement represented a watershed in postwar Slovak politics. It had profound implications for relations between Slovakia's Catholics and the DS, between the KSS and the DS, between the KSS and the Catholic Church, and between the Czech lands and Slovakia. The agreement all but guaranteed a DS victory in the May 1946 elections, while at the same time exposing the party as never before to Communist attempts to have it labeled as a nest of fascist collaborators and treated in accordance with that reputation. The Communist pressure on the DS increased during the election campaign and reached a new level of intensity after the large DS electoral victory. Over the ensuing months, the DS was on the defensive from Communist attacks, while the Catholic Church sought to defend itself from continuing pressure from a secularizing state. These developments continued through to the end of 1946 and beyond, when the trial of Jozef Tiso for war crimes increased both the intensity and the complexity of the interrelationship between Catholics, Democrats, and Communists.

In the spring of 1946, the DS faced the immediate challenge of selling the April Agreement both to its own party and to Slovakia's Catholics. On April 5, the DS's Executive Committee approved the agreement, but not without opposition from several leading Democrats, including Milan Polák, Ján Ambruš, Ján Lichner, and Martin Kvetko.[1] Lichner opposed the fact that the agreement was put in writing, something the Catholics insisted upon, fearing that the Communists would use the agreement against the DS.[2] The

Catholic signatories to the agreement, meanwhile, took on the task of winning the approval of Slovakia's bishops. With the exception of Vojtaššák, who was adamant in his desire for a separate Catholic party, the bishops greeted the agreement with approval.[3]

It is not surprising that the April Agreement ultimately won the bishops' approval. It was easier for Catholics to place their hopes in an already well-established party, and one that was promising to defend Catholic interests and in which Catholics would hold a majority of the key positions, than in the chimera of an independent Catholic party. Such a party would have to start from scratch and be hamstrung by the conditions under which the SNF accepted its application. Furthermore, the agreement brought with it a virtual guarantee of an electoral victory in May.

Soon after the April Agreement was publicly acknowledged on April 7, the DS began the job of justifying the agreement and selling it to the Catholic population. On April 11, *Čas* carried an editorial that outlined the DS's defense of the agreement.[4] The author presented the April Agreement as a corrective to the political structure of Slovakia as it emerged after the war, in which Catholics were without a party to represent their interests. This structure, whereby the only permitted parties were the KSS and the DS, *Čas* regarded as an overreaction to the clericalism of the wartime regime, and one which carried with it the danger of Catholic dissatisfaction. The April Agreement, however, was leading Catholics from destructiveness, bitterness, lethargy, and apathy to democracy, responsibility, and positive work for the republic. By bringing Slovak Catholics and Protestants together, it stood in the tradition of Štefan Moyses and Karol Kuzmány, prominent Slovak patriots of the mid-nineteenth century who cooperated despite their religions differences.[5] On April 21, in the Easter edition of *Čas*, Lettrich referred to two further reasons for the April Agreement. He presented the agreement, accurately, as an attempt to preempt efforts by those seeking to destroy the DS by promoting a Catholic secession from the party and pointed to the failure of the KRS to live up to the expectations of its founders.[6]

In its efforts to win Catholics over to the April Agreement, two of the most important Slovak Catholic political figures at the time, Cvinček and Kempný, helped the DS. Cvinček issued a leaflet entitled "In the Spirit of Democratic Unity." Here, he referred to the fact that those Catholics hoping to found an independent Catholic party became disillusioned by the actuality of having to compromise or abandon key principles in order to win official approval for such a party.[7] Though recognizing that the DS had made mistakes in the past that alienated Catholics, he argued that such concerns must retreat before the vital need for "democratic unity." Kempný, in an article in *Čas* of May 9 entitled "In Order That It Is Clear on All Sides," gave a more detailed account of the failure of the KRS, noting that elements began to adhere to it which did not support its goals and that the delays it faced in getting SNF approval left it with insufficient time to prepare for elections. He pointed out the gains in position and influence achieved by Catholics via the April Agreement. Like Cvinček, Kempný placed great stress on the need for all democratic (i.e., non-Communist) forces in Slovakia to stand together in the face of threats to democracy and Christianity that would ensue were the DS to lose the elections.[8]

The April Agreement, as well as the entire effort to found a Catholic party that led up to it, forced the bishops to deal with an issue that had long been on the minds of Slovakia's Catholic hierarchy—the question of priestly involvement in politics. Already in August 1945, the Bishops' Council had agreed that clergy should not participate in partisan political activity, but allowed local bishops to make exceptions.[9] This enabled Cvinček, for example, to engage in Democratic politics, but also made it harder for bishops to prevent clergy like Straka from cooperating with the KSS. With impending elections, and the weekslong campaign preceding them, the bishops resolved in April that no priest may hold a seat in parliament or appear at campaign rallies, for any party.[10] The justifications were that priests were needed to focus on their pastoral duties, and that there were sufficient numbers of lay Catholics available to defend the church's interests in politics. Still, the ban was quite limited. First, it did not prevent priests from holding seats on the SNR, or positions on the Board of Commissioners or in the government. Nor did it prevent them from engaging in politically oriented journalistic activities, including the writing of campaign leaflets. Second, the ban on clerical participation at campaign rallies was violated by clergy on both sides.[11]

While the DS, and in particular its leading Catholics, were trying to sell the April Agreement, the KSS was countering with efforts to discredit the agreement, the DS, and the Catholics who were party to the pact. Husák addressed the matter in the Provisional National Assembly on April 12, calling the agreement a dangerous first step, bringing back into Slovak political life those forces against which the Slovak resistance had struggled during the war. He labeled the agreement an attempt to misuse the religious feeling of Slovaks for reactionary political goals and denied that these "reactionary activists" had the right to speak for the tens of thousands of Slovak Catholics who were in the KSS.[12] Writing the lead editorial in *Pravda*'s Easter edition (yes, Communist newspapers had Easter editions, and Christmas and Pentecost ones as well), Husák went further in his assault on the April Agreement, likening it to the Žilina Agreement of October 1938, in which the precursors of the DS made a pact with the Populists.[13] To Husák, the April Agreement was not in the tradition of Moyses and Kuzmány, but of Hlinka and Rázus, the respective leaders of the Slovak Catholic and Lutheran nationalist camps in the 1920s and 1930s. He anticipated opposition to the agreement from within the DS, particularly from antifascist Partisans unwilling to tolerate the "ludakization"[14] of their party, and from Protestants who would not appreciate being the target of a "*numerus clausus*." Seen through the Marxist-Leninist lenses of the KSS, the April Agreement was "a reactionary plot to maintain bourgeois-capitalist institutions."[15]

In responding to Communist attacks on the April Agreement, the parties to the agreement pointed out Communist hypocrisy in a number of ways. Kempný mentioned how, in the months before the signing of the agreement, he and his Catholic cohorts were being courted by the Communists, who regarded them as good patriots and lamented that they were being marginalized in the DS.[16] When the Democrats sought to accommodate these disaffected Catholics, however, Communists changed their line at once and began to pillory the deal as an alliance of "big landowning agrarianism and clerical reaction."[17] Kornel Filo, responding to Husák's charge in the Provisional National Assembly, argued that before the April Agreement, the KSS attacked the DS as a Lutheran party that excluded Catholics from positions of influence. With the April Agreement, however, the KSS changed its stance abruptly and presented the DS as trying to sow religious division within Slovak society through an alliance with reactionary Catholics.[18] The DS also exposed the hypocrisy in the Communist charge that former Populists were somehow unreliable, antistate elements. *Čas* and Kempný both cited a comment made by Husák, as deputy chairman of the SNR, on August 5, 1945: "I know that among the Populists were many honorable people, very many good Slovaks. The Populists wanted Slovaks to be lords in Slovakia, and many of them honorably tried to solve social questions. Up to 1938, they fought for autonomy."[19] Kempný used this admission by Husák to announce that he was not ashamed of his own political past in the HSĽS, for he was fighting precisely for that Slovak autonomy now stipulated in the Košice Agreement of 1945.[20]

The bitter controversy over the April Agreement belies the fact that the Slovak parties had agreed to conduct the campaign leading up to the May 26 elections "in an appropriate manner and without personal attacks."[21] On February 28, the SNF set up a commission of two Communists and two Democrats to monitor the campaign speeches and party press with this goal in mind. On March 23, the parties agreed to conduct the campaign "in harmony with the principles of the Košice government program," to develop their programs "positively" and to refrain from "polemics of personal defamation unconnected with principles." Party leaders were obliged to discuss any violations of this agreement should they occur. The parties additionally agreed to cooperate with each other after the election, regardless of their outcome, in forming a government.[22] In May, the parties of the SNF reiterated their commitment to this agreement "in the interest of consolidation and the unity of the Slovak nation" and resolved to issue directives to their organizations and agents along these lines.[23]

Despite these agreements, the election campaign was fought aggressively and bitterly, and nowhere more so than over issues connected with the Catholic electorate. Those Catholic voters in Slovakia who were not enticed by the April Agreement and the arguments of the DS had three basic alternatives—vote for the KSS, vote for the new, ostensibly Catholic, Party of Freedom, or vote with so-called blank ballots (*biele lístky*), the latter being a way to register one's disapproval with all of the parties. The KSS's strategy was to weaken the DS by drawing Catholic voters away from it, preferably to vote for the KSS, but also for the Party of Freedom or with blank ballots.

The question of blank ballots was a very controversial one in Czechoslovakia in the first months of 1946 right through the elections. The idea was first proposed by KSČ leader Klement Gottwald in the Czechoslovak National Front on January 16, and immediately opposed by the DS and Czechoslovak National Socialist Party, who saw it for what it was, an effort to deprive these parties of votes.[24] As the National Front was unable to resolve the matter, the Provisional National Assembly settled the issue in favor of blank ballots by a 155 to 131 vote. This meant that the DS would have to convince Catholic voters not to exercise this option. DS efforts in this regard also had to take into account propaganda from the Slovak underground, which was urging Slovaks to vote with blank ballots, and to mark them with a cross, to show their refusal to recognize Czechoslovakia's new political order as legitimate.[25]

In fighting against the use of blank ballots, DS spokesmen had to point out that such ballots represented not only wasted votes, electing no one, but also played into the hands of those who wanted to splinter and thereby weaken the Catholic and Democratic camps.[26] A writer in *Čas* urged Slovaks to "Watch out! Blank ballots are a bait that lures those who are blinded by narrow partisan hatred," a reference to those Catholics who remained loyal to the Populist spirit and shared the underground's hostility to the Democrats as traitors.[27] There was also the fear, expressed in a DS leaflet and the party's internal newsletter, that should a large number of Slovaks vote with blank ballots, the Communists would use this to present Slovakia as a hotbed of reaction in order to justify harsh measures of control there.[28] That blank ballots served Communist interests was best expressed in the slogan of the time, "White ballots turn red in the ballot box." In attempting to dissuade Catholic voters from using the blank ballots, DS spokesmen pointed to, among other things, Pope Pius XII's Easter message of 1946, in which the Holy Father reminded Catholics of their moral responsibility to vote, with the implication that voting with a blank ballot was not what the pontiff had in mind.[29]

Despite the considerable controversy over the blank ballots, the DS won a victory in that relatively few Slovaks exercised this option in the May elections. Only 12,724 of a total 1,612,216 ballots cast were blank.[30] A DS situation report from the region around Topoľčany noted in early May that once the April Agreement was concluded, the movement for blank ballots collapsed in that heavily Catholic part of Slovakia.[31] Nevertheless, the DS victory was a Pyrrhic one. After the elections, the KSS opted to present the low proportion of blank ballots as evidence not that Slovakia had few reactionaries, but that its many reactionaries were voting for the DS.

Another alternative for Slovak voters feared by the DS and fostered by the KSS was the Party of Freedom. At its core were those Slovak Catholics who did not accept the April Agreement and followed through on plans to secede from the DS.[32] The party's raison d'être became to attract Slovak Catholics away from the DS, but it met little success. It openly trumpeted its support for policies supported by the church, including religious education in the schools. On May 15, its newspaper *Sloboda* even called for the return of parochial schools, which evidently touched a nerve with the regime, because that same newspaper two days later came out in support of the nationalization of education.[33] Its leader, Šrobár, had a long record of hostility to traditional Slovak Catholicism and nationalism, and most Slovak Catholics viewed the party as an affiliate of the Czechoslovak National Socialist Party.[34] The party also had little time to organize, and the Slovak bishops made it clear that it did not have their endorsement.[35] Nevertheless, the DS regarded it as a danger and publicly urged Slovaks to avoid its blandishments, meager though they were. For example, in a leaflet of May 16, Cvinček accused the Party of Freedom of dividing the democratic front at a time when Slovakia's future was being decided and reproached the new party for supporting blank ballots and not attacking the Communists in its press.[36] The Communists, for their part, presented the Party of Freedom in a positive light. In distinguishing it from the DS, *Pravda* reported that it was founded by "responsible elements" from the DS.[37] As an alternative for Slovak Catholics, the Party of Freedom was almost a complete failure. In the parliamentary elections, it received only 60,195 votes, or less than 4 percent of the Slovak vote.[38]

While the KSS placed some of its hopes in the blank ballots and the Party of Freedom, a full frontal assault on the DS combined with a vigorous appeal to Catholic voters was the keystone of Communist electoral strategy. The Slovak Communists ventured, in word and deed, to portray themselves as friends and defenders of Christianity, and of Catholicism in particular. Communists gave themselves credit for getting an increase in salaries for clergy, for opposing the separation of church and state, and for fighting to overcome "religious prejudice."[39] In an article in *Pravda* on May 1, Novomeský praised Slovak Catholicism for its "magnificent Slavic Cyrilo-Methodian tradition" and its efforts over the ages with respect to the social question, "which corresponds to the most beautiful and glorious tradition of Christianity."[40] He expressed the party's disinclination to wage a Kulturkampf against the church, preferring instead a harmony between state and church. A key part of Communist propaganda was to minimize the differences between Communism and Catholicism, or even to present the two belief systems as ideologically complementary. Husák, while attacking the DS in parliament over the April Agreement, pointed to the tens of thousands of Catholics who were in the Communist Party and argued that a majority of the soldiers and Partisans in the Slovak National Uprising were Catholic boys, among whom there were also Catholic priests.[41] On May 5, 1946, *Pravda*'s regular featured column for working women was entitled "I Am a Catholic and a Communist." It consisted of an account by a Slovak Catholic woman who, impressed by the respect a Communist speaker showed her faith, joined the KSS. She writes, "Hearing her words I felt: I can be a sincere Catholic, and, if I want, in accordance with my faith, to live to help people, as my mother taught me, it would be good to join the Communists, who are helping people. I applied to the party and they accepted me. I am therefore a Catholic and a Communist, and thus, I can best serve my family, the working people, and God."[42] In a leaflet written to appeal to the peasant population, the KSS's central secretariat wrote, "Religious feeling is not in schism with the political program of the Communist Party of Slovakia. In the KSS is a great majority of members who are at the same time good Communists as well as good Catholics or Lutherans. In the KSS are also Roman Catholic and Lutheran clergy."[43]

Personifying this harmony of Catholicism and Communism was Straka, whose views were featured in a front-page appeal entitled "Sincere Words to Slovak Catholic Clergy and People," appearing in *Pravda* shortly before the elections.[44] Straka opened by accusing the DS and Party of Freedom of misusing the religious feelings of the Slovak people by falsely presenting themselves as the only representatives of Slovak Catholicism, thereby taking the Lord's name in vain in violation of the second commandment. He warned Slovak Catholics to be leery of the religious slogans of the DS, because its leaders had at one time supported the separation of church and state. Such misuse of religion, behind which stood the personal and avaricious interests of politicians "who have nothing in common with Catholicism" could only damage Slovak Catholicism, as the church was harmed in the past when the HSĽS pulled her into the political arena. According to Straka, it was only thanks to the Communists that Slovak Catholicism was not equated with the "Tiso-Tuka fascist regime,"[45] and revenge taken against the church and her clergy. The church can also thank the Communists for preventing the separation of church and state and for raising the pay of clergy. In fact, Straka argued that the KSS from the start had always been for full freedom of religious life, "for the support of the fulfillment of the mission of the Roman Catholic Church." Thus, anti-Communism could not be founded on religious reasons; it must have baser motives. By bringing religion into politics, according to Straka, the DS and the Party of Freedom were dividing the nation. Thus, he lamented that Roman Catholic priests sympathetic to those parties were violating their bishops' ban on clerical engagement in election campaign politics. Cvinček in particular was singled out in Communist electoral agitation, mainly because of the public support he gave the DS in his leaflet "In the Spirit of Democratic Unity."

Communist efforts to reach out to Christians on the local level can be seen in a leaflet put out by the District Committee of the KSS in Považská Bystrica, advertising a KSS rally for May 19. In a paragraph entitled "Christians!"—which is worth quoting at length—the KSS showed the degree to which it was prepared to go to court the vote of religious believers, and how it blended class-based tensions with religious rhetoric:

> Therefore, Slovak Christians, have no fear of Communists, who want you, as good Christians, to enhance yourselves socially! If it is moral among those who are frightening you to wear new clothes on every major holy day and earn a good income, it is decidedly unchristian when these people shun you because you are poor and wretched. Yes, we want you to go to church in better clothes, and to go not only to ask God for things in your prayers, but also to thank Him for what He's blessed you with, like those who are frightening you can do, because they have everything they need. Those who are trying to divide you according to religion need only your votes; they need power in their hands and would rather see you humbly praying at the doors of the church, so they could throw you a penny, than inside the church with equality! Therefore, beware! Working Christians, you must not be afraid of Communists, because you yourself will have the word in the KSS.[46]

The DS did not stand idly by while the KSS sought Slovak Catholic votes. Rather, it produced a slew of reasons for why Slovak Catholics should regard the DS as their own. With respect to the past, DS writers both stressed the Slovak Catholic role in the resistance and defended supporters of the wartime regime from the charge of collaboration. Like the Communists, *Čas* pointed to the large number of Catholics taking part in the resistance: "Slovak Catholics, in the overwhelming majority, took part in the resistance to Hitlerite tyranny."[47] At the same time, the DS was careful not to alienate those Slovaks who supported not the resistance but the HSĽS. Kempný, in an article in *Čas* on May 9, wrote that he was not ashamed of his political past as a Populist, because he had nothing of which to be ashamed. He was working, then as now, to solve the Slovak question within the framework of the Czechoslovak Republic.[48] By quoting Czech publicist Ferdinand Peroutka, who opined that the struggle against Slovak Catholicism was one of the biggest mistakes the government made during the First Czechoslovak Republic, *Čas* gave further succor to former Populists.[49]

As far as the present was concerned, DS spokesmen placed much stress on their party's Christian worldview.[50] The elections were presented as a fateful plebiscite between not just two political parties but two worldviews—a Christian versus a materialist understanding of democracy. Only the former could guarantee fundamental human rights. If the latter were to put its stamp on Czechoslovakia's new constitution, civil rights, personal security, and parochial education would be doomed. With the stakes so high, Slovak Catholics had a moral obligation to vote and were reminded of this by *Čas*.[51] It was particularly important that Slovakia's Christian forces remain united in this struggle and resist Communist attempts at *divide et impera*.

Like the Communists, the Democrats also tried to appeal to women on religious grounds. In an article entitled "A Word to Women," it was argued that "it is to the credit of the DS alone . . . that we can freely carry out our religious obligations."[52] Because the DS advocates Christian moral education in the schools, the Slovak family, "living according to Christian principles, lives and falls with the DS." The article praised the Slovak woman as "the guardian of our Christian family life, which in the past preserved our nation from destruction and in the future will be the fundamental pillar of our national life. Thus, the battle of Slovak Christianity with non-Christian Communism is in the first place the battle of Slovak women."

The DS appeal to the defense of religion was closely tied to education, an issue in the forefront of the minds of many Catholics. A DS campaign leaflet cited a Communist commentary on Soviet education, which stated that "the school should train militant atheists, who not only don't believe in God, but who will lead a systematic and persistent struggle against religion of every kind."[53] The leaflet went on to attack the "red priest" Straka, who, as a functionary in the Commission of Education, allowed the Our Father, the Hail Mary, and religiously derived greetings "*Pochválen*" and "*S Bohom*" to be removed from the schools. In an appeal to voters on the front page of the May 14 issue of *Čas*, the DS emphasized that "we recognize the age-old right of the Church to found and maintain its own schools, dormitories, and religious clubs," and expressed its support for school reforms and laws that took into regard "the interests of the family, the Church, and the state."[54] The appeal called for religion to be an obligatory course in elementary, secondary, and vocational schools, and for the teaching to be carried out in a Christian spirit. Among other things, the appeal asserted that textbooks should not contain interpretations that oppose Christian feelings, that students be free to venerate Christian symbols and take part in religious ceremonies, that bishops have the authority to oversee religious teaching and curriculum, and that teachers of religion receive adequate compensation. These positions were essentially identical to those taken by Slovakia's Catholic bishops.

Part of the DS's approach to Catholics was to expose the hypocrisy behind Communist attempts to woo Catholics. Democratic periodicals regularly pointed out cases where Communists presented themselves as friends of Catholicism, misusing the symbols of religion in accordance with the slogan "the end justifies the means."[55] *Čas* repeated the observation of Pope Pius XI, in his 1937 encyclical *Divini Redemptoris*, that Communists have learned to moderate their programs and mask their hostility to religion whenever the situation warrants it.[56] Straka in particular was cited as a Catholic Judas in service of the Communists, working toward this end.

The KSS kept close tabs on Democratic electoral campaign propaganda and actions, primarily in order to demonstrate that the DS was violating the preelection agreement against negative campaigning and harboring elements disloyal to Czechoslovakia, its people's democratic regime, and the Košice program. Communist archives contain much data that the party collected on Democratic campaign slogans, leaflets, and speeches, as well as accounts of conversations allegedly overheard by Communist informers. The KSS kept specific track of manifestations of anti-Communist, anti-Soviet, anti-Red Army, anti-Czech, and antistate sentiments by DS speakers and supporters, including Roman Catholic clergy. KSS files include numerous descriptions of things such as anti-Communist graffiti, anti-Communist sermons by priests, physical assaults on Communists, priests pressuring voters to vote against the KSS, and so forth.[57] Included in this data are accounts of priests and DS activists claiming that the KSS intends to close churches, expel catechism classes from the schools, and carry out other attacks on Christianity. Given that their aim was to paint as bleak a picture as possible of the DS with respect to its loyalty to the present regime, these documents are not especially reliable and may contain exaggerations and even fabrications.[58] Furthermore, some of the more vehement expressions of anti-Communism reported were as likely to have come from the Slovak underground as from Democrats. Nevertheless, this material serves as an indication of the KSS's great interest in finding evidence that could cast aspersions on the DS, and of the lengths to which some of the DS's detractors would go to provide such evidence. In one of the more egregious of numerous affidavits submitted to Communist Party officials by informers, a woman from Kural'any wrote, "After a speech on May 18, 1946 by Commissioner Kvetko, a supper was organized by members of the DS. I listened from beneath the window and learned that their conversation was directed against the Soviet Union and the celebrated Red Army, because, among other things, I heard it said that the Red Army was uncivilized [*nekultúrna*]."[59]

While most of the conflict and animosity between the KSS and the DS was manifested in propaganda attacks on the other, at times physical violence was part of the campaign. On several occasions, KSS members or sympathizers attacked DS rallies and functions. On May 19 in Žilina, for example, a group of armed Partisans disrupted and vandalized a DS rally.[60] Local animosity between Communists and Democrats also led to a handful of violent assaults on individuals, including murder. In May, a local Democratic activist in Dolný Kubín was shot and killed by a Communist activist, and that same month in Čáry (Skalica district) a member of the DS shot and killed the local KSS chairman. The latter incident resulted from a fight over the posting of Communist placards. In an internal party document, a local Communist alleged that the local Roman Catholic priest may have been responsible for the murder on account of his unrestrained anti-Communist agitation.[61]

While the KSS and DS were slugging it out, the Catholic Church tried, with varying degrees of subtlety, to provide guidance to an electorate faced with a choice between Communists, Democrats, the Party of Freedom, and a protest vote registered via blank ballots. The Catholic bishops, five days before the elections, issued a proclamation to the Catholic public which stressed the great importance of the upcoming elections and the obligation of every Catholic to cast a valid vote (i.e., not a blank ballot). While not explicitly appealing on behalf of any political party, the proclamation stated that "although, as is known, Slovak Catholics were not permitted the sort of party they demanded, yet we are obligated by our conscience to cast our vote for a party that stands on a Christian basis and whose candidates will provide a guarantee that they will defend the freedom and rights of the Church, especially her right to schools and to the training of youth (i.e., dormitories), freedom of the Catholic press, and Catholic clubs."[62] The proclamation went on to deny allegations then current in some parts of Slovakia that Slovak bishops had joined the Party of Freedom.

Several of the major themes of the proclamation were being developed in the Catholic press at this time—that the elections were of enormous significance for the future of Slovakia and the church; that they represented a clash of two distinct worldviews; that Catholics were morally obligated to choose between them and not waste their vote on blank ballots;[63] and that Catholics should choose the party and/or candidates which would best serve Catholic interests.[64] That this was not the KSS went without saying.

As a technically nonpartisan newspaper, *Katolícke noviny* was not permitted to endorse political parties or candidates. Its authors tended to depict the Slovak political situation as confusing and any choice that Slovaks might make as the lesser evil. Nevertheless, the DS was Catholics' best hope for championing issues close to the heart of the church—the legalization of parochial schools and religious dormitories; a Christian spirit in education; greater freedom for the Catholic press; permission for a Catholic organization for youth; and restoration of confiscated church property. The KSS was, and remained, hostile to these desires, while the Party of Freedom was too small, weak, and constrained by the circumstances of its establishment to promise much in this regard. Thus, a Slovak Catholic who followed the directives and recommendations of his bishops and press was most likely to opt for the DS.

And opt for the DS they did. On May 26, the Democrats won a resounding electoral victory, obviously due to the Catholic vote. With 62 percent of the vote, totaling 999,622, the DS more than doubled the Communist share of the vote in Slovakia (i.e., 30.37 percent, 489,596). The Party of Freedom, which sought to lure the Catholic vote away from the DS, drew a paltry 3.73 percent (60,195 votes), while blank ballots accounted for less than 1 percent (12,724).[65] The DS won all nine of Slovakia's electoral regions (*kraje*), from 68.36 percent in Liptovský Svätý Mikuláš to 52.72 percent in Banská Bystrica, drawing as high as 94.89 percent in some of Slovakia's eighty electoral districts (*okresy*) and never below 37 percent. Conversely, in no region did the KSS do better than 39.26 percent (Banská Bystrica). In no district did the Communists reach 60 percent, and in Námestovo they drew as little as 3.05 percent of the vote.[66]

The election results in Slovakia were a marked contrast to those in the Czech lands, where the KSČ won 40.17 percent of the vote, making it the strongest of the four permitted Czech parties by far. A distant second and third were the National Socialist Party and the Czechoslovak People's Party, with 23.66 percent and 20.23 percent, respectively. Though the Social Democrats came in last, with 15.5 percent, combined with the Communists they gave the Marxist parties nearly 56 percent of the Czech vote. This was one of the very best showings for Marxist parties at a time when the Left was running strong in number of European countries.

It is worth comparing the results of the May 1946 elections in Slovakia with the last parliamentary elections in Czechoslovakia, almost exactly eleven years earlier. In 1935, Slovakia's two most popular parties, the HSL'S and the Agrarians, drew approximately 30 percent and 17 percent of the vote, respectively, accounting for nearly half of Slovakia's vote. The KSS drew only 13 percent. By 1946, however, the electoral situation had radically changed. A number of Slovakia's inhabitants were disenfranchised—Germans, Hungarians, and those Slovaks charged with war crimes or with being "politically active" supporters of the Slovak state.[67] Moreover, the HSL'S and the Agrarian Party were outlawed, along with the Hungarian nationalist parties who themselves had drawn 14 percent of the vote in 1935. Meanwhile, the DS had emerged both to take up the banner of the Agrarians and, thanks to the April Agreement, to bring the former Populists back into Slovak political life. Two previously inimical forces in Slovak political life had come together, and for the first time in Czechoslovakia's existence a majority of Slovaks had voted for a single party in a free election. The KSS also made significant gains, from 13 percent to 30 percent of the vote, thanks both to its role in the Slovak National Uprising and to the outlawing of its former chief competitors, but these were no match for the Democrats' electoral tally of 62 percent. The April Agreement had proved to be a success—Catholics and Lutherans, former Populists and former Agrarians, now stood in one camp.

The electoral results came as a great disappointment to Slovakia's Communists. Rather than spend time licking their wounds, however, the KSS, in hand with the KSČ, went on the attack immediately. At the first postelection meetings of the KSČ and KSS Central Committees, held on May 28 and 29 respectively, the Communists resolved to set conditions that the DS would have to meet if it wanted membership in the government.[68] The Communists' goal was in effect to undo the results of the election in Slovakia, by shifting power in the state to an even greater degree to the central government in Prague, by isolating the DS from the other non-Communist parties, and by sowing divisions among the Democrats. In order to accomplish these objectives, the Communists tried to create the impression that Slovakia was infested with fascists, who were let back into public and political life in Slovakia thanks to the April Agreement.

In what was from the beginning a virtual all-out assault on the DS, and its supporters among the Catholic hierarchy and clergy, the Communists used a variety of weapons and approaches. Prominent among these were a press campaign against the Democrats and their Catholic allies; tendentious investigations into the situation in Slovakia by those police organs under Communist control; and the restructuring of relations between Slovakia and the Czech lands to the benefit of Prague. The Communists also sought to compel the DS to identify itself with positions that could alienate its Catholic members and voters, and keep the Democrats from achieving a position in statewide and Slovak organs that would be commensurate with the magnitude of their electoral victory.

No sooner were the election results announced than the Communist press sought to cast aspersions upon the Democratic success. *Pravda*, in a column entitled "After the Elections," attacked the DS for its alleged goal of winning at any price, misusing the religious feelings of the Slovak people, allowing people with a fascist and Germanophile past to set the tone in the party, and taking its antistate, anti-Communist, and anti-Soviet slogans almost literally from the period of the "Slovak State."[69] *Pravda* charged the highest church authorities with violating their own decision to maintain neutrality in the elections and coming out in favor of the DS in the last weeks of the election campaign, thereby once again making Slovakia's pulpits into "places of undignified partisan propaganda." *Nové slovo*, in its first postelection issue, echoed these criticisms and more. Daniel Okáli's lead article charged the DS with allying with clerical reaction, with "the beasts of knavery and murder hiding behind the mask of religion."[70] He reminded his readers that Tiso had decorated murderers with a *Te Deum* (a reference to a Catholic Mass honoring those who helped suppress the Slovak National Uprising), and noted that ex-fascists were wearing crosses. Equating the DS victory with the triumph of Tisoite fascists, Okáli claimed that after learning of the election results in prison, Tiso and his supporters sang "*Hej Slováci*"[71] and shouted "We won!" Okáli concluded his combined attack on the DS and Catholic Church by calling for the seizure of church lands and abolition of certain vestigial feudal privileges still enjoyed by the church.

In the same vein, that same issue of *Nové slovo* included an article by Ladislav Simovič, charging that the old HSL'S was now legally existing under the guise of the DS. Simovič drew a parallel between the Žilina Agreement of October 6, 1938, and the April Agreement, charging that both were made by the same people. He lamented how, with the April Agreement, the DS in one day went from a party of freethinking Lutherans to defenders of Christianity and the church, "more Catholic than the Pope himself." He accused the DS of trying to win Catholic votes by declining to condemn Tiso publicly, and argued that the Democrats' anti-Communist attitude attracted former Populists and Guardists.[72] In order to bolster the impression that an explosive mixture of reactionary Catholicism, Tisoite Populism, and the DS was a threat to the people's democratic regime in Slovakia, *Nové slovo* published the text of two documents—the Piešťany Manifesto of the Young Autonomist Generation of January 14, 1945, and a letter of January 8, 1946, sent by Slovakia's bishops to the presidium of the Slovak National Council on behalf of Tiso.[73] The former document, an avowal of young Slovak intellectuals of their allegiance to the existence and values of the wartime Slovak Republic, was published in an effort to discredit one of the leading Catholic activists in the DS, Jozef Kempný. Even though Kempný was not involved with the Piešťany Manifesto, the Communists took his assertion that he was not ashamed of his Populist past as an invitation to tar him with any purportedly disloyal actions taken by adherents of that movement in the past.

Crucial to Communist efforts to depict their opponents as reactionary threats to the existing order were the actions taken by the police, in this case, the Communist led Ministry of the Interior in Prague and Commission of the Interior in Bratislava, especially its notorious Sixth Department, a center for Communist influence and intrigue.[74] Immediately after the elections, Communists raised the question of DS disloyalty and called for investigations into that party's alleged abuses both during and after the elections. At an extraordinary session of the Czechoslovak government held on May 27, Deputy Prime Minister Široký argued that reconstructing the Slovak National Council on the basis of the electoral results would be tantamount to "putting the administration of Slovakia into the hands of the underground."[75] In reference to the Catholics Bugár and Kempný, he claimed that two of the DS's general secretaries were working to destroy the Republic. Minister of

Information Václav Kopecký, a Czech Communist, labeled the DS as a separatist and anti-Czechoslovak united front of the followers of Hodža, Tiso, and Tuka, reactionary church circles, and out-and-out enemies of the Czechoslovak Republic.[76] Such rhetoric was designed to raise fears of Slovak separatism among the non-Communist Czech parties, and thus to win the support of the democratic Czech parties for strict measures against the DS. On this occasion, the strategy succeeded to the extent that the government resolved to authorize the Interior Ministry to investigate the behavior of the DS during the election campaign.

Not surprisingly, that Communist led ministry soon produced a tendentious report, arguing that the "Populists" were the lords of the situation in Slovakia and proposing measures needed to bring Slovakia back into line.[77] Among these were a strengthening of Prague's control over Slovakia's administrative and security organs, a purge of Slovakia's public and political life, and the prosecution of those politicians who fused their parties into the HSL'S back in October 1938, when the Populists became Slovakia's only legal party. This latter proposal would personally affect Lettrich and Ursíny, both leading Agrarians of the time. The report also called for the transfer of potentially disloyal military units out of Slovakia to the Czech lands.

The DS had serious objections to the report, both procedurally and substantively. At a series of meetings of the Slovak National Front in June and July, Lettrich complained that the DS was being unfairly being singled out, that the Interior Ministry was not cooperating with the SNR and local security organs, and that charges were being made against his party without evidence to back them up.[78] When the venue for deciding about police investigations and measures in Slovakia was the government in Prague, the Communists could get their way, as they could effectively control the discussion and win at least the acquiescence of the Czech parties to some of their proposals. However, when the discussion shifted to the organs in Slovakia, the Democrats had a stronger position and could not be so easily outmaneuvered. Thus, the Democrats were able to make the case that all Slovak parties, not just the DS, should be investigated for alleged electoral campaign abuses, and the Slovak National Front resolved to set up a four-member commission to look into the mutual partisan recriminations over election campaign conduct.

Communist police influence in Slovakia, however, was strong even without help from Prague. The Commission of the Interior, led by the Communist Viktory, produced its own politically colored reports on the situation in Slovakia. At the same time, its Sixth Department was conducting its own investigations, without official authorization, and arresting people it alleged to be collaborators.[79] Nevertheless, despite the strong Communist position in the Slovak security organs, one of the Communists' main weapons against the DS was the strengthening of Prague's control over Slovakia. To this end, the support of the Czech democratic parties was crucial.

In vying for Czech support in their assault on Slovak self-government, the Communists tried to create the impression that Slovakia was pervaded by an atmosphere of unrest. They pointed to an assortment of incidents in Slovakia, some real, some fabricated, some exaggerated, some Communist inspired, designed to show that Slovakia was neither stable nor loyal, and hence needed the strong arm of Prague, and in particular the Interior Ministry, to keep it in line. Communists pointed to disturbances at a soccer game on May 30 in Bratislava, in which fans, including soldiers from Slovakia, ran onto the field three times during the game between Slovakia and the Czech lands; to whistling by students during a performance of *Tartuffe* at the Slovak National Theatre; to Tiso's alleged singing of "*Hej Slováci*" upon learning of the DS victory; to calls in Slovakia for Tiso's release.[80] Communist controlled groups organized protest rallies in Slovakia; Communist dominated trade unions threatened a general strike and carried out a typesetters' strike at the publishing house that produced the Democratic Party's daily newspaper *Čas*; and pro-Communist Partisan organizations threatened forceful interventions of their own.[81] These developments, trumpeted and magnified in tendentious reports by the Interior Ministry, persuaded the non-Communist Czechs in the government to side with the Communists with respect to issues of Slovak autonomy and security, thereby effectively isolating the DS.

With the upper hand, thanks to Czech support, in the government and Czechoslovak National Front, the Communists insisted that the DS meet certain conditions before it be allowed to participate in the new postelection government. Above all, these were to include DS support for a restructuring of relations between the central government and Slovak national organs, for a purge in Slovakia, and for the punishment of "traitors and collaborators."[82] From this point until the Communist takeover of February 1948, Communist calls for a purge of "neo-Populists"—that is, the Catholic wing of the DS—would be incessant. Those very Catholic intellectuals and political activists whom the KSS wooed until April 1946 were now the number one target and enemy in Communist eyes.

A key part of the Communist strategy was to discredit the DS by compelling it to sign on to documents that could both legitimize Communist charges against that party and damage its reputation in the eyes of its Slovak voters, particularly the Catholic ones. One such document was the so-called National Front Proclamation to the Slovak Nation and Czechoslovak Public, signed by Slovakia's parties on June 26, 1946. The document, drafted by the KSS and modified during discussions with the DS, asserted that "in recent months we are witnesses of the fact that irresponsible elements are trying, in Slovakia, to undermine the foundations of the renewed Republic in the spirit of the defeated Populist political ideology."[83] In addition to recommitting themselves to the Košice government program, the values of the Slovak National Uprising, and friendship and alliance with the Soviet Union, the parties agreed on a number of things that could not but upset significant portions of the Slovak Catholic electorate. The parties demanded "a just and severe trial of all agents of the so-called Slovak State, beginning with Tiso, Mach and Tuka, as decisively and quickly as possible."[84] They pledged to support a purge of "traitors, collaborators, and fascist elements" in public life, the army, the whole state apparatus, and the church. In what was clearly an allusion to the April Agreement and the Catholic Church's support for the DS, the proclamation declared that "Slovak political parties most decidedly condemn the misuse of religious conviction for political goals and the breaking up of the nation into hostile religious camps. Let the operation of the churches serve exclusively their mission of moral education, the free performance of which is guaranteed by law." Though the document made no explicit defense of the nationalization of schools, such was implied in its support for the Košice government program. A KSS report from mid-July explains the Communist rationale behind the proclamation:

> By signing it, the representatives of the DS are indirectly recognizing the correctness of the campaign that we are leading against neo-Populism and disavowing the promises which were given to antistate and Populist elements in the preelection period. Even if the Proclamation itself naturally cannot solve the complicated tasks involved in a purge, its political significance lies mainly in the fact that it helps to create the atmosphere necessary for the execution of a purge and facilitates our favoring of contact with the democratic and anti-Populist part of the DS for a common course of action against Guardist and antistate elements.[85]

Thus, the KSS conceived of the Proclamation as a means to sow discord within the DS and alienate the Catholic voters who brought that party its electoral victory in May.

Another document designed to hamstring the DS was the so-called Third Prague Agreement, which laid out stipulations governing the relationship between the central governmental and administrative organs in Prague and those in Slovakia, at the expense of the Slovak organs. The Third Prague Agreement strictly limited the competence of the SNR, subordinating it to the central government. The government received the power to decide whether a particular matter could be left to the SNR, or whether it had statewide significance and thus fell under Prague's purview. Ministers in Prague also got the power to operate in Slovakia, provided they informed the appropriate Slovak commissioner. The government assumed a voice in certain appointments in Slovakia, including the power to approve the SNR's choice for chairman of the Board of Commissioners. By erasing the line separating the jurisdiction of Slovak organs from those of Prague, and leaving it up to the government to decide ultimately whether an issue would be dealt with by the Slovak or the central organs, the Third Prague Agreement crippled Slovakia's capacity for self-government.[86] For example, from June 27, 1946, when the Czechoslovak National Front approved the Agreement, to May 10, 1947, the SNR sent thirty-two proposals to the government for approval; only three were approved unconditionally, and nearly half were denied approval altogether. Like the Proclamation of the National Front, the Third Prague Agreement was designed to bind the DS to positions that most of its voters would find distasteful. Though the leading champions of self-rule for Slovakia, the Democrats suffered the indignity of seeing that self-rule restricted rather than expanded in the wake of their electoral victory. At the Communists' insistence, and with the backing of the other Czech parties,[87] acceptance of the Third Prague Agreement was made a condition for Democratic participation in the government, and DS leaders acquiesced rather than fight a battle they believed, probably correctly, they could not win.[88]

At the heart of Communist measures against the DS was a desire to undo the effects of the April Agreement. On June 11, the Czechoslovak National Front set up a commission to investigate security measures needed in Slovakia, which later reported: "The Commission confirms that a continual source of threat to the security of the Republic in Slovakia, via the legalization of Populism, is the agreement between the leadership of the Democratic Party and the representatives of the Populists under the pretext of an agreement with Catholics. It therefore recommends that the Government take measures toward the abolition of this agreement, which runs counter to the constitutional principles of our democracy as well as to good morals, and measures toward the elimination of the consequences of this agreement."[89] For the Communists, such measures meant above all a purge of leading Catholics from key positions in the DS. The focus was on two of the most prominent and important Catholic activists in Democratic politics, Kempný and Bugár. Aside from press attacks on them and other Democratic Catholic activists, the KSS threatened to challenge the presence of Kempný, Bugár, and two other Democratic parliamentary representatives at the first session of the newly elected national assembly on the grounds that compromising material had been gathered concerning their alleged collaborationist activities.[90]

Due to the vigorous Communist attacks, and the at least tacit Czech support for them, the DS began paying the price immediately for its April Agreement–aided electoral victory. The Democrats' situation was somewhat analogous to that of the Smallholders' Party in Hungary after it won 57 percent of the vote to the Communists' 17 percent in the November 1945 parliamentary elections. It was said at the time that the Smallholders' leader, Zoltán Tildy, was like someone who had won a lion in a lottery and was afraid to bring it home.[91] Lettrich, too, had brought home a lion, and at once had to go to great lengths to keep his party from being devoured by it. At a series of SNF meetings, Lettrich complained of Communist misuse of the police, unjust press attacks, the parliamentary action being planned against Kempný and Bugár, and the fact that the DS alone was being singled out for alleged election campaign abuses.[92] At the same time, he and other leading Democrats, feeling they had no choice but to acquiesce in the Communist sponsored Third Prague Agreement and National Front Proclamation, had to negotiate a modification of the texts of those agreements in an effort to make them less unpalatable. As a way of defending against Communist attacks, the DS sent a circular to its local secretariats urging caution as to whom to let into the party.[93] The Democrats were especially fearful of Communist agents and infiltrators, as well as people with dubious pasts who could easily be exposed as reactionaries, fascists, or Hitlerite collaborators. At the same time, the Democrats had to make sure that they were delivering on their promises made to Catholics. On June 3, the DS presidium instructed its local and district secretariats to implement an immediate reorganization of the party in accordance with the proportion of Catholics and Lutherans among the local population.[94]

Key battlegrounds where the DS had to fight for a practical realization of its electoral victory were the negotiations over the composition of the Czechoslovak government and the Slovak organs of administration and government. In the central government, the DS obtained four seats to the KSS's three, despite having defeated the latter by a two-to-one margin in the elections.[95] Moreover, the overall influence of Slovakia was diminished, with only seven seats being held by Slovaks, down from the previous nine. On the Board of Commissioners, the proportion of Democrats to Communists reflected the electoral results (i.e., eight Democrats to four Communists), but with two important qualifications that represented Communist successes. The chairmanship of the board was given to the Communist Husák, and the Commission of the Interior, which the DS claimed as the dominant party, went to the nonpartisan General Mikuláš Ferjenčík, who did little to challenge the entrenched Communist control of the police.[96] Meanwhile, the SNR was reorganized in accordance with the electoral results, with the DS getting sixty-three of its one hundred seats, and the Communists thirty-one, accurately reflecting the two parties' electoral showing. Lettrich was elected chairman of the SNR, with the Democrats and Communists each holding two deputy chairmanships.[97]

In evaluating the DS's position after the elections, both in Slovakia and statewide, one is struck by the fact that a party that won handily in Slovakia, by a two-to-one margin, found itself immediately isolated and on the defensive. The DS ended up representing a Slovakia that was to have less political clout in Prague than before the elections, with the Slovak organs that it could control being effectively crippled by the Third Prague Agreement. That the DS could not translate its electoral victory into a chairmanship of the Board of Commissioners or control of the Commission of the Interior is an indication of how effective the Communists were in keeping the electoral results from being reflected in Slovakia's power relationships. The dilemma for the DS was that the very development that helped deliver it a crushing electoral victory, the April Agreement, also proved to be the party's Achilles' heel. Without it, the DS may not have acquired the Catholic support necessary to be Slovakia's numerically dominant political force. With it, the party opened itself up to charges of harboring pro-Tiso collaborators and elements disloyal to the people's democratic Czechoslovak Republic. Thus stuck between a rock and a hard place, the DS became an easy target for Communists seeking to subvert and overturn the results of the election in Slovakia.

With respect to Slovak Catholics, internal Communist party documents give some indication of differences within the KSS over dealing with the question of Catholicism in Slovakia. Široký represented the most aggressively anti-Catholic position. At the KSS Central Committee meeting of May 29, for example, he called for the arrest of bishops Škrábik and Vojtaššák as a way to frighten Catholic priests and keep them from mixing into politics.[98] Široký feared the church's influence, noting in a discussion at the Central Committee meeting of July 14 that the main cause of the KSS's electoral failure was that the peasant masses had succumbed to Catholicism.[99] The fact that Catholicism was popular in Slovakia, however, led other Communists to do some soul searching. An undated, unauthored KSS report dealt with the causes of that party's electoral defeat and proposed tactics aimed at improving Communist prospects in future elections. Alongside suggestions that the KSS promote folklore, in particular the cult of Jánošík,[100] and send Soviet autos to Bratislava capable of rivaling the American ones seen on Wenceslaus Square in Prague, the author proposed that the Communist press defend the KSS against charges that the latter was intolerant toward religion. The author went on to urge the KSS press to stop attacking the common Slovak people through its attacks on Populists and Guardists. The report reads, "We must take into account that 'the majority of our common and decent people were Guardists and Populists' (in the words of Marek Čulen in early May to party functionaries in Holíč). But what sort of activity were these Populists and Guardists involved in in the majority? They dressed up on Sundays in Guardist uniforms or just a Guardist cap, went to Church, then home, and that was that. The same was true for the great majority of Populists." Therefore, in the author's view, it was a tragic mistake to speak in the press of a purge of Guardists and Populists; rather, the talk should be of a purge of "lords, spongers, exploiters, and warmongers."[101]

During the summer and autumn of 1946, the KSS continued its efforts to discredit the Catholic Church. Attacks on the church were targeted at bishops and priests, with laypeople left alone unless they were leaders of the Catholic bloc in the Democratic Party. One particular avenue of Communist attack was to associate the Catholic clergy with the Populist movement and Tiso regime, and go on to present them as unreconstructed opponents of Czechoslovakia's new people's democratic regime. In an article in *Nové slovo* in September entitled "What Does the Catholic Clergy Want?," Ondrej Pavlík accused Catholic clergy of a negative stance toward present-day Czechoslovakia.[102] Pavlík complained that fewer than 25 percent of the clergy were engaged in the building of the new Czechoslovak Republic, which was hurting Slovakia's relations with the Czechs, tarnishing Czechoslovakia's image abroad, and facilitating the emergence of the underground campaign against Czechoslovakia's new regime. He concluded with the threatening rhetoric that was not uncommon in Communist attacks on the church: "Under the present situation, when it is necessary to exert all efforts, we must pronounce anyone who is not working [for the Republic] and is in a state of passivity as a saboteur and an enemy of the nation." At times, the Communists let the Catholics provide the rope with which, figuratively speaking, to hang themselves. For instance, in October, *Nové slovo* reprinted an article from *Katolícke noviny* of November 7, 1940, in which the Catholic paper defended clergy from attacks at the time that they were not supporting the new regime. The article trumpeted the Catholic clergy's support for the HSL'S, their financial contributions to its press, their involvement in its local organizations, their warm relations with its officials, and so forth. The article asserted that the Catholic clergy welcomed the Slovak State with great joy, made great sacrifices for it, and were the prime workers of the HSL'S.[103]

A particular target of Communist attacks was Bishop Vojtaššák. In the summer of 1946, a group of Czech journalists touring Slovakia called on him for an impromptu press conference. As a consequence, the Czech press reported that Vojtaššák refused to comment on whether he was for a united state of Czechs and Slovaks and on whether Tiso was a traitor; that he defended his refusal, in January 1945, to recognize the Beneš government when asked to do so by the visiting Vavro Šrobár; and that he had a picture of Hlinka in his office and one of Tiso in his bedroom.[104] Commenting on what had become a minor press scandal, *Pravda* called Vojtaššák "one of the greatest Slovak collaborators" who "did not hide his open sympathy for Tiso and his traitorous regime and negative attitude toward the renewed Czechoslovak Republic."[105] While Vojtaššák was indeed the most pro-Populist of Slovakia's bishops before and during the war, Communist efforts to discredit him were at times dishonest and absurd. For example, in November, an article in *Pravda* attacked him on the grounds that, eight years before the Munich Agreement, he sought German aid.[106] The evidence for this accusation was a letter written by Vojtaššák to HSL'S leader Hlinka in the early 1930s in which he welcomed cooperation between the HSĽS and the party of German Catholics. This disingenuous argument was based on the view that all Germans were Nazis, so that cooperation with non-Nazi Germans in Slovakia three years before Hitler came to power was deemed as collaborationist, playing a role in the "germanization of Slovakia." In another apparently dubious attack, the Czech Communist daily *Rudé právo* published allegations that Vojtaššák forbade a village pastor from ringing his church's bells on October 28, Czechoslovakia's Independence Day. *Katolícke noviny* published a refutation of the allegations by said priest and the chairman of the local national committee.[107]

In attacking the hierarchy and clergy of the Catholic Church, the KSS press at the same time took pains to draw a distinction between the evil, collaborationist clergy and the decent rank-and-file Catholics. *Nové slovo*, in June, in challenging Catholic accusations of persecution in Czechoslovakia, argued rather that it was Populists, not Catholics, who were being persecuted, and that it was time to disconnect Catholicism in Slovakia from Populism.[108] An article in *Pravda*, after attacking Vojtaššák, claimed that he and clergy like him were not representative of the great majority of Slovak Catholics. The author writes, "The Slovak Catholic people are, in the majority, loyal to the nation and Republic, as they showed during the Uprising."[109] Not just Slovak Catholics, but even Populists, found favor in Communist eyes. *Pravda*, in a column in early July entitled "Beware of a Trojan Horse!," which alleged Populist infiltration of Slovakia's governmental and administrative organs and economic life, added that these plans would find little resonance among "the great part of the minor adherents of the former HSĽS, whose interest and goal is to join in the building up of a new ČSR."[110] Even the church itself could be complimented in Communist efforts to avoid alienating Catholics. In a November article in *Pravda* attacking Slovak clergy for collaboration with the Nazis, the author noted that it is Tiso, Vojtaššák, and others, not the Catholic Church, that is guilty of these sins, and argued that Tiso committed his crimes as a politician, not as a Catholic priest and pastor. The article added that "the Catholic Church has, in its teaching, nothing in common with such crimes."[111]

In the wake of their electoral defeat in May, Slovakia's Communists sought to discredit the Catholic hierarchy and clergy as Nazi collaborators, but tempered these attacks in a couple of ways. First, they rarely appeared on page one of Communist publications; nor were they written by the party's leading lights, but usually by lesser-known journalists. Second, they made some efforts to convince common Slovak Catholic men and women that the mud thrown at Catholic bishops such as Vojtaššák was not meant for them. This approach reflected the ambiguities facing the KSS as it tried to undermine the Democratic Party by branding the April Agreement as a pact with the Populists, to weaken the influence of the Catholic Church, and to keep from alienating further Slovakia's Catholic population.

Spearheading the defense of the Catholic Church and its clergy was *Katolícke noviny*. In July, the Catholic weekly responded to systematic attacks on Catholic bishops and priests in several periodicals by contesting Communist attempts to decouple the clergy from the laity. According to *Katolícke noviny*, an affront to the priests was an affront to all Catholics.[112] In August, in response to Communist efforts to discredit the Slovak episcopacy for its behavior during the Second World War, the Catholic weekly published "almost the entire text" of the Slovak Catholic bishops' pastoral letter of March 8, 1943, on the Jewish Question.[113] The letter, which according to *Katolícke noviny* was received with thanks and praise by the whole democratic world, including Czechoslovak Radio in London, applied the teachings of both the natural law and Jesus Christ to the Slovak Republic's policies toward its Jewish minority. The bishops reiterated that no one should be punished without sufficient cause, that an entire group should not be punished for the deeds of some of its members, and that "we must raise our decisive and admonitory voices against measures which impinge upon the personal, familial, and proprietary freedom of our co-believers [i.e., baptized Jews] and co-citizens without the appropriate determination of the guilt of each individual." *Katolícke noviny* used other opportunities to present evidence to counter Communist charges of collaboration—for instance, that the local Gestapo in Nitra reproached the Slovak bishops for not helping the Germans against the Slovak National Uprising, or that those bishops resisted German pressure to issue a joint pastoral letter against the Slovak National Uprising and Bolshevism.[114] The Catholic weekly also rallied to the support of Bishop Vojtaššák in August, when the fallout of his interview with Czech journalists produced a number of press attacks on him. *Katolícke noviny*, for example, defended the fact that the bishop had a picture of Tiso in his abode by pointing out that said picture was in his private quarters, which also contained a large picture of former Czechoslovak President Tomáš G. Masaryk.[115]

The heart and soul of *Katolícke noviny* was a priest, editor, and journalist named Jur Koza-Matejov. Though a combative apologist for Catholicism and

Slovak nationalism, Koza entered the postwar period with the sort of credentials that would allow him to be publicly engaged. In 1925 he had left the HSL'S and his job on the editorial board of its daily *Slovák* in protest against the influence of the pro-Hungarian and later pro-Nazi Vojtech Tuka within the party. During the Second World War, Koza was persecuted for his opposition to the pro-Nazi faction of Šaňo Mach and Tuka. When, in September 1945, the Catholic bishops received permission to publish a Catholic weekly newspaper, Koza became its most prominent writer. A brilliant publicist, writing for a mass circulation weekly read by much of Slovakia's Catholic population, he staunchly and energetically championed Catholicism in frequent columns, in which, among other things, he defended parochial schools, demanded the expansion of the Catholic press, and repelled almost incessant Communist attacks on him and other openly anti-Communist Catholics.

The Communists very much regretted that Koza had gotten onto the editorial board at *Katolícke noviny*. Already in October 1945, the KSS lamented the fact that the Catholic daily was in the hands of men like Koza, instead of the docile Straka.[116] The Communist dominated *Hlas oslobodených* accused Koza of being a "guardist-fascist journalist," a loyal supporter of the Tiso regime engaged in treasonous activity and hostile to anything Czech.[117] Koza replied by citing his bad relations with the Hlinka Guard during the war and the fact that he was looked at with suspicion by the wartime regime, and he claimed to have wept for days in church over the demise of the Czechoslovak Republic. He also expressed his umbrage at the Communist habit of labeling any critics of Communism as "fascist." He told the story of a village woman who was accosted for wearing a "fascist symbol"—a cross. "She replied, 'But the cross is a Christian emblem. If Christ was a fascist, then I too want to be a fascist.'" To which Koza appends, "Yes, I too."[118] Such writing was Koza's response to the sort of violent, threatening rhetoric he had to face, as exemplified by this passage from *Hlas oslobodených* of July 5: "If the competent authorities do not put Koza-Matejov where he belongs, the honest antifascists together with the Partisans will take care of things. It is not possible that people of Koza-Matejov's ilk should further poison our democratic atmosphere. I stress—the patience of the antifascists has its limits. The day is coming when we'll put the traitors who are walking among us in their place, even if we must remove them at the price of incarceration."[119]

Nevertheless, Koza fearlessly advocated Catholic interests on the front pages of *Katolícke noviny*. He was particularly engaged, along with Bishop

Jantausch, in the Catholic struggle for a daily newspaper of their own, *Katolícke noviny* being a weekly that technically was forbidden to engage itself in political matters. As Koza expressed it, Catholics needed an independent, nonpartisan daily that could deal with all current questions, be they political or not.[120] The Communists, however, having enough trouble with *Katolícke noviny*, were hardly willing to allow an additional Catholic newspaper, particularly a mass-circulation daily that would engage political questions more directly. And given the April Agreement, it was easy to argue that defending Catholic interests could not be nonpartisan. The wide gap between *Katolícke noviny*'s self-representation and the Communist view of that newspaper was evident in a press polemic in September 1946. In response to Communist attacks, *Katolícke noviny* ran a front-page column, by Jozef Zadvorský, that stressed its independence of political parties.[121] To Communist charges that the Catholic weekly did not give the Slovak National Uprising its due on its second anniversary in August, *Katolícke noviny* replied that it was similarly reproached by the wartime regime for insufficient enthusiasm about Slovakia's March 14 independence day. Zadvorský went on to claim that *Katolícke noviny* was being attacked from both sides—for being insufficiently supportive of the state, or oppositional, and for being pro-state, or insufficiently combative. This latter reproach was an allusion to attacks on the Catholic press from the radical Populist underground, which regarded Czechoslovakia as totally illegitimate and worthy only of being resisted. *Pravda* seized on Zadvorský's attempt to equate those who, like the Communists, feared the misuse of Catholicism for political ends, with the fascist underground, to whom anything but hostile and aggressive opposition to people's democratic Czechoslovakia was anathema, citing it as evidence that the Catholic paper was cultivating an oppositional attitude toward the state.[122]

A Catholic daily newspaper was only one of the issues that concerned Slovakia's Catholic bishops when they met on August 8, 1946, in Belušské slatiny. Also on the agenda were questions connected with education, property, and detention of Slovaks alleged of past political crimes. Two weeks later the bishops submitted a petition to the SNR and Board of Commissioners, laying out the issues raised at their meeting.[123] With respect to education, the bishops asked for the return of all schools belonging to religious orders as well as those Catholic gymnasia, six in number, which served as early centers of seminary education. In addition, they called on the state to assume the debt of the schools it had confiscated. The bishops also called for the return of all

Catholic dormitories, especially Svoradov, along with the property of Catholic clubs and organizations, and those documents seized earlier from episcopal and parish offices that had yet to be returned. They also asked for compensation for endowments lost by the church during state seizures of its agricultural and forestlands, endowments that went toward helping poorer parishes cover their expenses. The bishops also petitioned for permission to publish a Catholic daily newspaper and for the lifting of the ban on the activity of the Association of Catholic Youth.[124] Finally, they called for the release of those citizens who had been detained for weeks or even months without a hearing, often accused of minor offenses, sometimes groundlessly, and who were not likely to flee the country if released. The bishops expressed their concern that many families were being hurt by the detention of their breadwinners, and that many Slovaks found these detentions unsettling.

In comparison with the bishops' demands of the summer and fall of 1945, the petition of August 21, 1946, was markedly restrained. Apart from the call for the release of detainees, and some demands pertaining to the Hungarian minority, the bishops mainly focused on the return of specific items of confiscated church property and the questions connected with it. This may have reflected a belief that limited, focused demands carried more likelihood of being met.

In fact, however, the bishops' requests had relatively little effect on Slovakia's administrative organs. The Commission of Education was manifestly unsympathetic to the bishops' petition. Aside from a few minor concessions regarding compensation for school property, the commission reiterated its views against parochial education and opposed the return of any schools to the Catholic Church.[125] The Commissioner of the Interior, Ferjenčík, agreed that confiscated documents could be returned to diocesan and parish offices if they were not needed in upcoming trials or hearings, and that those detainees under the Commission's auspices could be freed if they did not pose a threat to flee or engage in antistate activities. At the same time, however, he recommended against permitting a Catholic daily, expressing serious doubts that such a daily would be pro-state, given the political orientation of the bishops. He also opposed the reestablishment of the associations for Catholic or Protestant youth, seeing those organizations as threats to public peace and order.[126] Straka, in his function as head of the religious affairs department of the Commission of Education, urged the denial of a Catholic daily and youth organization.[127]

Straka continued to be a thorn in the side of the Slovak bishops in other ways as well. In the fall of 1946, he was appointed to the state commission responsible for certifying Catholic clergy.[128] He also kept up his service to the Communists through his press activity. In November, for example, he published an article in *Nové slovo* entitled "The Need for Religious Tolerance in Civil Life," which, among other things, asserted that the KSS supported the principle of religious toleration and full freedom of religious confession as well as respect for the feelings of Slovak religious believers.[129]

The case of Straka placed the Catholic Church in Slovakia in a difficult position. Here was a priest who had joined the Communist Party, was championing that party zealously in press writings aimed at a religious audience, and defending educational and cultural policies to which the Catholic bishops were adamantly opposed. Yet, Catholic authorities were reluctant to discipline or silence him. When Straka publicly claimed, however, that his membership and activity in the KSS were approved by church authorities, his bishop, Andrej Škrábik of Banská Bystrica, issued a statement refuting that claim.[130] While the Catholic Church felt free to dissociate itself from Straka, it was not confident enough, given the postwar situation, to run the risk of confronting the Communists head-on over his antics.

Alongside tensions between Catholics and Communists, it became increasingly clear during the summer and autumn of 1946 that the honeymoon between Catholics and the Democratic Party was winding down. At the heart of this problem was the perception on the part of many Democrats, especially Catholic ones, that their party was not taking full advantage of its electoral victory and was behaving too timidly in the face of Communist pressure. A Democratic Party document of August 2 reports that, in one unidentified locale, probably Bánovce, people were losing trust in the DS due to its failure to secure a proportionate degree of representation for itself in the government, SNR, and Board of Commissioners.[131] The report stated that the local population feared the Communists would get their way in deciding who would sit on the local national committee, as the DS was doing little to resist KSS dictates. The Communists were insisting on screening any Democratic candidates for local office, which caused resentment among local Democrats. A DS report of October 1946 from the region around Topol'čany refers to sharp local criticism of the DS due to failure to secure for itself the Commissions of Education and Interior on the Board of Commissioners.[132] A Democratic student group, in a resolution sent to their party's presidium, expressed its dismay that very little of the DS's promises had been realized, despite its smashing success in the elections.[133]

With the DS failing to deliver on its promises, including some of the stipulations of the April Agreement, Catholic discontent began to grow. Immediately after the elections, *Katolícke noviny*, in a front-page editorial, said that the time had come to find out whether the preelection wooing of Catholics on all sides had been sincere. The author mentioned that the DS electoral victory had brought the conditions for a solution to pressing problems connected with Catholicism's place in postwar Slovakia, but that "it is a question of whether the commitments and promises will be fulfilled."[134] Five months later, Koza would write in that same paper that Catholics feel disappointed, and even wronged, especially since the May elections promised more than they fulfilled.[135] Yet, despite a few press references, Catholic disillusionment with the DS, and the related tensions between Catholics and Protestants within that party, was kept largely behind the scenes. On July 22, Cvinček wrote a letter to Lettrich charging that the DS was not holding to the April Agreement.[136] He mentioned that he was receiving protests from Catholic voters who were upset with the candidate lists the DS had drawn up for the party's seats on the SNR. These lists had been drawn up by the party's executive committee, which was dominated by Protestants, rather than in the new presidium, a party organ founded in the wake of the April Agreement in order to give Catholics a majority position in governing the party. By arrogating for itself functions reserved for the presidium, Cvinček argued, the executive committee was keeping Catholics from having a say in the reconstruction of the SNR.

Catholics also felt that they were not being given a share of positions in the DS's administrative structure and economic enterprises in line with the April Agreement.[137] The April Agreement had also stipulated that the DS would hold a Party Congress no later than October 1946 and elect a new party leadership in accordance with a 7:3 Catholic to Protestant ratio. However, the Congress was postponed several times and not held until January 1948, giving another cause for Catholic discontent.[138] KSS documents from early 1947 mention tensions between Protestant and Catholic Democrats over candidate slates, positions in the party's economic enterprises, and influence at *Čas*.[139] By the end of 1946, there were even some Catholic Democrats who tried to revive the idea of a separate Catholic political party.[140]

The stipulations of the April Agreement regarding power sharing and administrative and economic positions for Catholics, essentially an "affirmative action" for Catholics, presented all the major political forces in Slovakia with dilemmas. Catholics had to decide how forcefully and how rapidly to insist on the implementation of the 7:3 ratio; Democrats had to contend with opposition in their party by those who opposed the stipulations; and Communists faced the difficult task of condemning the stipulations while not alienating Catholic voters. The KSS tried to finesse the issue, using it against the Democrats, but not making it a particularly prominent part of their attack. On the one hand, Communist commentators predicted that the DS would not be able to fulfill the promises it had made to Catholics (while the KSS was working energetically to make sure that this prediction would become a reality).[141] At the same time, the Communist press pointed out the problems with allotting a fixed quota of positions to Catholics—it revives confessional divisions in Slovakia, it keeps capable Protestants from finding suitable employment, and it puts unqualified people in key positions, thereby damaging the Slovak economy and nation.[142]

The position of the DS, squeezed between Catholic expectations and pressure against fulfilling those expectations by the Communists and some Democrats, can be seen in the way the trial of Croatian Archbishop Alojz Stepinac played out in the Slovak press in the autumn of 1946. Stepinac was the Archbishop of Zagreb and the leading figure in the Catholic Church in Croatia during the Second World War. Shepherding his flock through those turbulent years, Stepinac both worked with and criticized the fascist Ustaša regime. After the war, his refusal to collaborate with Tito's new Communist regime in Yugoslavia led to a Communist assault on the Catholic Church in Yugoslavia. The centerpiece of this assault was Stepinac's trial, a fraudulent exercise in Communist jurisprudence in which the accused was convicted on shaky evidence of a series of trumped-up charges and sentenced to sixteen years of hard labor for treason, collaboration, and conspiracy against the "Federal People's Republic of Yugoslavia." Slovakia's Communist press wholeheartedly supported Tito's policy and the verdict against Stepinac. *Pravda*, in July 1946, repeated charges by leading Yugoslav Communist Milovan Djilas that the Catholic Church in Croatia was aiding and abetting the fascist underground after the Second World War—housing secret Ustaša archives, hiding war criminals, keeping arms depots in monasteries.[143] A series of articles in *Nové slovo* in the fall of 1946 likewise tried to impugn Catholicism in Croatia, and Stepinac in particular.[144] Straka contributed by asserting the nonbiased nature of the Yugoslav National Court and refuting charges that Stepinac was being persecuted not for collaboration with fascism but rather for resistance to Communism.[145]

The Democratic press came to Stepinac's defense. In July 1946, *Čas* ran an article protesting *Pravda*'s distorted coverage of the situation of the church in Yugoslavia and of Stepinac in particular.[146] After the verdict against Stepinac had been passed in October 1946, *Nové prúdy* published an article on Stepinac that opened with a critique of the press coverage of his case in Slovakia, charging that almost all of it has been negative and very little of it neutral.[147] The author went on to provide considerable evidence in support of Stepinac—that he protected thousands of Jews, especially children, from deportation to death camps; that he wrote reams of letters to the Croatian government protesting against Ustaša atrocities; that he denounced Croatia's fascists in his Christmas radio address of 1942. Likewise, the article called for an understanding of the context in which Stepinac operated, one in which it would have been impossible to remain completely aloof from political and public life. Then, strangely, the author concludes by asserting that "Stepinac was a traitor and deserved his punishment." This article is quite telling with respect to the way the Democrats tried to handle this volatile issue—volatile because of the damage the party could incur should it been seen as siding too closely with a convicted fascist collaborator and prominent anti-Communist, or should it be seen as not siding closely enough with a prominent victim of Communist repression of the religion from which the Democrats drew most of their votes. The author, in affirming the verdict, sought to avoid being identified with Stepinac while at the same time using his professed desire to correct an imbalance in Slovak press coverage to present evidence on Stepinac's behalf. This cagey approach did not go unnoticed and was compounded four weeks later when *Nové prúdy* published a letter to the editor that pointed out just how strange the article was.[148] The letter noted that said article affirmed the verdict of the court of a totalitarian, one-party state, which by definition could not be independent and objective, while presenting only evidence of Stepinac's innocence.

The Stepinac case allowed Communists, Democrats, and Catholics to transfer their domestic conflicts and tensions onto a foreign object. Other issues of the autumn of 1946, however, brought the conflicts home in a more immediate way. The perennial question of educational policy tested Democrat resolve, and capacity, to meet their electoral promises to Catholics, while the intensifying debate over Sundays and religious holidays brought Communists and Catholics face to face over a question the latter regarded as fundamental.

Education was a particularly sensitive issue, fraught with dangers for the DS. It was an issue that many Catholics cared about very deeply, and one where the Communists were unlikely to budge. It was a big blow to the DS, and regarded as such by Catholics, when the Democrats failed to obtain the Commission of Education when the Board of Commissioners was reorganized in the summer of 1946. On August 9, the Democrats presented to the Communists a list of conditions under which they would be willing to abandon their claim to the Commission of Education, which they repeated in a letter to the KSS presidium on August 30.[149] The Democrats demanded that two notorious opponents of Catholic interests in education, Straka and Ondrej Pavlík, be removed from their positions on the commission.[150] The DS also demanded that the commission submit to the SNR a proposal for an amendment of the norms for nationalizing schools and dormitories, and that it see that only Catholic university students be housed in the historically Catholic Svoradov and only Protestants in the dormitory Štefánik. In reply, the Communists accused the DS of trying to politicize personnel matters and went on to put off any decisions on the demands because Novomeský was out of town.[151] In the end, very little was done to accommodate the DS's demands, while the commission itself remained in the hands of the Communist Novomeský.[152]

DS weakness in the face of the Communists was evident in an incident connected with state abuses against a school formerly run by the Sisters of Mercy of St. Vincent in Ružomberok. The provincial directorate of the sisters complained that the new director and inspector of the nationalized school, both Protestants at a school where all the students were Catholics, moved into their convent, taking spaces for themselves to which they were not authorized, dealing with the sisters in an arbitrary and unjust manner, and obstructing them in the performance of their religious and educational duties.[153] On October 20, Lettrich wrote to Novomeský asking him to correct the situation at once ("*hned*"), adding that it was damaging to the reputation of Slovakia's educational administration when it got into superfluous conflicts over living space with religious houses, especially when said administrators were not Catholics.[154] Despite this intervention by the chairman of the Slovak National Council, it took several more months before the problem was resolved and the convent vacated by the administrators.

The Catholic Church did not just wait for the DS to press its claims, but launched a drive of its own in defense of Catholic education. In the autumn of 1946, a new school law was being drafted in parliament. On October 4, the Catholic Educational Council (KŠR),[155] headed by Bishop Čársky, sent out a circular to all parish offices and Catholic associations, calling on them to send resolutions to the Czechoslovak Ministry of Education against the state monopoly of education.[156] The circular called for, among other things, the return of all those Catholic schools and dormitories that were nationalized, the right for the church to found more schools, state support for parochial education where needed, a rejection of pedagogical novelty, obligatory religious instruction at all schools, and an end to "the politicization of education."[157] Other Catholic demands expressed at this time were for chairs of Catholic philosophy and pedagogy at teachers' training colleges, Catholic representatives in all organs of the state education administration, and elected representatives of families on all bodies of educational administration.[158] *Katolícke noviny* prepared the way for the drive with a series of articles in defense of Catholic education, reiterating the chief arguments against the government's educational policies.[159] These articles stressed that the church had a natural right to found schools, and parents a fundamental right to educate their children according to their beliefs. The state's role was to protect and foster these rights, not to set up a monopoly of education and culture and compel Catholic parents to educate their children in violation of their convictions. One article anticipated the Educational Council's circular by expressing a skeptical attitude toward most modern pedagogical innovations, arguing that Catholic schools did not eschew all innovation, but rather employed only those innovations that were well grounded.[160] A September 8 editorial called for a referendum on education, something that the government surely feared and probably would have lost in Slovakia. The Communist press at the same time reiterated its defense of the nationalization of education. In an article in *Nové slovo*, Pavlík argued that confessional schools divided the nation, placed teachers under external influences and pressures, and subordinated them to nonspecialists who pursued narrow interests.[161] A secularized state system of education prevented the distortion, exclusion, or restriction of scientific and scholarly ideas, so that science was not presented in a medieval, obscurantist way. It was also an improvement fiscally and organizationally, being more efficient, and even helped parishes by freeing them from the expense of maintaining schools.

Along with education, the question of public holidays also struck at the soul of Catholic Slovakia. It became acute in the autumn of 1946 and was connected with the question of the postwar reconstruction of the country economically. Here the charge was led mainly from Prague, by the government, and nonparty but leftist organizations such as the trade union movement. Slovakia's Communists knew better than to antagonize Catholics over an issue like this. The government in Prague, as part of its efforts to encourage Czechs and Slovaks to work to meet the state's new two-year plan, resolved to modify the traditional two-day holiday of the first two days of November—that is, All Saints' Day on November 1 and All Souls' Day on November 2. Instead of two holidays back to back, All Saints' Day was to be a workday and All Souls' Day the holiday.[162] On October 31, the Board of Commissioners in Bratislava resolved that these designations be switched for Slovakia, in light of the fact that All Saints' Day was the more significant holy day for Catholics. The switch was made out of sensitivity to Catholic feelings on the issue, and *Katolícke noviny* regarded the solution as a reasonable one. More controversial was a call by the Revolutionary Trade Union Movement (ROH)[163] for all factory and office workers to work voluntarily on Sunday, October 27, not only the Sabbath for Catholics, but the feast of Christ the King as well. ROH equated failure to work with disloyalty to the state and disagreement with the two-year plan, charges that were practically tantamount at the time to that of war criminal. This presented a dilemma for Catholics, as the Communist controlled trade union association surely had hoped it would. If they worked on Sunday, they violated their church's and God's commandment about the Sabbath being reserved for rest. If they did not work, they risked being charged with disloyalty. As it turned out, few Catholics worked on October 27, though many made it up at another time. *Katolícke noviny* protested against this attempt to desecrate Sundays and stigmatize Catholics, and Czechoslovakia's bishops did likewise in a memorandum to the government. In defense of Sunday and holy day rest, Catholics argued that the practice of holy days was commanded by God, made venerable by a centuries-long tradition, and essential to the full development of the human person, giving one much-needed physical rest and opportunity for carrying out one's spiritual responsibilities. The success of the two-year plan would be threatened, argued authors in *Katolícke noviny*, if it was pursued via the desecration of Sundays and holy days. Such means would damage the morale of workers, who need and deserve a weekly day of rest, as well as alienate Catholic workers and prevent them from fulfilling their religious obligations. It would also mean that postwar Czechoslovakia was being built, like ancient Babylon, without God and against God, a situation that from the Catholic view would be laden with inauspicious implications.

A final issue of church-state conflict that became more acute at this time was the policy toward the Magyar minority. The government authorities were hoping to displace as many Magyars as possible from southern Slovakia, either by transferring them to the Czech lands to replace expelled Sudeten Germans, or by exchanging them for Hungarians of Slovak ethnicity living in Hungary who wished to immigrate to Slovakia. In the end, these operations caused the removal of approximately 89,000 Magyars to Hungary and some 40,000 to the Czech lands.[164] In August 1946, Slovakia's bishops sent a memorandum to the SNR's presidium and the Board of Commissioners that dealt in part with the minority question. The bishops asked that minority clergy who were otherwise loyal to the republic not be moved out of Slovakia.[165] The bishops pointed out that this would create a priest shortage, and one that would affect not just Magyars but Slovaks as well. Some Slovak parishes had priests of Magyar origin. Furthermore, Slovaks moving to Slovakia from Hungary often had a poor knowledge of the Slovak language, and in the bishops' view, should have access to Magyar worship services during the time that they were learning to master Slovak. Apart from these church-specific concerns, the bishops also reiterated their opposition to revenge, the persecution of the innocent, and unjust and inhumane actions during the transfers that violated "natural law." The commissioners of the interior and of education both rejected the bishops' request that priests be exempted from transfer as an unwarranted privileging of the clergy.[166]

During the winter of 1946–47, the state authorities began transferring Magyars, many against their will, to the Czech lands. The bishops met in December to discuss the matter and accepted Škrábik's suggestion that they voice their concerns in letters to state authorities, but not via the press.[167] Róbert Pobožný, the chapter vicar of Rožňava diocese, sent a series of protest letters to various government representatives in January and February 1947.[168] He informed the authorities that he had been made aware of a number of alleged abuses during the transfers—that people were being forced to sign requests for "voluntary" transfer; that children and the elderly were being transferred; that vengeful Jews were taking part in the transfers; that officials were corruptly enriching themselves off of Magyar property; and, above all, that the transfers were being carried out in the cold of winter, a "heartless and relentless" time of year. The plight of the transferees was so pitiable that even soldiers and police were weeping. Pobožný urgently called for a temporary halt to the transfers until the springtime. On February 1, Jantauch sent an appeal on behalf of Slovakia's bishops to President Beneš, Foreign Minister Jan Masaryk, and the SNR's presidium.[169] In the lengthiest of all episcopal documents on this issue, Jantausch noted a number of violations of legal norms in the process of transfer—people were being transferred without regard to age or sex, with children, the elderly, pregnant woman, those seriously ill, even right from Komárno's hospital, being transferred. He noted that this was being carried out in the winter, sometimes in cruel cold. Jantausch argued that the transfers were creating local labor shortages, with indispensable artisans, for example, being sent to the Czech lands. He protested that people were being left without means of existence, as pensioners, former state employees, and clergy were cut off from state support. He denounced the practice of blanket condemnation of Magyars regardless of their individual guilt, and the unjust deprivation of the innocent of their property. His letter drew parallels with the methods earlier used against the Jews and mentioned the bishops' wartime protest along these lines. He urged the state to "do unto others" with respect to the minority question.

As far as one can tell, these protests fell on deaf ears. The regime was determined to rid Slovakia of as many Magyars as it could and recognized that making that omelet would necessitate breaking more than a few eggs.[170] And while Slovakia's bishops did repeatedly protest to the regime against abuses against the Magyars, they took care not to give this issue much public prominence. Their interventions were largely behind the scenes and were largely rebuffed or ignored by the regime. Also, the bishops avoided condemning the idea of transfer per se, instead urging that it be carried out in a legal and humane manner, without coercion, without corruption, without cruelty. The bishops also informed the authorities that they favored the strengthening of the Slovak element in the recovered lands and were ready to cooperate toward that end.[171]

As mentioned previously, both of Slovakia's major political parties supported the state's minority policy. The Democrats, wanting to support state policy and remain in the bishops' good graces at the same time, made little public mention of the bishops' position, one way or the other. The Communists, on the other hand, would attack the bishops in their press for showing sympathy for the minorities, though neither frequently nor prominently.

The period from the April Agreement to the end of 1946 saw Democrats, Communists, and the Catholic Church deal with the implications of the April Agreement. For the Democrats, it meant an unimagined margin of victory in the May parliamentary elections, along with a fierce and incessant Communist attempt to discredit the DS as being ridden with former Populists. On the defensive, the DS found it impossible to translate its electoral gains into real power in Slovakia, and thus disappointed its Catholic voters and supporters. The party was also slow in implementing all the provisions of the April Agreement and soon found itself facing an insurgency from Catholics within, as well as counterpressures from Democrats who were leery of the pact with the Catholics. Thus, in any number of ways, the DS was in an unenviable position, despite capturing 62 percent of Slovak votes. The Communists, outmaneuvered by the April Agreement, were nevertheless able to play the anti-Populist card, and the fears it generated in Prague, in order to paralyze the DS in Slovakia. Most significantly, they kept the police out of the hands of the DS and maintained possession of the Commission of Education, from which they could easily prevent Democrats from delivering on their promises to Catholics in the realm of educational policy. Though the Communists saw their attempts to court Catholics turn to dust in the May elections, they nevertheless sensed that the realities of the Slovak situation demanded the continuation of a more nuanced approach to Slovakia's Catholic population. The KSS was careful to maintain its past distinction between the evil Populist collaborators, to whom the DS was pandering, and the basically decent Catholic common people, who were being misled. Thus, Communists would attack the DS for misusing religion for electoral gain while seeking to assure Slovaks that the KSS was indeed the friend of Catholicism. At the same time, the issues of contention between the Communists and the church remained on the table, as the Communists intensified their drive to weaken the church while the bishops and Catholic press continued their campaign to defend Catholic interests and prerogatives. Significantly, on the horizon for everyone was the impending trial of Jozef Tiso and other leaders of the wartime Republic, an event that promised all sorts of opportunities and dangers as the bubbling stew of Slovak politics, religion, and history would be given a big stir.

3

DEALING WITH THE PAST

The Trial of Jozef Tiso

THE trial, conviction, and execution of Jozef Tiso was a central event in postwar Slovakia, and one which had the effect of mobilizing and energizing forces across the Slovak political and social spectrum. The KSS had a strong interest in condemning Tiso, and with him the wartime regime, as a means of forcing the DS into a no-win situation. The Democrats could either defend Tiso, and risk being labeled as enemies of the Republic, or abandon him, and risk alienating the Catholic support they had won with the April Agreement. That is, the DS could become crippled either by police investigations and subsequent government enforced purges of its ranks or by the defection of the very voters that gave it a landslide parliamentary victory in May 1946. Partisan organizations and trade unions, in line with Communist wishes and seeking Tiso's demise, mobilized their forces in calls for his conviction and execution, while village and townswomen from some of Slovakia's most heavily Catholic areas, encouraged by clergy sympathetic to Tiso, engaged in antigovernment demonstrations. Slovak Catholic bishops urged calm while requesting clemency for Tiso from various government bodies. President Beneš and other non-Communist Czech political leaders had to decide whether to support clemency or ratify his execution, while the Slovak nationalist underground sought to stir up public unrest against Czechs, Jews, Communists, and Lutherans in connection with Tiso's destiny. From December 1946 to May 1947, Slovaks were caught up in the Tiso trial and its aftermath.

The issue of what to do with Tiso was present already during the war. In December 1943, during talks with the Soviet leadership in Moscow, Czechoslovak President-in-exile Edvard Beneš asked the Soviets to insist on the punishment of those Slovak leaders responsible for Slovakia's participation in the war against the Soviet Union.[1] In making this request, which Soviet Foreign Minister Vyacheslav Molotov declined, Beneš could put the onus on the Soviets, not the Czechs, for any prosecution of Slovakia's wartime leaders that would occur after an Allied victory in the war. Tiso, who in April 1945 fled to Austria, and then Bavaria, was arrested by the American army in early June, detained in the American POW camp at Garmisch-Partenkirchen for several months, and extradited to Bratislava in late October. Now in the custody of the Czechoslovak Republic, Tiso could expect to face trial for a series of alleged war crimes.

Because Tiso was a Catholic priest and former head of state of a regime that had close relations with the Catholic Church, his fate was a prime issue of concern for Slovakia's Catholic bishops. As discussed above, these bishops sent a letter on January 8, 1946, to the Slovak National Council, calling for a more complex, tolerant, and balanced understanding of Tiso's actions and the dilemmas and pressures he faced during the war. Slovakia's bishops stood almost alone in Slovak public life in saying some positive things about Slovakia's former leader.

The Vatican, not happy with Tiso's initial decision to assume leadership of wartime Slovakia, and upset with some of his wartime policies, such as the deportation of Jews from Slovakia to a grim fate in Nazi Germany, was cool to Tiso during the period leading up to his trial. A measure of the Vatican's reluctance to get involved in the Tiso affair is evidenced by the visit of Monsignor Amleto Cicognani, the Vatican's representative in Washington, D.C., to the Czechoslovak ambassador to the United States, Vladimír Hurban, on December 18, 1945.[2] Making his visit on papal orders, Cicognani reported that the Vatican had received much embittered correspondence from Slovakia's bishops and priests, alleging that there was the danger of nationalist disturbances in Slovakia on account of the Tiso trial. For that reason, His Holiness made two requests, neither of which, the monsignor stressed, were to be construed as an attempt to influence the course of the trial. These requests were, first, that Tiso not be interned in a prison, but in a monastery; and, second, that Tiso be given "due regards." Hurban promised to pass on the first request to Prague but asked for clarification about the second request, given its vague nature. Cicognani agreed that, indeed, his request was vague and promised to get clarification from the Vatican. In his report to Prague, Hurban noted that the embassy had reason to believe that the Slovak League of America was behind this action, most likely getting American Catholic bishops to write to the Vatican urging an intervention on behalf of Tiso. This might explain why the intervention was done in Washington rather than Prague. Czechoslovak foreign minister Jan Masaryk, at a government meeting of February 4, 1946, commented on Hurban's report and added that, from inquiries at the Vatican, he learned that the pope's action was not intended to be seen as an official intervention, but rather as an act taken on the basis of Christian love.[3] The timidity of the Vatican's intervention on behalf of Tiso is an indication that the Holy See had little willingness to defend Tiso beyond the basics required by Christian love and by the fact that he was a priest. Czechoslovak deputy prime minister Zdeněk Fierlinger confirmed this observation at a government meeting on the eve of Tiso's trial by sharing his impression, from an unofficial talk with the interim papal nuncio Saverio Ritter, that the Vatican would not intervene on behalf of Tiso during his trial.[4]

Far more interested in Tiso's fate than the Vatican were the Communists. The Tiso trial was a centerpiece of their political strategy in Slovakia, and they had been discussing issues pertinent to the trial for well over a year. The Communists' goals were several: to use the trial to totally discredit the former regime, thereby justifying the new people's democracy; to use any unrest connected with the trial to justify increased security measures in Slovakia as well as investigations of the Democratic Party for allegedly harboring Tiso's sympathizers; to discredit the DS in the eyes of Slovak Catholics by foiling any plans that party might have of getting Tiso's execution commuted to a prison sentence; to sow division within the DS between those Democrats who were hostile to Tiso and those who were not; and to weaken, and even force a purge, of Slovakia's Catholic bishops and clergy.[5]

As discussed earlier, the KSS had met already in November 1945 to work out its plan for the trial, including, in great detail, the role to be played by the propaganda and information organs. Through 1946, the KSS continued to discuss, plan, and monitor the trial preparations at its meetings. The Communists were especially interested that the DS be engaged in the political campaign connected with the trials.[6] On December 2, 1946, the joint Central Committees of the KSS and KSČ met to finalize plans for a common course of action.[7] In a joint resolution, both parties agreed that the Tiso trial was currently one of the most significant events in the Republic, and that "all necessary attention must be dedicated to its course, its correct political management, and its successful conclusion." A successful outcome of the trial would have considerable influence on the inner party relations of the DS. Among other things, the Communists agreed on the necessity "to take all measures so that public opinion is correctly influenced through the press, radio, or other means," and "to monitor carefully the entire press, especially the DS press, and intervene immediately against attempts to influence public opinion in favor of Tiso and company." The Communists also agreed to take certain steps aimed at isolating the DS politically. They planned to raise objections against Kempný, Bugár, and Staško, three of the leading Catholics in the DS, deliver these objections to all political parties, have the Communist controlled police investigate these allegations, and report on them to the government. The Communists would also launch an attack on the Democratic led Farmers Bank,[8] accusing it of subversive and reactionary economic mismanagement, in order to put the DS under strong political pressure during the period of Tiso's trial. Wide strata of the population (meaning, above all, the Communist led or influenced trade unions and Partisan organizations) were to be mobilized in these campaigns.

The Communist plan was to force the DS into the impossible task of navigating between the Scylla of angering its Catholic members and voters, who had hopes that the Democrats would rescue Tiso from a death sentence, and the Charybdis of being sucked into a police investigation for allegations of harboring reactionaries and defending war criminals. In pursuing this aim, the Communists tried to keep the DS integrated into broad political efforts to condemn Tiso, frighten it from speaking out on Tiso's behalf, and render fruitless its hopes of defending Tiso from execution. At the same time, they charged the DS with being a haven for Tisoite Populists and tried to pin excesses committed by the Slovak nationalist underground on the Democrats. Ideally, as a result of these policies, the DS would be discredited in the eyes of Catholics as an ineffectual and lukewarm defender of Tiso while concurrently discredited in the eyes of everyone else as a haven for reactionaries.

Developments in Czechoslovakia surrounding the Tiso trial thus put the DS in a quandary. The Communists alleged that the DS had promised, in a secret clause of the April Agreement, to use its influence to prevent Tiso's execution and reduce his sentence to something less extreme.[9] This charge was later denied by leading Democrats, and evidence that such an agreement existed has never been found. The matter of the secret clause is, however, a moot point. Regardless of what may have been agreed upon behind the scenes, the DS did act as though it felt itself obliged to at least make an attempt to protect Tiso from execution. Indeed, such an obligation would go without saying for a party intent on winning over Slovakia's Catholics into its political camp during this period.

After the elections of May 1946, the Communists were intent on making sure that the DS would disappoint any Catholics who thought the landslide Democratic victory would be good news for Tiso. The Communists insisted that the DS come out strongly against Tiso as a condition for entering the government. On June 12, the Czechoslovak National Front, to which all government parties had to belong, resolved that all member parties should agree with, among other things, "the condemnation and punishment of Tiso."[10] The DS reluctantly went along with this. Soon thereafter, the KSS involved the DS as cosponsor of the "Proclamation to the Slovak Nation," part of which stated, "we demand, as decisively and as quickly as possible, the conviction and sentencing of all agents of the so-called Slovak State, beginning with Tiso, Tuka, Mach, Gašpar, Kubala, et al., who already before Munich linked up with our eternal enemies, who then helped destroy the Czechoslovak Republic and threaten the honor and existence of the Slovak nation, when, in the service of the Nazi imperialists and Magyar irredentists, they placed Slovakia against the Slavic and other democratic nations, driving Slovak soldiers into a fratricidal battle against Poles, Russians, Ukrainians, and Byelorussians, declaring war on Great Britain and the USA, and introducing into Slovakia the system of fascist totality."[11] In signing on to these policies and sentiments, which the DS had to do to ensure its political existence, the DS showed a timidity in the face of the Tiso question, demonstrating an a priori admission of Tiso's guilt, even of the dubious charge of treasonous activity before Munich. This timidity extended to the DS press. One of the party's situation reports of December 1946 notes that in the region around Topol'čany, people were complaining that *Čas* was very cautious in its coverage of the Tiso trial, publishing only fragmentary official statements without its own commentary and reflections.[12]

While facing criticism from within its own ranks for being too timid on Tiso's behalf, the DS was at the same time prone to Communist charges that it was in complicity with underground actions for Tiso and against the state. The Slovak underground was never as large, as organized, or as dangerous as Communists and Slovak émigré nationalists, at the time or later, made it out to be. Its activity consisted mainly in disseminating leaflets, posters, and graffiti that were viciously anti-Czech, anti-Communist, anti-Jewish, and pro-Tiso. This was often done in campaigns timed to coincide with critical events. Tiso's return to Czechoslovakia in late October 1945, and the parliamentary election campaign of spring 1946 were such occasions. The Tiso trial was another, and in December 1946, in time with its opening, underground leaflet activity was stepped up, propagandizing on Tiso's behalf.[13] Some of these leaflets blamed Czechs, Communists, and Protestants for wanting to condemn Tiso against the will of the Slovak nation.[14] In a report on the security situation in Slovakia in November 1946, Commissioner of the Interior Ferjenčík reported that the underground movement in Slovakia was mainly composed of members of the better-placed social strata—civil servants, students, soldiers, priests, and shopkeepers, and was most active in the regions around Orava, Nitra, Topol'čany, Piešt'any, and Bánovce, less so in Protestant and in industrialized areas.[15] Its activities were limited to leafleting, whispering campaigns, and menacing graffiti. These actions intensified as the Tiso trial got under way. The Slovak political emigration also stepped up its propaganda activities during this period. Ferdinand Ďurčanský, as chairman of the Slovak Action Committee, issued a "Proclamation to the World Public on War Criminals," in which he denied that Slovaks had committed any criminal acts.[16] In January he wrote to the pope on Tiso's behalf, and in February he wrote the United Nations, asking that Tiso and his government be judged by an unbiased international court rather than a domestic one. Meanwhile, the illegal radio station Voice of the Slovak Republic, based in Italy, called for Slovaks to organize actions in defense of Tiso.[17] Czechoslovakia's Communists sought to link the DS with the underground support for Tiso, both domestically and internationally, and with efforts to prevent Tiso from receiving a harsh sentence. A report by Czechoslovak interior minister Václav Nosek, from late November, expressed concern over reports that the underground was spreading rumors that several leading politicians had made a commitment to get Tiso off with a light sentence.[18] At the government meeting where the report was discussed, Široký made the charge that Ďurčanský had instructed those Slovaks who were not politically compromised to enter the legal parties and work against the Czechoslovak Republic. He went on to target the Democrat Kempný as a prime example of this Trojan horse policy, a policy that the Democrats allegedly facilitated when, in accordance with the

April Agreement, they made Kempný one of their party's general secretaries.[19] As underground activity in Slovakia intensified over the next several months, the Communists used it to keep the DS on the defensive.

Also intensifying its activity was the other extreme in Slovakia, those largely pro-Communist resistance organizations. In mid-November, a Slovakia-wide Resistance Conference resolved to oppose what it regarded as attempts to influence the National Court, by which it understood any efforts on behalf of Tiso.[20] District and local organizations also publicly expressed similar intentions. On the eve of the trial, at the KSS's urging, the Union of Slovak Partisans stepped up its activities, demanding a speedy trial and the implementation of a harsh punishment.[21] Such groups would remain publicly engaged in the events surrounding the Tiso trial for its duration, in line with the KSS's policy of mobilizing wide strata of the population.

Practically right from the beginning, Slovakia's police and political parties sought to judge the popular mood with respect to the Tiso question. A number of reports noted that there was great public sympathy for Tiso, though the underground's success in translating this into public unrest remained limited. In November 1946, Slovakia's security organs reported on the public mood as they saw it, surmising that in approximately thirty of Slovakia's administrative districts (*okresy*), 50 percent or more of the population was opposed to the condemnation of Tiso.[22] These included a number of districts in Eastern Slovakia (including Michalovce, Bardejov, Prešov, Trebišov, Košice), Hlinka's hometown of Ružomberok, Tiso's former residences of Vel'ká Bytča, Bánovce nad Bebravou, and Nitra, and the strongly Catholic areas around Piešt'any, Trnava, and Orava. The report also speculated that approximately half of the membership of the DS opposed Tiso's condemnation. A report from the Commission of the Interior's Seventh Section, from December 1946, estimated that 50–60 percent of Slovakia's population was in support of Tiso, the rest against him.[23] There were also rumors circulating in Slovakia at this time that Beneš had said that Tiso ought to be condemned to death.[24]

Commissioner of the Interior Ferjenčík dealt with the mood in Slovakia in his report of November 1946.[25] According to his intelligence, a considerable and growing number of Slovaks expected Tiso to be convicted but not executed. Many Slovaks could not imagine that a priest would be hanged or shot. Tiso's well-wishers were encouraged by a number of factors: that the Tiso trial took so long in coming; the public's perception that the KSS and DS did not see eye to eye regarding the trial; the increase in the clandestine distribution of pro-Tiso leaflets and collections and prayers on Tiso's behalf; the relatively mild verdicts in the earlier trials of alleged collaborators from the Protectorate of Bohemia and Moravia;[26] and the belief that Peter Zat'ko and Imrich Karvaš, high-ranking officials in the wartime regime who aided the Uprising and on that account were freed from postwar detention, had Tiso's approval in working against the Germans.

Police speculations must be taken with a grain of salt. Nevertheless, there is no doubt that many Slovaks were opposed to the trial of Tiso. It is too simple a dichotomy, however, to divide Slovakia into those for and against Tiso. Certainly there were plenty of Slovaks who regarded him as a war criminal deserving of death. The Communists and members of Partisan organizations fell into this category. For them, Tiso stood for the former regime and its anti-Communist and anti-Semitic policies, collaboration with Nazi Germany, suppression of the Slovak National Uprising, and clericalism. Among Tiso's supporters, views varied. Some saw him as a hero, a saint and martyr acting on behalf of the interests of the nation he loved. To others, he deserved reverence and respect above all because he was a Catholic priest. To still others, he had the misfortune of living in interesting times and was the victim of events beyond his control.

Given the indications that many Slovaks were sympathetic to Tiso, and the fact that a Slovak underground was clearly engaged in illegal propaganda activities, the Czechoslovak authorities took security measures in Slovakia in connection with the Tiso trial very seriously. The Czechoslovak government, at its meeting of November 28, 1946, discussed the matter and authorized the Ministry of the Interior, the Ministry of Defense, and the Commission of the Interior to take all necessary measures to ensure order in Slovakia during the trial.[27] At this and other meetings of Czechoslovak and Slovak organs, the Communists insisted on the most stringent security preparations for the trial.

In Slovakia, security forces were instructed to step up intelligence work on the local level, taking note of the mood among the population, noting any suspicious persons, and keeping an eye out for pro-Tiso leaflets and activities.[28] Special attention was to be devoted to the activity of the Roman Catholic clergy, professors' and teachers' councils, students, and intellectuals, as those groups formerly most committed to the Tiso regime. Security forces were to submit daily reports to Section Z of the Commission of the Interior and keep heightened watch on the border for the infiltration of foreign agents. All crowds assembling due to the Tiso trial were to be dispersed and guards posted at important state institutions and enterprises to protect against sabotage. A list was to be made of all persons regarded as unreliable, who in the event of unrest or the justified fear of unrest were to be detained. The Czechoslovak army, along with security forces from the Czech lands, was to assist the Slovak police in implementing these measures. In addition, Slovakia's Board of Commissioners authorized the Commission of Justice to see that the press was strictly monitored and that intervention was made against any periodicals stepping out of line.[29] Finally, the KSS held local membership meetings across Bratislava, where the necessity of heightened vigilance during the Tiso trial was discussed.[30]

Hanging over the trial was the question of the political use of the judiciary. As elsewhere in Central and Eastern Europe, the Communists saw the courts as weapons to use against their political enemies. Communist proclamations proceeded from the assumption that Tiso and his codefendants were guilty and needed only to be condemned and punished. Already before the opening of the Tiso trial, there were indications of discontent over the politicization of justice. On October 17, 1946, L'udovít Rigan, the head prosecutor at the Slovak National Court, wrote to Husák, the chairman of the Board of Commissioners, responding to the latter's expressed wishes that the cases before the court be dealt with "more quickly and more radically."[31] Rigan pointed to a growing distaste among the public for the way in which "people's justice" was being carried out, argued that by law the death penalty was to be used only in exceptional cases, and expressed his refusal to expedite cases involving heavy penalties (i.e., execution or imprisonment). The prosecutor noted that it was his official, professional, and human obligation to point out that a radical course of action conflicted with his legal convictions and the whole of his personality. Rigan threatened to resign rather than accede to Husák's wishes, noting that his resignation would also eliminate the unfavorable situation whereby both the Prosecutor's Office and the National Court were headed by a Protestant, a situation causing strife between Catholics and Protestants in Slovakia and giving occasion for talk that Protestants were using the court to exact revenge against Catholics. Here once again, religion was figuring in Slovakia's political developments.

While Rigan's dispute with Husák was limited to a correspondence between the two, another controversy over the question of politicization of the judiciary brought about a clash between Communists and Democrats within Slovakia's governing organs. At issue was the person of Igor Daxner, who as president of the Senate was appointed to serve as head of the National Court that tried Tiso. Although a year earlier the KSS itself had had reservations about Daxner and favored his removal from the National Court, by the time of the Tiso trial, the Communists appeared as staunch defenders of Daxner against DS attempts to have him replaced.[32] The issue came to a head at the meeting of the presidium of the Slovak National Council of November 8, 1946, where DS representatives Polák and Cvinček raised a number of objections against Daxner.[33] They stressed that he was regarded as politically biased, and that there was speculation in Slovakia that he had made a deal with Beneš to have Tiso condemned to death. They also pointed out that, since Daxner was a Protestant, it made a bad impression in Slovakia that both judge and prosecutor were non-Catholic.[34] Since the trial needed to be convincing, the Democrats argued, it needed a different judge. They also expressed dissatisfaction with the job he had done in previous trials. The Communist representative Karol Šmidke came vigorously to Daxner's defense, and even threatened to boycott further meetings if Daxner was removed. Šmidke argued that to replace the judge would be an affront to a man who had made considerable sacrifices for Czechoslovakia. Daxner had served as a Legionnaire during the First World War and as a Partisan in the Slovak National Uprising, and was persecuted during the Tiso regime. He was, in Šmidke's view, highly competent and of high moral qualities. For the Slovak National Council to decide on such a matter would constitute an undue interference in the judiciary's sphere of competence.

Democratic objections against Daxner also turn up in a confidential report to President Beneš dated November 22, 1946, which outlines the Democratic case against Daxner. The report presents three allegations against Daxner: (1) that he was telling people he had received an order from Beneš to condemn Tiso to death, and as such talk spread through Slovakia's rumor mills, it was having a detrimental affect on the public mood; (2) that he was telling people he would be named as general consul in Kiev after the trial; and (3) that he was ill, suffering from progressive paralysis. The Democrats offered to provide medical testimony to prove their third allegation. The report's conclusion noted that the Democrats expressed a willingness to accept anyone but Daxner and threatened to withdraw their delegates from the Senate if he was not removed.

Despite their objections and efforts, however, the Democrats ultimately failed to procure Daxner's removal. The KSS would not budge on the issue, and Beneš, as much a defender of Daxner as the Communists were, was hardly moved by the Democratic arguments. For the Communists, the primary objective was to get a conviction and execution of Tiso, not to assuage Slovak public opinion. Anything less than Tiso's execution would redound to the favor of the DS, while an execution would expose the DS as ineffectual, unable to deliver on the hopes its May 1946 electoral victory had raised among Slovak Catholics. It would demonstrate that, in a Slovakia that was approximately 80 percent Catholic and where 62 percent of voters chose the Democrats, a Catholic priest could still be hanged.

As the Tiso trial was getting under way, Slovakia's Communists launched their planned propaganda offensive in conjunction with the trial. They sought to bring public and political pressure on the DS with charges of corruption and mismanagement aimed at the Democrat led Commissions of Food and Supply (Kornel Filo) and Agriculture (Martin Kvetko), and the Farmer's Bank, and they sought to blame the Democrats for food shortages, the black market, and the high cost of living in Slovakia.[35] In addition, the Communists focused on institutions that were allegedly harboring former Populists or under the influence of the anti-Communist, anti-Czechoslovakia Populist ideology. The prime targets were the DS and the Catholic hierarchy. *Nové slovo* opened the new year with a cover article by Husák, in which he alleged that the pro-Populist element in the DS hung over the party like the sword of Damocles, hampering the Democrats' freedom of decision and causing the party to deviate from the progressive program it had inherited from the Slovak National Uprising.[36] Thanks to the DS, according to Husák, close friends of émigré traitors were sitting in protected positions and exerting important influence in Czechoslovakia. In a subsequent series of articles under the pseudonym Historicus, Husák continued to assault the DS. In early February, for example, he pointed to the widespread support the HSL'S had among the clergy in the past and alleged that Ďurčanský, when the wartime Slovak Republic's demise was imminent, laid plans for a "fifth column" of Populists to operate in postwar Slovakia. Husák, in line with Communist plans to discredit leading Catholics in the DS, implied that Catholic Democrats Kempný and Staško were part of a plan to infiltrate parliamentary, administrative, economic, and party organizations under the people's democratic regime.[37] In early March, *Nové slovo* published the text of the April Agreement, accompanied by an article by Historicus entitled "Agreement for the Legalization of Populism."[38] Calling the April Agreement an attempt to create an Agrarian-Populist anti-

Communist bloc, Husák likened the agreement to the earlier collaboration between Agrarians and Populists in the wake of the Munich Agreement in autumn of 1938. Like the earlier marriage of convenience, where Tiso shared some power with the Agrarians in exchange for their support in managing the newly autonomous Slovakia, the same process was at work, but with the roles reversed. The Democrats, descendants of the Agrarians, were sharing power with the ex-Populists in order to win Catholic votes. As they had always done, the Populists were masking their political agenda behind the cause of Catholicism.

While Husák's articles focused mainly on the DS and attacked Catholics only to the extent that they were in league with the Populists, in other places the KSS took on the church more directly. During the period of the Tiso trial, a number of references appeared in *Nové slovo* attacking Slovakia's bishops, in particular the three who testified in Tiso's trial—Kmet'ko, Buzalka, and Škrábik. For example, a feuilleton quoted an article that Buzalka had written for the August 26, 1941, issue of *Slovenský vojak*, in which the bishop both defended Slovakia's participation in Germany's war against the Soviet Union and condemned any cooperation with Communists.[39] *Nové slovo* also noted that Buzalka asked permission to offer his hand to Tiso at his trial, and added its interpretation that this symbolically represented Buzalka's friendship with Tiso and desire to pull him out of a ditch.[40] An article of March 15 discussed Škrábik's anti-Communist booklet of 1925, *Red Slovakia*, which blamed Jews for Bolshevism and portrayed Soviet Russia as a hotbed of sexual perversion and abuse.[41] Kmet'ko was attacked for some aspects of his trial testimony, namely his views on Czechs and his purported refusal to reject outright the possibility that Christianity and Nazism could be harmonized.[42]

Having to deal with Communist media assaults from many directions and on a variety of issues, and operating in an atmosphere of anxiety, lest defense of beleaguered Catholic clergy and politicians be branded as support for Tiso, DS attempts to defend their leading Catholics were mild and intermittent. A front page article in *Čas* in mid-January entitled "Important Work of the Clergy" stressed the positive and important role played by the clergy in Slovak history.[43] The article, authored by a Democratic member of the SNR, credited the clergy with helping improve the social, economic, and cultural conditions of Slovak peasants during the period of Hungarian domination, with supporting the Slovak National Uprising, and with contributing to Slovakia's liberation and reconstruction during and after World War II. The author opposed efforts to exclude the clergy from public life and to sow distrust of them among Slovakia's working-class population. In February, *Čas* provided a venue for Kempný to defend himself against leftist attacks, particularly those coming from the Social Democratic newspaper *Hlas práce*.[44] Kempný denied allegations that he was engaged, during the wartime regime's waning months, in conspiring with Ďurčanský in preparing plans for Populist underground activity after liberation. In his speech at a DS district conference in Holíč in early March, Rudolf Fraštacký, a top-ranking Democrat and deputy chairman of the Slovak Board of Commissioners, asserted that the great majority of Slovak Catholics had nothing in common with the treason of 1938 and that the whole Catholic camp should not be maligned due to the political pasts of certain individuals.[45] The above examples, which are among the few found on the pages on *Čas* during this period, demonstrate that the DS limited its media activity to airing generalized statements of blanket support for clergy, providing venues for Catholic Democrats to respond to attacks, and commending the loyalty to the state of the great majority of Catholic rank and file.

A press polemic involving *Katolícke noviny* gives a good indication of the problems a media organ could face if it defended beleaguered Catholics too assertively, and illustrates the continuing Communist efforts to dissociate their attacks on Populists, leading Catholic Democrats, and Catholic bishops from the Catholic religion and population in general. In its March 2 issue, *Katolícke noviny* responded to an article on Tiso by Lutheran pastor Juraj Chochol in *Svobodné noviny*. Among other things, Chochol distinguished between two types of nationalism in post-1918 Slovakia—the constructive Protestant kind and the destructive Catholic kind. In a front-page response entitled "Is Catholicism Destructive?," author J. Š. Čierny argued that some people were using Tiso as an excuse to condemn the Catholic Church.[46] He then went on to defend Slovak Catholics' support for autonomy for Slovakia in the interwar period, seeing it as a result of discrimination against Catholics in favor of Protestants. Finally, he pointed to postwar seizures of Catholic schools, dormitories, organizations, and property under the pretext of combating treason, collaboration, fascism, and reaction. *Nové slovo* then joined the fray, reporting on the polemic and marshalling evidence of the destructiveness of Populist nationalism.[47] The Communist journal noted a letter by the Bishops' Council of November 15, 1943, in which Kmeťko wrote, "The Catholic clergy has a lion's share in the formation of the Slovak state and wants to be its most devoted citizens," and accused the bishops of not distancing themselves from the Tiso regime and the atrocities of the time. Lest these charges be seen as an attack on Slovakia's Catholic population in general, the author asserted that, "if by Catholicism we mean the hundreds of thousands of common people, then it is not and will not be a question of destructiveness. These were the people who fought against and defeated Tiso." The author accused *Katolícke noviny* of rousing Populists to fight under the banner of defense of Catholicism and pronounced that war criminals have no right to talk about persecution of religion, as it is their crimes, not their religious affiliation, for which they are being punished. He concluded, "The sooner Catholicism in Slovakia unbinds itself from Populism, or from political life altogether, the more quickly will better and more peaceful conditions for our development occur." A further aspect of this polemic was the authorities' seizure of the pertinent issue of *Katolícke noviny* in Bratislava and parts of the Slovak countryside on account of Čierny's article.[48] On March 1, the provincial court in Bratislava ruled in the Catholic organ's favor, on the grounds that its writing did not exceed the criticism allowed in democratic states. *Katolícke noviny*, in reporting on the confiscation and court ruling, addressed those of its readers who thought the paper was not aggressive enough in defending Catholic interests, presenting the difficult circumstances as evidence for why the paper's room for maneuver was limited.

While the Democratic and Catholic media in Slovakia avoided directly commenting on Tiso and his trial during this period, underground elements in Slovakia sought to stir up the Slovak population in Tiso's defense. One step they took was the so called name day action. In February, Tiso's well-wishers were asked, through underground leaflets, to send cards and telegrams to Tiso on the occasion of his name day on March 19. According to a KSS situation report of the time, several thousands of letters and over a hundred telegrams were sent as part of this initiative.[49] Communist informants alleged widespread complicity on the part of postal workers in this action, for example, by failing to notify the police, by taking no cognizance of who was sending the telegrams, by passing on the mail even without postage. In the leaflet launching the initiative, Slovaks were reminded that March 19 was the name day of their "dishonoured and imprisoned but well-loved Leader (*Vodca*) and President."[50] Noting that he would be condemned and probably executed in March, it asked, "Can the brave majority allow this loathsome revenge purposefully directed against Catholics? Is it possible that Communist tyrants and Lutherans full of venom judge the honorable Catholics who led the nation to success?" The leaflet called on the "sheepish, prattling, and imprisoned Slovak nation" to raise an outcry against Tiso's execution and instructed readers that it was their duty as patriotic Slovaks to send the following greeting to Tiso:

> Mr. President! On your name day, the day of St. Joseph, patron of the Holy Church and our defender, we wish you, as our beloved Leader, an abundance of God's blessings, care and help. We believe that, as the unjustly imprisoned Joseph of Egypt became a benefit to Egypt and his family, so also you will again become our Joseph of Slovakia, because without you we are orphans. For your freedom and the freedom of all those imprisoned.

As with much pro-Tiso sentiment, the appeal for the name day action combined Catholic piety, Slovak nationalism, anti-Communism, hostility to the existing regime, and combativeness. The negative reference to Lutherans, an allusion to the fact that the chief judge Daxner was of Lutheran background, identifies the leaflet with the Populist underground, which also attacked the DS from time to time for the strong Lutheran influence within it.

In addition to the name day action, underground sympathizers of Tiso used leaflets, graffiti, and whispering campaigns in an effort to produce a Slovak revolt on Tiso's behalf. Despite their efforts, Slovakia remained surprisingly calm during the trial. Nevertheless, some demonstrations did break out in mid-March in certain regions, namely in Piešt'any, Nové Mesto nad Váhom, and in the district around Topol'čany. These places, along with Tiso's hometown of Bánovce nad Bebravou, were particularly sympathetic to Tiso and especially agitated by his trial. DS internal reports note the mood in Topol'čany during the trial, where residents expressed upset with the DS over its excessively cautious press coverage, especially when juxtaposed with the Party of Freedom's more opinionated paper *Sloboda*.[51] DS reports also noted that a DS rally in Bánovce on March 16 became a manifestation in support of Tiso's release, and that a local DS speaker was attacked by party rank and file from the region for the DS's apparent failure to come to Tiso's defense.[52] There were sporadic examples of support for Tiso elsewhere in Slovakia as well; for example, several petitions on Tiso's behalf were signed by dozens of Slovaks in locales near Žilina and Prievidza.[53] However, it was the demonstrations that broke out in mid-March that were the most dramatic manifestations of support for Tiso, and which gained the most attention of the authorities and the public.

The occasion for the demonstrations was the conclusion of Tiso's trial on March 19, which also corresponded coincidentally with the Feast of St. Joseph, Tiso's patron saint. As Slovakia's population awaited the verdict and sentence, pious and patriotic sentiments toward and concern for Slovakia's former priest-president were running high. At the initiative of Vojtech Žilinčan, a Catholic priest in the village of Krakovany, the local Association of Catholic Women organized a Catholic Mass at the Jesuit church in Piešt'any on Tiso's behalf. Attending the Mass on the morning of March 19 were mainly women from Piešt'any and the surrounding countryside. Afterward, around eighty to one hundred women congregated on the town square, from where they proceeded to march to the local headquarters of the district national committee chairman, the highest state administrative official in Piešt'any. Along the way, hundreds of onlookers accumulated, so that the demonstration grew to anywhere from one thousand to fifteen hundred participants and spectators. During the march, demonstrators sang religious and nationalist songs and chanted various slogans, most on Tiso's behalf, though some observers noted shouts against Czechs and Jews, on behalf of Mach, and in defense of Catholic schools. At the district national committee headquarters, a delegation of seven women presented the chairman, Chrenko, with a request that Tiso be freed. The chairman, a Democrat, rejected the request and warned the women to disperse, finally calling on police units to put an end to the demonstration by early afternoon. Aided by firemen and soldiers, the police succeeded in getting the crowd to disperse peacefully. More than thirty main protagonists of the demonstration were arrested, with more to follow, and they spent the next several weeks in a labor camp. Žilinčan spent eleven months in prison.[54]

Considerably smaller demonstrations on Tiso's behalf broke out in several places on March 20. On the evening of March 19, a couple hundred people congregated at the local parish church in Nové Mesto nad Váhom (almost certainly to hear a Mass on Tiso's behalf), deciding to demonstrate the next day when they hoped for a larger turnout. Early the next evening, several hundred (estimates range from four hundred to eight hundred) people met at the town square, an estimated two-thirds of whom were women and children. The crowd shouted pro-Tiso slogans until a local police unit moved in and succeeded in dispersing them, again without violence.[55] Twenty-three people were arrested, twenty of them women, most of whom ended up spending several weeks in a labor camp.[56] The same day, at Chynorany in the district around Topol'čany, a crowd gathered in the evening outside the local cinema after a film, then began to march to the railroad station singing nationalist songs, including songs of the wartime Hlinka Guard, and shouting pro-Tiso slogans. At the railway station, they wrote these slogans on railroad cars. The police intervened to arrest a dozen people, eleven of them male.[57] The occupations of those arrested indicate a feature of the mid-March demonstrations everywhere, that the participants were overwhelmingly common people. Among the twelve people arrested in Chynorany were three peasants, two carpenters, one mason, one building supervisor, one shopkeeper, one housekeeper, one carpenter's apprentice, one shoemaker's assistant, and one painter's assistant.[58] After the rally at the railway station was dispersed, approximately half of the demonstrators began marching to the nearby village of Žabokreky nad Nitrou. Some demonstrators reportedly stopped automobiles in transit, asking if Jews or Czechs were inside. The police intervened, arresting seven of the main protagonists, thereby causing the march, composed mainly of women and children, to disperse.[59]

Certain features characterized the Piešt'any, Nové Mesto nad Váhom, and Chynorany events. The events were connected with Catholicism. This was particularly the case at the largest demonstration, at Piešt'any, as evidenced by the roles of Žilinčan and the Association of Catholic Women, the singing of religious songs, as well as by the fact that Catholic Mass was the focal point for congregating and a Catholic feast the ostensible occasion. In addition, the events were largely the work of women, both in terms of organization and participation. This certainly reflects the fact that rural women historically were particularly strong supporters of the HSL'S and devoutly Catholic in these areas. It may also reflect the feeling among women that they were less likely to be treated brutally by the police, particularly if they had their children in tow. The demonstrators were overwhelmingly common people—local peasants, shopkeepers, artisans, and menial workers. And, judging from the songs sung and slogans shouted, overlapping sentiments of Slovak nationalism, Catholicism, and sympathy for Tiso both as symbol and person characterized these manifestations. The authorities took few chances and, in all cases, intervened more or less quickly with security forces that proved to be sufficient. In all cases, the suspected perpetrators were arrested, detained, and sent to labor camps for short terms. In no case did the demonstrators resist violently. Some Slovaks may have been willing to express publicly their sympathy for Tiso, but few were eager to clash with the state's security forces over the issue. For their part, the authorities also sought to avoid bloodshed. At both Piešt'any and Nové Mesto nad Váhom, the authorities refrained from asking for support from Partisan organizations whose members were on hand behind the scenes and ready to intervene if asked.[60]

In the wake of the demonstrations of March 19 and 20, several steps were taken to assure calm and order in Slovakia. Government and administration at all levels stepped up security measures. Additional security forces were authorized for Slovakia, and the Commission of the Interior intensified its scrutiny of the press; banned any sort of meetings, rallies, or gatherings without its permission; and authorized the arrest of anyone calling for Tiso's release or, in a measure clearly aimed at Catholic clergy, preaching and praying in his favor. Government employees who took part in or cooperated in antistate activities were to be punished with loss of employment.[61] Both DS leaders and the Catholic hierarchy appealed for calm and asked Slovaks to refrain from such demonstrations in the future. The DS asked the Slovak bishops, and the bishops asked the Slovak priests, to use their influence to keep Catholics from taking part in similar disturbances, which they regarded as counterproductive.[62] Bugár, the DS's general secretary for organizational affairs, instructed the party's regional and district secretaries on March 20 to inform the local membership of the harmfulness of such demonstrations and to take steps to prevent them.[63]

Slovakia's two leading parties responded to the demonstrations, as might be expected. The Communists sought to implicate the DS, the Catholic Church, and lax security while arguing that the disturbances were not just pro-Tiso but also antistate and hence a danger to be taken seriously. They also portrayed the demonstrations as attempts to restrict the independence of the judiciary, and, as directed against the republic, the government, the president, Czechs, and Jews. Husák, writing in *Nové slovo* as Historicus, noted that the demonstrations only confirmed what he had written back in the February 8 issue—that is, that there was a Populist fifth column active in Slovakia.[64] He accused the DS of sheltering antistate elements in order to get votes and pointed to the unrest as the fruits of that ill-conceived policy. He also presented the demonstrations as closely tied to the Catholic Church, claiming they were inspired by priests, whose Masses and sermons on Tiso's behalf helped incite the population. The Piešt'any demonstrators, noted Historicus, assembled at a church and sang Marian hymns along with antistate slogans while marching. *Pravda*, in an implicit attack on the DS, argued that the laxity of state officials made the demonstrations possible, a view also found in internal KSS reports.[65]

The Communist press also addressed the role of women in the demonstrations, writing of the "immoral misuse" of "simple village women" by the antistate provocateurs, who cowardly sent these women to the front lines.[66] While alarmed at the forces they regarded as being behind the demonstrations, the Communists had little fear of the rural women who made up the bulk of the demonstrators. As Husák wrote in his New Year's article in *Nové slovo*, "Even the political novice knows that in the decisive moments, sociological quality counts as well as numbers. Twenty village grandmas, who vote the way their parish priest tells them, do not count for as much as one class-conscious factory worker."[67]

The Democrats' response to the demonstrations, and to Communist intimations that the DS was at least partly to blame, was to calm the population, condemn the disturbances, dissociate the DS from them, and point out possible motives that could implicate the party's enemies. *Čas*, in a page-one column, appealed for calm and condemned the demonstrations as counterproductive.[68] The author, expressing regret and moral indignation over the events, argued that it did not help Slovakia if others saw it as a hotbed of disorder. This could lead to a backlash that would deprive the Slovaks of the benefits they were currently enjoying in the Czechoslovak Republic (freedom and democracy, for example). Hence, the people behind the protests were selfish and shortsighted and playing into the hands of those who wanted to deviate from the normal democratic path in pursuit of their goals. In another article in *Čas*, efforts were made to find the fingerprints of the Communists and the Party of Freedom on the causes and use of the demonstrations.[69] For example, it was pointed out that the Party of Freedom was active in regions where the disturbances took place and for months had been wooing former Populists with a more radical program that criticized the DS as too moderate, not implementing the promised share of spoils for Catholics stipulated in the April Agreement, and not effectively defending Catholic schools and organizations. Implicit here was the insinuation that the DS was unwilling or unable to effectively defend Tiso. In this view, the events at Piešt'any were above all an attack on district national committee chairman Chrenko, a Democrat, for betraying Catholic interests. At the same time, since Democrats were a majority in the district and a Democrat headed the district administration, Communists could use the demonstrations as a club with which to beat the DS—for its alleged laxity in taking precautions against unrest and harboring of subversive elements who fomented disturbance. It was also argued in *Čas* that the police agents and their informants dealing with the events at Piešt'any were exclusively Communist, and hence biased against the DS.

It is worth noting that some Communists on the local level were actively sympathetic to Tiso. *Čas* quoted the Communist representative at a meeting of the four political parties in Piešt'any held in the wake of the demonstrations who stated, "We cannot reproach the women who demonstrated—there were female members or wives of members of all political parties. There were female Communists and wives of Communists there."[70] The DS district secretary in Topol'čany reported in March that the local KSS chairman in Chynorany signed a resolution of the local National Front on March 20, the morning before the disturbances there, calling for Tiso's release.[71] The local DS chairman, after consulting with superiors in his party, opposed the resolution and had it voided.[72] It is difficult to tell whether these Communists were simply caught up in the local enthusiasm for Tiso, or were afraid of public opprobrium if they did not appear sympathetic to Tiso, or whether they were following orders from party higher-ups geared at provoking disturbances.

As soon as news spread through Slovakia of disturbances in Piešt'any, Slovak Partisan groups organized rallies in a number of locales. As the capstone rally, these organizations, along with trade unions and four political parties, held a demonstration of "Loyalty to the Republic" in Bratislava on March 21.[73] Each of the six organizers contributed a keynote speaker to the event. For the DS, the rally was a way to distance itself from the pro-Tiso demonstrations, which the speakers and participants severely denounced. For the Communist Party, it was a way to implicitly condemn the DS and simultaneously court and threaten Catholics, as well as a vehicle for attacking the Catholic Church through the Communist influenced trade unions and Partisan organizations. Speaking for the Union of Slovak Partisans, the Communist Samo Falt'an called for political parties to purge their ranks of "antipeople" elements and stop coquetting with fascists and parasites. This was clearly an implicit attack on the DS, as was a reference by the KSS speaker, Secretary-General Bašt'ovanský, to ex-Populists making their way into political parties in Trojan horse fashion. Bašt'ovanský warned those who were taking advantage of the indulgence and magnanimity the Czechoslovak Republic had hitherto shown toward its enemies. Near the end of his speech, he appealed to the minor adherents of the former HSLS not to be misled by irresponsible elements into catastrophe, but rather to engage themselves in the work of rebuilding the country.

Catholicism and the Catholic Church did not go unmentioned at the rally. The Partisan organizations, for example, read the following resolution: "We appeal to the conscience and responsibility of church officials that they do not permit their churches and pulpits to be used for antistate agitation and that they prevent the misuse of the religious feelings of the people for goals hostile to the Slovak nation, the Czechoslovak Republic, and the Church itself. Away with antistate subversive activities from the houses of God!"[74] Such words against the church, presupposing a big clerical role in the disturbances, were seconded by Bašt'ovanský, though couched in the terms Communists had been using for the past couple of years in their attempts to woo, or at least disarm Catholics. Bašt'ovanský concluded his speech by stating: "In the same way we expressly confirm that our manifestation and our behavior is not directed against the Catholic Church or against the Catholic clergy. We are and will remain to the full extent for religious freedom, toleration, and confessional cooperation, but in no case can we or will we allow places, set aside for religious ceremonies and functions, to be misused for the breach of public order and for incitement against the state."[75]

Katolícke noviny, though trying to tiptoe cautiously through the minefield of the Tiso trial and Piešt'any demonstrations by keeping commentary on these developments to a minimum, felt compelled to respond to charges against the Catholic Church both at the Bratislava rally and in the Communist press. The author of a March 30 article noted that Slovakia's Catholic bishops had repeatedly expressed their support for the Czechoslovak Republic, both in pastoral letters and in memoranda to the president or government, and that they had sent circulars to parish offices urging priests to contribute to the maintenance of calm and order.[76] The article went on to declare that if individual Slovak priests were engaged in antistate activity, they should be specifically identified and prosecuted; instead, the Communists were making sweeping insinuations about the clergy as a whole.

It was not in *Katolícke noviny*, however, but in *Čas* where the most forceful and controversial Catholic response to the pro-Tiso demonstrations appeared. On April 1, Cvinček, who as deputy chairman of the DS and deputy chairman of the Slovak National Council was the leading representative of Catholic interests in the DS, wrote a front-page appeal entitled "To Slovak Catholics of Good Will."[77] The appeal opened with an elaboration of the persecution of Catholics in the Czechoslovak Republic over the past two years, interpreted by Cvinček as attempts to provoke Catholics into thoughtless violence. He pointed to the repeated accusations that Catholics were enemies of the Republic and not willing to engage in reconstruction work; to the searches and seizures at Catholic bishops' offices; to objections to Catholic nominees to Slovak government and administrative organs; to fabricated stories about mass Hlinka Guard rallies, unreliable Slovak army regiments, underground arms depots in monasteries, and planned assassinations of leading Czechoslovak statesmen. In the face of these actions, Cvinček noted, Slovakia's Catholics maintained a positive attitude to the new state. He went on to imply that the pro-Tiso demonstrations were the work of provocateurs, who saw the end of the Tiso trial as their last and best chance to rile up Slovakia's population and provoke illegal actions, which would then justify a crackdown on Catholics in Slovakia. He objected to attempts to ascribe those disturbances to the church or Catholicism, and blamed them on shortsighted youths, political adventurers, and pious women. Cvinček concluded by appealing, "don't allow yourselves to be used and misused against your own interests, the interests of the Slovak nation and of the Catholic Church." He argued that this was not simply a question of the fate of the DS, but of the nation and the church, two values which now hung in the balance.

The Communists professed to be extremely offended by Cvinček's article. On April 3, the KSS's general secretary, Bašt'ovanský, responded in the lead front-page article in *Pravda*.[78] He vented his objections to Cvinček's claim that Catholics were being persecuted in Slovakia and accused Cvinček of consciously and maliciously lying to incite Slovak religious believers. Bašt'ovanský argued that any measures taken against Slovak Catholics, such as searches and seizures of church offices or objections against certain nominees for official posts, was not due to their Catholicism, but rather to suspicions of illegal activities or questions about their political reliability. He expressed indignation at Cvinček's insinuation that agents provocateur were behind the pro-Tiso demonstrations, and at his apparent refusal to admit to the strong presence of underground and aboveground enemies of the state in Slovakia. Bašt'ovanský went on to criticize the DS for running such a column in its party newspaper and called into question the propriety of having a man "who has such a dishonest and insincere relation to the security of the Republic and who defends anti-state subversives" holding the position of deputy chairman of the Slovak National Council.

While the Democratic and Communist presses had long been sniping at each other, the furor over the Cvinček appeal was one of the few times that such leading figures in these respective parties had exchanged views in such prominent fora. The Communists were taking Cvinček's action very seriously. An internal party document of April 1947, reporting on the political situation in Slovakia, interpreted Cvinček's appeal as a message to Populist sympathizers to avoid making public disturbances and leave it to the more effective responsible agents in legal positions to defend Tiso.[79] In other words, public unrest on behalf of Tiso could undermine the DS's efforts to mitigate his sentence.

Meanwhile, Slovakia's bishops were trying to defend Tiso during and after his trial. Several of them testified at the trial, namely Kmeťko, Škrábik, and Buzalka. In the course of lengthy interrogation, producing testimony that ranged rather wildly chronologically and thematically, the bishops made the case that the Slovak Republic was the lesser evil, given the other options of the time (i.e., German occupation and status as a Nazi Protectorate or occupation by Hungary), that Tiso was far preferable to the extremely pro-Nazi Tuka, and that Tiso saved many Jews by using his presidential prerogative to exempt them from deportation, often at the request of individual Slovak bishops.[80] On March 31, after Tiso's trial had concluded but before the verdict was rendered, Bishop Jantausch, on behalf of the Slovak Bishops' Council, sent a letter to President Beneš, Prime Minister Gottwald, the government's presidium, and the Slovak National Council requesting clemency for Tiso in the event he be sentenced to death.[81] Jantausch, eschewing the lengthy argumentation of the bishops' letter of January 1946, limited his argument to the potential impact of Tiso's execution on Czech-Slovak relations and the reconstruction of the state. He argued that clemency would strengthen Slovak Catholics in their devotion to the state. Such a display of religious toleration would engender closer and more fruitful cooperation between Czechs and Slovaks and help to consolidate the Republic all the sooner. Tiso's execution, on the other hand, would shake the efforts at postwar rebuilding to their foundations.

The DS also lobbied on behalf of clemency for Tiso. Concerned about the outcome of the Tiso trial and hoping to stave off an execution of Slovakia's wartime leader, Lettrich invited the three prosecutors of the Tiso trial, Anton Rašla, Ľudovít Rigan, and Juraj Šujan, to meet with him.[82] On March 12, Lettrich and the prosecutors discussed the matter for nearly four hours. Lettrich argued that the execution of Tiso would evoke hatred in Slovakia against Protestants as well as against Czechs. As a way to avoid such consequences, Lettrich argued that, though Tiso should be condemned to death, the sentence should not be carried out. In making his case, Lettrich pointed to the wisdom of Yugoslav Communist leader Josip Broz Tito, under whose regime Archbishop Stepinac did not receive the expected death sentence, but rather sixteen years in prison. Šujan and Rigan agreed with Lettrich that the prosecutor should recommend clemency after Tiso's sentence was handed down.[83] Rašla, a one-time Social Democrat turned Communist, staunchly supported the execution of Tiso. He doubted that clemency would win Populist elements over to the Czechoslovak Republic, because they would object to the fact that Tiso was condemned at all. He also stressed the didactic purposes of execution—to overthrow a potential idol for Slovakia's younger generation. Regarding the Yugoslav model, Rašla pointed out that Stepinac was condemned for his activities *after* liberation, not during the war, and hence was in a different situation than the war criminal Tiso.

In the course of the meeting with the prosecution, Lettrich mentioned that he had discussed the matter of clemency for Tiso with Beneš on two occasions, and that Beneš's position was noncommittal—that is, that he would not take a stand so as not to encumber the situation in Slovakia and that he would allow the government's decision on the matter to guide him. Because it was up to Beneš, according to Czechoslovakia's Constitution, to make the final decision regarding clemency, his position on the Tiso case was of critical importance. Ursíny claims in his memoirs that in fall of 1946, Daxner asked Beneš how he should handle the Tiso case, to which Beneš replied, "I think that he deserves death, but this is the affair of an independent court."[84] Despite these indications of Beneš's position that came the way of the DS's top leaders, the party continued to make efforts to influence him. On March 21, the political clerk of the Democratic Minister of Transportation Ivan Pietor met with Beneš's secretary, Škarvan, apprising him of the situation in Slovakia and presenting clemency as an unusual opportunity to oblige recalcitrant Slovak Catholics.[85]

Defending Tiso was going to be an uphill battle for the DS. The KSČ, KSS, and Czechoslovak Social Democratic Party were dead set on seeing

Tiso's execution carried through, as were Slovakia's leftist dominated Partisan and trade union organizations. Daxner was openly biased against Tiso from the start, both for personal and political reasons. Daxner was a veteran of the Slovak National Uprising, imprisoned for a time under the wartime Slovak regime, as was his brother, the latter ending up in Mauthausen, where he contracted ailments that would cause his death in June 1945.[86] Moreover, the Vatican proved no help to Tiso. Before the trial began, Archbishop Josef Beran of Prague returned from a visit to Rome and spread reports that the Vatican was not interested in Tiso.[87]

On April 15, the National Court convened to announce the verdict against Tiso and his codefendants, Ďurčanský and Mach.[88] Daxner, as chairman of the court, opened by mentioning that the judgment against Mach was postponed on account of health reasons. Mach, claimed Daxner, drawing from official medical reports, was suffering from tuberculosis and in need of hospital care. Daxner then rejected a proposal from Tiso's defense attorney that the trial be continued. Next, he went on to read the judgment, with Tiso found guilty of 95 of 113 points of accusation, including treason, betrayal of the Slovak National Uprising, collaboration with the Nazis, and deportation of Slovakia's Jews. His punishment was death by hanging. (Ďurčanský, too, was convicted and sentenced to death by hanging in absentia.) After reading the grounds for the judgment, Daxner asked Tiso if he requested clemency. Tiso stood up and replied that he requested it "out of moral obligation." His attorney Ernest Žabkay then submitted a written request for clemency to the court.

The request for clemency set in motion a chain of events, long prepared for on both sides yet difficult to predict, that would involve critical decisions both by the Slovak National Council and the Czechoslovak government and by President Beneš, with whom the final decision lay. These events would severely strain the DS, putting to the test its capacity to resolve the dilemma the party had been living with since the April Agreement—how to satisfy its Catholic constituency, many of whom placed their trust and hopes in the Democrats' capacity to spare Tiso from execution, without giving ammunition to those, like the Communists, who sought ways to brand the DS as a party infested with fascist sympathizers, thereby removing or paralyzing it as an obstacle to Communist dominance of Slovakia and the Republic. With little room for maneuver, and in the face of enormous pressure, the DS had little choice but to face this challenge, hyperintensified by the burning question of clemency.

The initial response to the verdict in the DS press supported the court's decision while condemning any who would try to use it for their own divisive ends. A front-page column in *Čas* on April 17, by an author identified as Dr. A. Z., stressed that the trial was fair and just.[89] The author praised the court for its success in differentiating between the activity of Tiso as a priest and his work as a politician, condemning him only for the latter. The author asserted that, on the one hand, the DS most decidedly opposed any attempt to implicate the church or religion in the trial and its verdict. On the other hand, the Democrats "oppose those fanatics who want to accuse the leadership of the state of intentionally weakening the influence of Catholicism on our people, or of evoking religious conflicts by presenting [the verdict] as an act by Protestants against Catholics." Thus, in its first editorial comment on the verdict, *Čas* pronounced pox on the houses of both anti-Church and antistate elements.

Pravda, of course, also praised the trial. Šmidke, in a column recounting Tiso's crimes, called it an act of "inexorable historical justice," which all decent Slovaks accepted with satisfaction.[90] A column on April 18 mentioned that telegrams and petitions were flowing in, in support of Tiso's execution from Catholics and non-Catholics alike. The author noted that Tiso was not on trial for being a priest, but for being the leader and president of a fascist state, and quoted *Čas*'s praise of the court on the previous day for its success in making this distinction.[91]

No sooner were the verdict and sentence announced than groups and individuals across Slovakia intensified their efforts to weigh in on the controversy. The president's office, the government, and the Slovak National Council were flooded with telegrams, letters, and petitions from supporters and opponents of clemency. Resistance and Partisan groups held rallies throughout Slovakia, passing resolutions against clemency. Such groups also organized delegations to Bratislava and Prague, where they sought to present their views, or more accurately pressure the Slovak National Council and the government. The Vatican, on the other hand, tried to stay out of the controversy. On the day the verdict and sentence were announced, the Holy See's charge d'affaires told Beneš's secretary Vaněk in confidence that he had been instructed by Pope Pius XII to limit all interventions on Tiso's behalf exclusively to "the question of charity" and to avoid any sort of political intervention, a consequence of Vatican disapproval of Tiso's rejection of Vatican urgings to resign at the time of the deportation of Slovakia's Jews to Nazi death camps.[92]

The first formal step on behalf of clemency for Tiso was taken by the prosecutor Rigan, who submitted a request to that end to the court.[93] Rigan was alone among the three prosecutors in making such a request. In asking that Tiso's sentence be commuted to life imprisonment, Rigan pointed to a number of mitigating circumstances. He argued that the interwar Republic had a number of serious problems that undermined it (corruption, bureaucratic incompetence, extreme partisanship, ineffective leadership, insufficient time to consolidate, and failure to solve the Slovak question). Its demise could not be laid at the feet of Tiso. Rigan asserted that Tiso, like many other politicians in Europe, misunderstood the situation within which he operated and the dangers of the rise of Nazism. He noted that Tiso's narrow parochial outlook kept him from seeing the full ramifications of his choices. Rigan gave some credence to the arguments of Tiso's defense, that he was acting with good intentions and preventing a greater evil by committing a lesser one. He argued for Tiso's patriotism, claiming that Tiso maintained a consistent anti-Hungarian attitude, opposing Hungarian plans to annex Slovakia, and that he did not indulge the maximal demands of his German allies, only those demands which could not be avoided. Rigan also stressed, as have later historians of the period, the distinction and rivalry between the relatively more moderate Tiso and the extreme pro-Nazi orientation of Tuka and his followers.[94] Rigan noted that Tiso worked to blunt the influence of the extreme Germanophile Tuka while choosing people of character and relative moderation as his collaborators.[95] Finally, as a technicality, Rigan noted that documents to which Tiso would have liked to have appealed were not at his disposal, having been taken by the Red Army at the time Bánovce was liberated and transported to Moscow, where, despite promises to the contrary, they were not available to the court.

Tiso's lawyers, Ernest Žabkay and Martin Grečo, also submitted an official request for clemency, asking for a more "appropriate" sentence for their client.[96] Here, far more than in Rigan's request, the grounds stressed legal technicalities. Tiso's lawyers argued that the defense was not allowed to speak with the accused without the security organs present—a violation of a fundamental principle of criminal trial procedure—and that the defense did not have certain archival materials at its disposal, while the prosecution did. Furthermore, records of testimony were not made available within the requisite three days, but lagged by nearly two months, thereby making it impossible for the defense to cite testimony made after January 15 in its concluding statements. In addition to these and a number of other technicalities, Tiso's lawyers argued that the trial was politically biased, both because Daxner himself was biased, as the SNR itself had recognized in the past, and because, despite a legislative order calling for political parity on the court's senate that would judge Tiso, no members of the DS took part in the judgment. Tiso's attorneys also argued that Tiso was being punished for events beyond his control. They claimed that he did not prepare for Slovakia's independence in 1939, nor help cause it, and that he showed no initiative and intentionality in his cooperation with Nazi Germany. Rather, he simply tried to make the best of a bad situation that was thrust upon him. Finally, Tiso's attorneys, in the only argument that the DS would make its own, argued that clemency would strengthen Czech-Slovak relations, eliminate the threat of enmity between Slovakia's Catholics and Protestants, and strengthen ties between Slovak emigrants and their motherland.

The National Court quickly decided against recommending clemency for Tiso and passed Tiso's request on to the Slovak commissioner of justice, Ivan Štefánik, a Democrat. Štefánik in turn supported Tiso's request and submitted a proposal to the presidium of the SNR, which read, "I propose that the death sentence of Dr. Jozef Tiso be commuted to life imprisonment."[97] The proposal was to the point, absent the argumentation included in Tiso's request, and unlike Tiso's request, allowed for no sentence less than life imprisonment. On April 16, the SNR's presidium met to consider Štefánik's proposal, along with some other matters connected with Tiso's trial.

When the presidium convened, it was already under enormous pressure. By law, Tiso's execution had to be carried out within forty-eight hours of the announcement of the verdict, so matters had to be considered quickly. Moreover, the government in Prague was meeting later that day to discuss clemency and was eagerly awaiting the views of Slovakia's leading organs on the matter. Adding to the pressure was the fact that the presidium received the 214-page judgment against Tiso only shortly before its meeting.[98] In addition, telegrams and petitions, for and against clemency, were pouring in, while anti-Tiso rallies were staged across Slovakia by Partisan and labor organizations, and delegations from trade unions, housing estates, and especially resistance organizations arrived in Bratislava to add their presence to the deliberations.[99] Though there were no reported cases of violence, it is not difficult to imagine the presence of these groups, encouraged if not orchestrated by the Communists, adding a menacing character to the already intense pressure on the presidium, or, more precisely, its Democratic members. For example, a consortium of major resistance organizations issued a declaration on April 16 that condemned clemency as a "shameful defilement (*popl'uvanie*) of all the sacrifices of our national struggle" that could embolden Tiso's supporters into provoking unrest in Slovakia aimed at undermining the Republic.[100] If clemency was granted to Tiso, these organizations promised to assess the situation and consider what means to employ in defense of the Republic and the gains of the Slovak National Uprising.

The composition of the presidium, whose five members consisted of three Democrats (Lettrich, Cvinček, Polák) and two Communists (Šmidke, Horváth), favored the DS. Nevertheless, the presidium did not endorse Štefánik's proposal for clemency; rather, it resolved to submit the proposal to the government without comment. In his memoirs, Ursíny argues that Lettrich went into the meeting with the intention of avoiding debate over clemency, a position Ursíny strongly advised against.[101] Lettrich's behavior at the meeting does betray the actions of a man intent on avoiding debate.[102] First off, most of the meeting's discussion dealt with Democratic dissatisfaction with Daxner's handling of the trial and with the postponement of the verdict on Mach. When the presidium did get around to the Tiso verdict, Lettrich made it clear that he felt that the pressure of time made it impossible to acquire sufficient knowledge to take a position on clemency and that any recommendation would thus have to be "political." The Communist Horváth then proposed that the presidium take no stand, but simply pass on Štefánik's proposal to the government, without comment. He argued that a recommendation from the SNR was neither required by the pertinent agreements, nor necessary, for it was the government and Beneš whose views would be decisive. According to Horváth, since the Communists were opposed to clemency, they would be unable to support Štefánik's proposal, and hence any vote in the SNR would be on a partisan basis, setting a bad precedent for future Communist-Democratic cooperation. When it came time to vote on Horváth's proposal, the presidium accepted it unanimously. Before examining why the Slovak National Council, or more specifically its Democratic members, opted not to recommend clemency for Tiso, let us track the proposal's course to Prague and ultimately to Beneš.

The day before the government met to discuss clemency for Tiso, Beneš sent a note to Prime Minister Klement Gottwald, laying out his position on the issue.[103] Beneš noted that he was prepared to grant clemency to Tiso on humanitarian grounds, but that since this was also a political question, he would do whatever the government recommended. At the same time, Beneš made it clear that he had no sympathy for Tiso, whom he regarded as an accomplice in the murder of innocent people and as one who lied during his trial in an effort to shift the blame onto others. Though the Communists interpreted Beneš's note as an attempt to pressure the government to vote for clemency,[104] it seems rather that Beneš was instead letting the government know that if it wanted to see Tiso executed, it had better recommend that and not pass the buck to the president. Beneš almost certainly wrote his note knowing that the anticlemency forces were in the majority in the government. The Communists and Social Democrats were openly hostile to Tiso, and the nonpartisan ministers, Ludvík Svoboda (Defense) and Jan Masaryk (Foreign Affairs), could be expected to be so as well. Together, these constituted fourteen of the twenty-six members of the government, and enough to tip any vote to Tiso's detriment. On top of that, the Czech National Socialists were at best ambivalent. A number of leading National Socialists opposed clemency and wanted their party to vote against it, or at least not vote for it.[105] However, Minister of Justice Prokop Drtina, one of the party's top leaders, had earlier assured Lettrich that he would support clemency, provided the Slovak National Council did.[106] In the last of a series of meetings on the issue, held right before the government session began, Drtina managed to convince his colleagues to agree to the following position—to vote against clemency, but only after first proposing that the request for clemency be returned to the presidium of the Slovak National Council for that organ's recommendation.

The government meeting opened at approximately 5:15 P.M., after a delay of over an hour as they waited for reports from Slovakia.[107] Within ten minutes, a delegation of representatives from the Union of Czechoslovak Partisans and some other similar organizations asked to be admitted. Since the National Socialists had yet to arrive, making their last-minute plans in a nearby room, the meeting was adjourned for forty-five minutes while the Partisan organizations were given the opportunity to pressure the ministers to vote against clemency.[108] Once the delegations had their say and engaged some of the ministers over the issue, and the National Socialist ministers had arrived, the meeting was reconvened.

Gottwald began by sharing two pieces of information he had just received from Slovakia—the memorandum from the SNR's presidium passing on Štefánik's proposal for clemency without comment, and a telegram from Husák as chairman of the Board of Commissioners. Husák noted that Štefánik's proposal did not reflect the views of the Board of Commissioners or its presidium, whose standpoint Štefánik did not seek, and should therefore be regarded as his own personal proposal. Husák added that he did not agree with the proposal. Thus, the meeting opened with reports from Slovakia's two chief political organs, neither of which endorsed clemency. Gottwald then proposed that, since the National Court in Bratislava recommended against clemency, and the presidium of the SNR did not recommend for it, the government resolve against clemency. In a long and sometimes passionate debate, ministers from both sides weighed in on the question, with positions breaking down along party lines.

The Communists led the charge against clemency. Vladimír Clementis, the state secretary in the Ministry of Foreign Affairs, read a KSS declaration that laid out the Communist position. The declaration stressed the didactic function of the trial—that is, its purpose in discouraging enemies of the republic. A death sentence could do that far better than a life sentence in this respect. Clemency, on the contrary, would only encourage enemies of the state and sympathizers of Tiso and his regime. Reaction, as before, was trying to take over Slovakia "even at the price of the Republic."[109] The declaration argued that clemency would evoke distrust in the judicial system. Veterans of the Slovak National Uprising would be upset with the departure from the ideals of the resistance; people would note the injustice of lesser criminals having been more harshly punished than Tiso; and politics would be seen once more as "*pánske huncútstvo*."[110] The declaration noted in particular that Tiso showed no remorse for his crimes and, in fact, gave succor to the Republic's enemies in his concluding statement at his trial. Much of what Clementis read was identical to the declaration made a day earlier by Slovakia's resistance organizations, testifying to the commanding role Communists played in those organizations and the success the party had in coordinating various social organizations on behalf of its objectives. Indeed, both declarations concluded with the same threat to assess the situation and consider what means to employ in defense of the republic and its character. Czech Communists also spoke out against clemency, asserting that Tiso was a traitor and war criminal, and that failing to execute him would be a blow to Czechoslovakia's unity and independence. Communists speakers also argued that it was the will of the Slovak people that Tiso be executed, as evidenced by the position of the National Court, Slovak National Council, and Board of Commissioners, all organs composed entirely of Slovaks and representing Slovakia. This was why, Václav Kopecký noted, the DS would not speak up for clemency on the SNR's presidium.

The Social Democratic ministers were just as opposed to clemency as the Communists, and no less assertive about their position. Zdeněk Fierlinger, the leader of that party and a deputy prime minister, argued that a vote for clemency would upset Czechoslovakia's allies in the Slavic world, in part because it would fuel Slovak independence, which itself threatened Czechoslovakia's border with the Soviet Union. Fierlinger even remarked that how one voted on the clemency question was a test of one's patriotism. With respect to the religious dimension of the question, the Social Democratic leader asserted that Tiso's being a priest was not a mitigating circumstance, but rather one that made matters worse. He noted that it was not good for the Catholic Church to encumber itself with Tiso. While Fierlinger represented the pro-Communist left wing of the Social Democratic Party, that party's right wing was no less vehement about Tiso. Václav Majer, the leader of the right Social Democrats, referred to the Slovak priest as one of the chief war criminals, guilty of mass murder.

The most extensive attack on Tiso and argument against clemency, however, came not from the ministers of the leftist parties, but from the ostensibly nonpartisan (albeit closet Communist sympathizer) Minister of Defense Svoboda. As a Czechoslovak hero of both the First and Second World Wars, Svoboda's words carried a certain cachet. Svoboda spoke at length about why Tiso must die. He came out strongly against so-called half solutions; at hand was a definitive historical question with long-term implications that should not be judged according to the needs and mood of the moment. Tiso was not just a war criminal; he was the symbol of Populism, fascism, treason, and collaboration. To grant clemency to Tiso, according to Svoboda, would render his trial useless and superfluous. If alive, Tiso would remain around to poison cooperation and unity between Czechs and Slovaks; clemency would encourage his supporters while disappointing others. Like many speakers and writers of the time, Svoboda noted that Tiso showed no remorse. He called for a firm and resolute action against him as a means of strengthening Czechoslovakia's international position and prestige. To those who argued that Tiso should be spared because he was a priest, Svoboda declared, "We are not judging a priest, but a traitor, a destroyer of the Czechoslovak state and a criminal. That Tiso is a priest only makes matters worse; he profaned the priestly office and

Church at a time when thousands of other priests fought valiantly against Nazism and perished in concentration camps and prisons."

On the other side of the equation were those ministers who championed clemency, in the ranks of which were only the Democrats and Czech Populists. Here the most prominent speaker was Ursíny. The Democratic deputy prime minister argued that clemency would improve relations between Czechs and Slovaks, Lutherans and Catholics, and aid in the overall consolidation of the postwar Republic. Such a goodwill gesture might also win over some of Czechoslovakia's enemies. Ursíny noted that religious feelings ran strong in Slovakia, where the execution of a priest was a serious and potentially upsetting matter. He pointed out that many good people were for clemency, including some bishops and high functionaries in the Lutheran church, a church that itself had suffered under Tiso's regime.[111] The Democratic Minister of Transportation Ivan Pietor also spelled out a number of reasons for clemency. He argued that Tiso was popular among the majority of Slovaks and that the prevailing majority of Slovaks would vote for clemency if given the chance, though this did not mean they agreed with Tiso's politics. He, too, noted that important Lutheran leaders sent fervent appeals on Tiso's behalf in the interest of the peaceful development of Slovakia and Czechoslovakia. The given political situation, according to Pietor, demanded statesmanlike thinking and wisdom and sensitivity to the prevailing political conditions and mood. In such a context, clemency would be a gesture to win over hearts in Slovakia and bring the Czech and Slovak nations together. While the court may have unanimously established Tiso's guilt and called for his execution, that was a judicial decision, not a political one. What the Republic now faced was a manifestly political question, and the task of the government was to settle it in accordance with political considerations.

The Czech Populists, as members of a Catholic party with moderate inclinations, also supported clemency. Minister of Post František Hála, himself a Catholic priest, presented clemency as the most suitable solution for Czechoslovak and Slovak interests. The Populist Minister of Health Adolf Procházka remarked that clemency was the desire of most Slovaks, and of the Lutheran church leadership. Jan Kopecký, a minister without portfolio, supported clemency as a way to consolidate the Republic and reminded his ministerial colleagues that life imprisonment was not tantamount to acquittal.

In making his case, Ursíny contended that the SNR did not recommend against clemency; rather it was not the presidium's function to express a position on the proposal, but only to pass it on to the government. Technically, he was correct in that the Second Prague Agreement of April 11, 1946, the statute under which such matters were regulated, stated that the commissioner's proposal be submitted to the government "via the Presidium of the Slovak National Council."[112] However, this strict construction is not the way the SNR had hitherto been dealing with proposals. Gottwald snidely noted that the presidium had suddenly decided in this case to limit itself to the role of a post office, and along with Fierlinger, he regarded Ursíny's explanation as sophistry. They were not buying the Democrats' claim that the presidium's position was not a failure to endorse clemency.

It was the centrist parties, however, that expressed the most anger over the SNR's silence regarding clemency, a silence that, because the DS had a majority in the presidium, was clearly blamed on the Democrats. A number of National Socialist and Populist ministers voiced their indignation at the SNR's attempt to pass the buck. Jaroslav Stránský, the minister of education, said that he wanted Ursíny and his friends to recognize the situation into which they had gotten the government, which thanks to them now had to decide on a matter about which it did not have sufficient knowledge. Now the government could be blamed if Tiso did not get clemency, thereby being burdened with what was primarily a Slovak problem. Drtina, similarly, said he was perplexed by the presidium's unexpected course of action, one which now put the government in a difficult situation. He proposed sending the proposal back to the presidium for its opinion, in accordance with the Second Prague Agreement. Following suit, Hubert Ripka noted his party's astonishment at the SNR's action—how it limited its role to that of a mailbox in the way it interpreted the Second Prague Agreement. He remarked that Slovakia's self-proclaimed leading organ did not have the courage to express itself on a question of such importance for the future and fate of the Slovak people. According to Ripka, it was clear that the SNR presidium wanted to shift the responsibility for Tiso's fate onto the government. He now insisted that the presidium express itself on the issue, and as quickly as possible. Hála, speaking for the Czech Populists, echoed the sentiments of the National Socialists, noting that the presidium's action greatly surprised him and that it seemed to want to pass responsibility on to the government.

While the National Socialists and Populists expressed agreement with Drtina's motion to return the proposal to the SNR, the leftist parties adamantly opposed it. Gottwald, Fierlinger, and others argued that the SNR had already taken a position by failing to endorse clemency, and that further delay of Tiso's execution would only drag things out, sustain a state of tension, and provoke and evoke supporters of Tiso, as well as open the floodgates for clemency for others sentenced to death. When Drtina's motion to return the proposal to the presidium of the SNR came to a vote, it was defeated thirteen to ten. The voting broke down according to party: the National Socialists, Populists, and Democrats supported the proposal; the leftist parties and nonpartisan ministers opposed it.

While the Czech Populists may well have sincerely believed that the best remedy for the crisis would be for the SNR to voice its opinion on the matter, we know that the National Socialists made and supported the motion simply for cosmetic purposes, hoping that it would fail. The Democrats, of course, were in a quite unenviable position. The motion's failure meant that they would not be given a second chance to make a stand for clemency in the presidium. At the same time, it is not certain that they would have known what to do with a second chance; the factors that kept them from endorsing clemency the first time around were still operative.

As the debate over Štefánik's proposal resumed, the National Socialists now came out against clemency and sought to present the anticlemency position as the one identified with Slovakia. Drtina, noting that the government was not fully informed of the details of the case, thought the matter should be best settled by Slovakia, as it indeed was—a Slovak court securely established Tiso's guilt and unanimously rejected clemency, which the SNR also failed to recommend. Ripka, demonstrating the sort of Czech ignorance of Slovakia that rankles Slovaks, claimed that Tiso, long before 1938, was as bad or worse than Tuka. Because the consequences of Populism had not yet disappeared from Slovakia, clemency should be rejected. Ripka not only came out against it, but also appealed to the DS and Czech Populists to abstain on the vote, so the government could present a united front in its rejection of clemency. He addressed the Democrats with the rebuke that, if they did not vote for clemency in Slovakia, they should not now at the governmental level, where the domestic and international ramifications of such a vote were greater.

After more discussion, the government ultimately passed a resolution voicing its opposition to clemency, on the grounds that the National Court in Bratislava had recommended against it, and that the presidium of the SNR did not endorse it when passing Štefánik's proposal on to Prague. The vote was seventeen in favor, six against. All ministers rejected clemency except those from the DS and Czech People's Party. The meeting was adjourned at 8:50 P.M.

Shortly thereafter, Gottwald took the government's recommendation to Beneš, who accepted it and informed Slovakia's Commissioner of Justice that his request for clemency had been officially denied.[113] Upon learning of the decision, Lettrich made a last-ditch intervention, telephoning Beneš's chancellery with a message, stating his position that the government's standpoint was in conflict with Article 1, Letter B, of the Second Prague Agreement, which stipulates that, if the government had objections against a proposal from Slovakia, it was to return that proposal to the SNR's presidium, not pass it on to Beneš with a recommendation.[114] Lettrich warned Beneš of possible "immense political consequences" that could result from a rejection of clemency, and for which the DS could not accept responsibility. Lettrich concluded by noting that the DS had an absolute majority in the SNR and its presidium, and along with the Party of Freedom, fully agreed with Štefánik's proposal, considering clemency as in the state and national interest. Beneš received the message early the next morning, instructing his chancellery to tell Lettrich that he had gone to the countryside and would discuss the matter with Gottwald if Lettrich so desired.[115] Ursíny too attempted an appeal on behalf of clemency, and also found out that the rejection of clemency was an accomplished fact and that Beneš was incommunicado.[116] Štefánik himself made a final attempt on Tiso's behalf on April 17, asking the National Court that Tiso be transferred to the jail of the Office of the Public Prosecutor, so he could be questioned regarding some other cases. This the National Court rejected on the grounds that Tiso could be just as easily questioned at its own jail.[117] With all avenues for clemency now exhausted, Tiso was hanged early the next morning, officially pronounced dead at 5:30 A.M.

It was no surprise that Tiso was found guilty, or that he was sentenced to die. Nor was it astonishing that the majority of ministers in Prague rejected the recommendation for clemency and that Beneš acted in accordance with their position. But what was puzzling was the behavior of the DS—supporting clemency in Prague, but not in Bratislava; desperately appealing for clemency on the eve of Tiso's execution while letting the issue pass right through the hands of the SNR presidium, on which they held a majority a day and a half earlier.

Did the DS want the appeal for clemency to fail? Such a view can be found in the police record, where a report mentions that Lettrich was opposed to clemency for Tiso.[118] Like many scenarios sketched out by police informants, however, this one seems without much grounding. First, Lettrich lobbied Tiso's three prosecutors on behalf of clemency and got Minister of Justice Drtina to promise his support for clemency as well. These are hardly the actions of a man desiring Tiso's execution. Nor does such an alleged desire harmonize with Lettrich's agitated attempts to lobby Beneš at the eleventh hour. Other explanations must lie behind the timidity of Lettrich and the DS at the notorious SNR presidium meeting of April 16.

Historians who have examined the meeting, and the issue of clemency overall, have come up with a number of explanations, which will be discussed here in ascending order of plausibility and influence.[119] Most dubious is the view that the Democrats trusted that Beneš would grant clemency regardless of the recommendations he received. While there apparently was public speculation that Beneš might spare Tiso, the DS leadership had little reason to put their trust in such suppositions. Beneš had already given Lettrich and Ursíny quite clear indications of his opposition to clemency.[120]

Another of the weaker arguments for why the SNR did not take a stand on clemency was the one the DS itself used to explain itself at the government meeting of April 16 and thereafter—that is, that the Second Prague Agreement stipulated that the SNR's role in the process was simply to pass proposals on to the government and not to comment on them, and that if the government had objections to Štefánik's proposal, it would solicit the SNR presidium's views on it. This explanation holds no more water upon reflection than it did at the time. A party that believed Slovak organs should speak for Slovakia, and a good bit of whose appeal was based on its advocacy of autonomy for Slovakia, is behaving out of character when it surrenders to Prague the prerogative to decide on a matter so close to the hearts of so many Slovaks.

Another explanation put forth by the DS was that it lacked sufficient time to study the documentation pertinent to the Tiso trial. While on the surface this is factually correct, still, the SNR was not being asked to render a legal or judicial judgment, but a political one. In the latter case, the party could have made up its mind on a position long before the verdict, as the Communists had.

More convincing are the views that the DS was simply afraid that a vote for clemency would prompt the KSS to provoke a political crisis in Slovakia, halting cooperation within the SNR, mobilizing resistance and trade union groups against the Democrats, and forcing Prague to step in. Indeed, such threats and pressures were already evident on the Slovak political stage for over a year and were common everywhere else in East Central Europe where Communist parties were active. In this view, the DS simply lost its nerve and opted to pass the matter on to Prague rather than deal with it in Bratislava. This explanation seems valid enough in that Communist pressure was always an influence. However, if fear of repercussions were the main thing keeping the DS quiet, why did Democrats vote for clemency at the government sessions in Prague? Was it to give public assurance to their constituents that they opposed clemency, but at a venue where they did not have to worry about their vote carrying any influence and thereby provoking a clemency-induced crisis back home? This question is moot, given the influence of the most significant factor of all.

A final explanation is the most convincing and crucial one—that the DS could not count on its own representative on the presidium, Milan Polák, to vote for clemency. Polák's record, both before and after 1947, placed him on the left wing of the DS. A former Partisan, and leader in the Partisan veterans' movement, Polák collaborated with the Communists during and after the February coup of 1948.[121] Unable to count on his vote, Lettrich preferred no vote on clemency to one in which Polák would abstain or vote no. Thus he chose the least painful but still damaging option. While many of Slovakia's Catholics would be upset if the presidium, on which the majority of members were Democrats, failed to take a stand on clemency, they would be even more outraged should the presidium outright reject clemency, or be unable to muster the three votes needed for it to pass. Ursíny's memoirs provide further evidence for this explanation. Ursíny reports that, when on a visit to the United States in the fall of 1967, he spoke by telephone with Lettrich, who told him that he wanted the SNR to avoid the issue of clemency because Polák would not have voted for it.[122]

As Tiso's corpse was removed from the scaffolding and preparations made for his burial, it remained to be seen how Slovakia's Catholic population would respond to the execution and how they would regard the DS's failure to stand up for clemency in the SNR presidium. It also remained to be seen how the DS would explain itself to those voters who had placed their hopes in its capacity to translate a booming electoral victory in Slovakia into protection for Tiso and defense of Catholic interests. Finally, it remained to be seen how the Communists would deal with a DS that, on the one hand, was weakened by its failure to protect Tiso, while at the same time, by publicly identifying itself with support for clemency in the government and elsewhere, had become an even more conspicuous target for those seeking to implicate it as a haven for war criminals and other elements disloyal to the Republic.

4

CONSPIRACIES

Plots against the State and the Democrats

THE period from Tiso's execution through the autumn of 1947 saw the most aggressive and comprehensive assault on the DS and its leading Catholics to date. The Communists thwarted an attempt by the DS to remove Daxner from the court, thereby quashing a Democratic initiative aimed at restoring that party's standing among Catholics in the wake of Tiso's hanging. They also worked to further restrict Slovakia's autonomy and pushed to cement the state monopoly of education in a new school law. Their rhetoric and policy proposals took on a sharper edge of class conflict during this period. Pro-Communist Partisan, labor, and peasant organizations intensified their pressure on the Democrats. The KSS and its allies in the police used the uncovering of a bush league antistate conspiracy in Slovakia to implicate several of the DS's leading Catholics and even succeeded in entangling Ursíny in the affair. The DS, already fraught with growing internal tensions and damaged in the eyes of many Catholics for its behavior during the fight for clemency for Tiso, scrambled to survive this series of blows. The Catholic Church, whose leadership was also targeted by the Communists as, like the DS, harboring elements disloyal to the regime, likewise tried to protect itself and its interests, above all by continuing its defense of parochial education and trying to distance itself from the Communist induced security crisis in Slovakia.

In the immediate aftermath of Tiso's execution, Slovakia was calm, a fact noted by the KSS itself in both its internal reports and public pronouncements.[1] A combination of appeals by the Catholic bishops and the DS for calm, along with extensive security precautions and perhaps a fatalistic acceptance on the part of the Slovak population that there was little they could do to change the course of events, accounted for the lack of serious unrest. Police reports, however, do note some minor incidents—attacks on Czechoslovak and Soviet army graves in Humenné, a rock thrown through the window of Communist headquarters in Sabinov, sporadic appearances of antistate graffiti and nasty underground leaflets.[2] Generally, though, to the extent that there was opposition expressed to the execution of Tiso, it was done legally and passively—men wearing black armbands or black ties, women wearing black kerchiefs, the display of mourning banners, Requiem Masses celebrated for Tiso's soul (though without his name being mentioned).[3] On April 20, many Slovak Catholics went to church, and that afternoon a relatively sizable number (eventually totaling around five hundred) congregated in St. Martin's cemetery in Bratislava at what was alleged to be Tiso's grave, praying and singing.[4]

Katolícke noviny tried to give voice to some of the sense of frustration, grief, and powerlessness felt by many Slovak Catholics. In its report on Tiso's execution, it stressed the prayerfulness of Tiso's last hours on earth. In assessing the implications of his execution, an issue that could land the editors in hot water, the paper elected to reprint an article from *L'Osservatore Romano*, which lamented that, by denying clemency, the state lost an opportunity to strengthen relations between Czechs and Slovaks.[5] In the May 4 issue of *Katolícke noviny*, the indomitable Koza-Matejov wrote a front-page column entitled "Povedte nám, čo máme robiť?" ("Tell Us, What Should We Do?").[6] He portrayed Slovak Catholics as "orphans," who were encouraged to be politically active and then condemned for their activism; who were told not to mix into politics but then denied a nonpartisan daily newspaper; who were attacked for taking part in demonstrations but also attacked for remaining "suspiciously" calm when they did not. Defiantly, he stated, "We are not afraid of the court of the people, because we believe in the court of God." Slovak Catholics had done their best, according to Koza, and the future would bring them vindication.[7]

Though Slovakia remained calm after Tiso's execution, the feelings of sadness, bitterness, and frustration expressed by Koza were no doubt felt among much of the Catholic population and were directed not just at Czechs and Communists but also at Protestants and at the DS itself. Immediately after

Tiso's execution, there were mass resignations from the party, though these fell precipitously by the second day.[8] There had been since 1945 tensions within the DS between Protestants and Catholics, between ex-Agrarians and ex-Populists, and between those members who had resisted the Tiso regime and fought in the Slovak National Uprising and those who had served the wartime regime.[9] Diehard Partisans from the former group were unhappy with the April Agreement; staunch Catholics were equally unhappy with lapses and delays in implementing that agreement. While police reports on conditions within the DS were often exaggerated or misinformed, they were correct in discerning these inner party tensions. Already in the summer of 1946, Cvinček wrote to Lettrich on behalf of Catholics disgruntled that they were not being given the degree of influence and positions within the party promised in the April Agreement.[10] At issue was the fact that the party's Narrow Presidium, where Catholics had a majority, was being circumvented in deciding the selection of the party's candidates for high state office. Instead, such decisions were being made by the party's Executive Committee, where Catholics had less influence. Divisions in the DS were significant enough to cause the repeated postponement of its party congress, which the April Agreement stipulated would occur by the end of 1946; in the absence of a party congress, the DS was unable to make some of the structural and personnel changes that would accommodate Catholic demands. Bugár later explained that Protestants in the party leadership favored relatives and ex-Agrarians in assigning positions and influence.[11] Ursíny testified in court in 1948 that the April Agreement was not being consistently followed in the allotment of positions in the party's economic and administrative life.[12] By the time of the Tiso trial, there was even talk of Catholics splitting off to found their own party or defecting to the Party of Freedom.[13] In early 1947, Ivan Pietor, a Catholic Democrat, tried to sell the idea of a Catholic party to Slovakia's Bishops' Council, but to no avail. The bishops were lukewarm to the idea, and Vojtaššák was outright hostile, distrusting Pietor as a former member of the secular and pro-Czech National Socialist Party and a disciple of Šrobár.[14]

It was a DS marked by such tensions that chairman Lettrich had to guide and hold together through postwar Slovakia's biggest political crises, which began at the close of the Tiso trial and continued on through to February 1948. The DS's first task was damage control in the face of anger directed at it by Catholics for its failure to prevent Tiso's execution. Of central importance in this respect was the notorious meeting of the SNR presidium of April 16, when a Democratic majority failed to recommend clemency for Tiso. In the April 23 issue of *Čas*, the DS explained itself in a front-page column entitled "How Was It in Reality?" ("Ako to v Skutočnosti Bolo?", hereafter referred to as "How Was It").[15] This issue of *Čas* was then confiscated by the authorities due to the article's content. In response, the DS's press office sent a circular to all regional and district offices of the party, instructing them to inform voters of the party's views as expressed in the offending article. The text of "How Was It" accompanied the circular.[16] Local Democratic leaders set up meetings where they expressed the party's position.[17] In this way, the content of the article became known throughout Slovakia.

"How Was It" began by making two points designed to stave off charges that the DS was thinking and acting to the detriment of the Republic. First, the article pointed out that the DS was only bringing up the details surrounding the matter of clemency for Tiso because of the "tendentious and malicious" information being spread in the press by their enemies, a reference to articles that had been appearing in the Czechoslovak press insinuating that the DS was complicit in Tiso's execution. Second, the DS made it clear that it rejected Tiso's policies and recognized his guilt, supporting clemency only out of regard for the interests of the republic—that is, as a way to consolidate relations between Czechs and Slovaks and smooth the way for reconstruction and the drafting of the new constitution.

At issue was why the Democrats, if they indeed opposed Tiso's execution, did not make a stand in the SNR presidium, where they held a three-to-two advantage, and pass a resolution endorsing the request for clemency. In a somewhat contradictory explanation, *Čas* made several points: that the circumstances made it extraordinarily difficult to take such a stand; that the SNR presidium did indeed take a stand for clemency for Tiso; and that the SNR presidium expected the government to return the proposal to the presidium if it had objections to it. With respect to the first point, *Čas* noted that the presidium received the lengthy judgment against Tiso only ten minutes before the meeting and had to make a decision quickly, as the government was meeting to discuss the matter in just a few hours and Beneš was to make the final decision that evening. Compounding this pressure were deputations of workers and resistance veterans, a flood of telegrams, and the (accurate) perception that the Communists were spoiling to produce a serious political crisis if they did not get their way. With respect to the second point, *Čas* argued that the fact that the SNR presidium submitted the proposal to the government undeniably constitutes "*the agreement of the SNR presidium with the proposal* [emphasis in original]," so that a specific resolution to that effect was unnecessary. If the presidium disagreed with the request for clemency or did not want to take a position on it, it would have stated so in its resolution. The article noted that such a procedure was indeed a departure from past practice, in which the presidium voted on proposals before passing them on, but that it was nonetheless valid. No explanation for why no position was taken was included, though one could surmise that a key factor was the difficult circumstances of the meeting. The third point is connected with the Second Prague Agreement of April 11, 1946, which stipulated that "the President of the Republic grants clemency in Slovakia . . . at the suggestion of the Commissioner of Justice, who submits it via the SNR Presidium to the Government—The Government will return the proposal to the SNR Presidium if it has objections against it from the perspective of statewide interests; otherwise, it will submit it to the President of the Republic." According to *Čas*, the presidium expected that the government would return the proposal if it had any objections.

By passing it on to Beneš, the government was violating the Second Prague Agreement. In conclusion, *Čas* argued that some political circles were distorting the facts as a way to attack the DS, its chairman, and the SNR presidium, but that such attacks would not free their attackers from the responsibility they took upon themselves.[18] The article also noted the urgent but fruitless efforts taken by Lettrich at the last minute to convince Beneš to grant clemency.

"How Was It" set off a storm of protest in Slovakia, most of it produced by the KSS. On April 23, Šmidke presented a KSS declaration at the meeting of the SNR presidium, in which he accused *Čas* of presenting falsehoods concerning the discussions of April 16.[19] According to Šmidke, the SNR Presidium did not support clemency for Tiso but rather resolved unanimously not to take a stand. Moreover, the SNR passed on the proposal to Prague without any expectations that it would be returned to the SNR. Šmidke went on to chastise the Democrats for fleeing from responsibility for their refusal to support clemency, which had the effect of shifting responsibility for the execution away from Slovakia and onto the shoulders of the government in Prague and President Beneš. This in turn has encouraged anti-Czech elements and feeling in Slovakia. Šmidke concluded by asserting that the DS's views, as expressed in the offending article, were incompatible with participation in the government, and that the DS had seriously threatened the possibility of constructive cooperation with the KSS in the future.[20]

At the same time, the Coordinating Committee of Resistance Units in Slovakia issued a resolution about the article in *Čas*. In a rhetorical assault clearly aimed at sowing division within the DS, the resolution lamented that "we cannot believe that such a text was published with the agreement and knowledge of actual Democrats, who fought hand-in-hand with us in the Czechoslovak army abroad, in Partisan units, in the Czechoslovak army in Slovakia, and in the underground resistance."[21] The resolution expressed dismay that *Čas* crudely and rudely attacked Partisan units in its "treacherous and perfidious" article. It claimed that Lettrich was personally opposed to clemency for Tiso and even open to accepting assistance from resistance units against the ex-Populists in his party; however, he ultimately capitulated to pressure from that wing of his party. The resolution concluded by asking the DS whether it agreed with the content of "How Was It," whether it agreed that the execution of Tiso was a transparent effort to compromise the leadership of the DS in the eyes of its members, and whether the DS wanted to pursue its Partisan interests even "at the price of the Republic." If the DS answered yes to these questions, then the committee would call for an investigation into whether such a party can still be regarded as pro-state, the resolution concluded.

Communist agitation over the *Čas* article even made its way to the government chambers in Prague, where Gottwald raised the matter at a meeting of April 25.[22] In a sharp debate over the offending article, Gottwald and Široký asserted that the DS's actions were not compatible with membership in the government. Ursíny replied that the whole controversy was started not by the DS, but by allegations in the press that the DS took no stand on clemency and was washing its hands in the manner of Pontius Pilate. Behind it all, according to Ursíny, was an effort to split the DS. Ursíny argued that the article was meant for internal party consumption. The Communists, on the contrary, charged that it was a matter of state security and promised to take the issue to the National Front.[23]

Both at the time and in retrospect, the case made in "How Was It" was quite flimsy. It is hard to imagine anyone believing that the SNR presidium's failure to take a position on clemency for Tiso could be regarded as the agreement and endorsement of clemency by that organ. Nor was the letter of the Second Prague Agreement a sufficient answer. The DS's refusal to bring clemency to a vote in the presidium was a radical departure both from past practice, where such proposals were regularly voted upon, and the DS's own Slovak autonomist ideology, which put much stock in Slovakia's organs of self-government, and self-administration and jealously guarded their prerogatives. Such an uncharacteristic step by the Democrats had to have another cause, as explained earlier. It was this cause that really put the DS in a bind when it came to justifying itself, and led to the production of the dubious explanation in *Čas*.

Why did the DS come up with feeble excuses rather than a compelling explanation for its actions on April 16? What explains the transparent sophistry of "How Was It?" The problem lay in the fact that Polák was opposed to clemency, and thus the DS would have lost had a vote come up. As speculation increased as to the DS's actions on April 16, the party felt compelled to offer an explanation, but it could not tell the truth. It could not explain to Catholic voters that it failed to come out on behalf of clemency for Tiso in the SNR presidium because one of its three members would not have supported it. Once accusations began to fly at the DS for its course of action on April 16, the party was left with only two options: be a silent punching bag for enemies who were trying to discredit it in the eyes of Catholics or come up with some less than compelling excuses to explain its behavior. While neither of these options was likely to inspire confidence in Catholic voters, the DS chose the latter. This then opened it up to a further barrage of assaults by enemies intent on dividing and destroying the party.

The KSS had long been aiming to foment conflict within the DS in hopes of splitting the party, along with the accompanying goals of discrediting the DS in the eyes of Slovakia's Catholics while at the same time portraying it as a haven for ex-Populists and other disloyal elements. At its meeting of May 12 and 13, the KSS's Central Committee discussed and specified its latest means toward achieving these goals. In his concluding report, Chairman Široký stressed that the Communists could not simply wait for the DS to fall apart under the weight of Tiso's execution; they had to take action.[24] He went on to outline three directions in which Communist activity should move: increase pressure from below, meaning organize a people's (*l'udové*) movement against the DS; employ the state's organs against the DS (to facilitate this, the Communists needed to emphasize that the character of the DS as an "Agrarian-Populist coalition" was no longer a matter of Communist-Democratic relations but a question of state interest); and battle the DS in the economic domain (this would entail uncovering the DS's "sabotage" of the economy and advancing the social-economic needs of the working people). In conclusion, Široký called for a "mobilization from below, an attack in the Board of Commissioners, and an intervention from the side of the government."

The spring of 1947 saw these Communist methods to assault the DS manifested in a number of ways, even before, but especially after, the May 12–13 meeting. Pressure from below meant that resistance organizations and trade unions would intensify and sustain a steady flow of anti-DS propaganda, proclamations, delegations, and rallies. With respect to using state organs against the DS, the Central Committee of the KSČ resolved at its May 19 meeting to authorize Interior Minister Nosek to investigate underground groups in Slovakia and come up with a list of "Populists" in leading places.[25] The authorities were then to demand that the DS purge these disloyal elements, and if they refused, the Communists were to engineer the expulsion of the Democrats from the government or provoke a crisis in Slovakia through the resignation of Communist members from the Board of Commissioners.[26] Soon, the Communists would set these mechanisms in motion in a process that would keep the DS fighting for its political life, and ultimately even to keep some of its members from arrest and prison. Regarding economic pressure on the DS, the Communists had for months been blaming the Democratic Commissioners Filo (Food) and Kvetko (Agriculture) for food shortages, the black market, and inflation. Communist propaganda in spring 1947 also began to raise class issues with respect to the DS more than it had in the past. For example, in *Pravda*'s Easter issue, Straka attacked "the betrayers of Christianity" who "under the mantle of Christianity want to gain profit only for themselves, who want to exploit the poor and weak. They are the Pharisees of today, or the money-changers."[27] In a similar vein, the Communist Miro Hysko wrote in a column in *Pravda* that the DS was using Slovak national organs to serve the class interests of individuals instead of the interests of the nation.[28] He went on to charge the Farmers' Bank, as a financial organ under the auspices of the Democrat controlled Commission of Agriculture, with failing to defend national properties.

Seeking to recoup its losses in the aftermath of Tiso's execution, and facing an enemy intent on doing its utmost to remove it from the political stage, the DS was in an unenviable position in May 1946. The sparks were still flying over "How Was It" when the DS made another move that caused an even bigger stir in Slovak and Czechoslovak politics and society, and triggered a crisis that nearly overwhelmed the party. At issue was the person of Igor Daxner, chairman of the National Court. The DS had long been upset with him; it had lobbied hard in November 1946 against his fitness to preside over the Tiso trial. Since then, the DS had additional reasons to seek his removal. Lettrich and other Democratic leaders were upset with Daxner for leaving them out of the loop with respect to the verdict against Tiso. Lettrich believed that he had Daxner's assurance that he would consult the SNR presidium before announcing the verdict.[29] Instead, the Democrats learned of the verdict from the press as a fait accompli. This evident betrayal of trust led to a complete breakdown in communications between the DS and Daxner. The DS was looking for ways to burnish its tarnished image in the eyes of Catholics, who could not help but notice the party's failure to champion clemency for Tiso to the hoped for degree. Engineering Daxner's downfall was about the most the DS could do at this point, and the party had good reason to hope that the recall of Daxner would be a success—not only were his horrid relations with the DS an obstacle to the smooth functioning of Slovakia's retribution trials, but his handling of the Mach case both upset DS leaders of all political stripes and looked bad to the Slovak population. Chief Prosecutor Rigan, who was not liked by the KSS, was willing to resign in what could be presented as an implicit quid pro quo for Daxner's removal. It was Rigan who protested to Husák back in October 1946 over the political interference in Slovakia's retribution trials, threatening at the time to resign, and who presented a request for clemency for Tiso immediately upon hearing the verdict.

When Daxner announced the verdict against Tiso and Ďurčanský on April 16, he prefaced his remarks by noting that the verdict on Mach would be postponed for health reasons. The DS, like many Slovaks, was suspicious; the evidence that Mach was too ill to stand trial was highly questionable, and the postponement of his verdict looked like part of a Communist plot to protect him in return for help he gave certain Communists under the wartime regime, as well as to avoid a situation whereby Tiso could be accorded clemency in an effort to distinguish him from Mach.[30] It was suspected that Mach would not be condemned to death but receive a lesser sentence. Announcing this on the same day as Tiso's death sentence would be scandalous, as Mach's wartime reputation, by any measure, was far worse than Tiso's. The interior minister for the Slovak state, Mach was one of the most radical of Slovak nationalists. He was extremely pro-Nazi and an energetic force for aligning

Slovakia closely with Nazi Germany and its ideology and policies.[31] The less radical Tiso had to spend the wartime years wrestling with the Mach-Tuka faction of his party, staving off their efforts to Nazify Slovakia and gain supremacy in the Slovak state with German backing. Thus, to condemn Tiso to a more severe punishment than Mach would appear a travesty of justice and ran the risk of riling up Slovakia's population.

That Daxner was apparently conspiring with the Communists on behalf of one of Slovakia's worst war criminals looked to the DS like an issue they could play for all it was worth. At the first SNR meeting after Tiso's verdict was announced, that of April 16, Lettrich opened discussion with an angry tirade against Daxner.[32] If ever there was a cause that would not be in the Communists' interest to champion, it would be Mach. However, when the Democrats called for Daxner's removal in the SNR presidium, the KSS representatives resisted. Though the Communists themselves did not think much of Daxner, they were set to rally round him once he became the Democrats' scapegoat for their own failings in the campaign for clemency for Tiso. As Lettrich put off a definitive vote in the SNR until mid-May, both Gottwald and Široký warned him not to take the step of recalling Daxner.[33] Nevertheless, Daxner's announcement on May 15 that Mach would receive a prison sentence of thirty years only confirmed Democratic suspicions of the KSS, exacerbated their disgust with Daxner, and encouraged their hopes that they could see his removal through. On May 17, *Čas* ran a page-one column alleging a Communist plot to spare Mach the death sentence.[34] On May 19, Democratic members of the SNR plenum interpellated the SNR's presidium about the Mach affair.[35] The Democrats used the occasion to present the case against Daxner. They alleged that Mach's verdict was postponed not on account of some purported illness, but to avoid the scandal of giving him his milder sentence on the day Tiso was condemned to death. Such a step by the National Court, according to the Democratic representatives, caused great agitation across Slovakia and strongly shook public trust in the objectivity of Daxner and the political neutrality of the court.[36]

The day after the interpellation, at the meeting of the SNR presidium, Lettrich proposed that Daxner be recalled from his post.[37] The Communists Šmidke and Horváth vehemently opposed the recall. They argued that it was a concession to reactionaries and a demonstration against the government and president for their handling of the Tiso case. It would jeopardize the status of the SNR in Czechoslovakia's upcoming constitution and retard the conclusion of Slovakia's retribution trials that they had hoped to see concluded by August. They warned that if the resolution passed the KSS members would cease their participation in the SNR presidium. In the Communist view, the matter should be decided by the Czechoslovak National Front (where they would have a greater chance of success).

Lettrich, Cvinček, and Polák came out strongly in support of the proposal.[38] They noted that nothing could retard the retribution process more than the fact that none of them were on speaking terms with Daxner, and that a more cooperative chairman of the court would expedite the process. They noted that a number of judges said that they could not work with Daxner. Far from encouraging antistate elements, the Democrats maintained, Daxner's removal would deprive such elements of a handy weapon in their agitation. In no way was Daxner's recall meant as a statement against Beneš or the government; it was not they, but the SNR, who had appointed Daxner and who had the authority to remove him. Their opposition to Daxner was not due to any actions taken in Prague, but because he had kept them in the dark regarding developments at the National Court, and because of his handling of the Mach case. Lettrich pointed out that the Communists had twice expressed agreement to Daxner's removal in the past but were once again reneging.

When it came to a vote, the resolution carried three-to-two, along party lines. The SNR presidium resolved to recall Daxner as chairman of the National Court and appoint Ivan Vesel, a court counselor (*súdny radca*), in his place.[39] The Communists then left the meeting in protest.

The Democrats had thrown down the gauntlet, and Daxner, the Communists, and the government in turn picked it up. On May 22, Daxner sent a protest telegram to the SNR presidium.[40] He refused to accept the recall decision, calling it illegal and hence not in force. In Daxner's view, the DS was violating judicial independence, a cardinal principle of democratic states enshrined in Czechoslovak law. What motivated the Democrats, according to Daxner, was his refusal of Lettrich's request that he meet with the SNR presidium before announcing the Tiso verdict. Because Daxner rejected this attempt to interfere in Tiso's trial, he argued, the Democrats had been planning his removal, a blatant violation of judicial independence.[41]

The KSS immediately took up Daxner's cause publicly. The May 23 issue of *Pravda* featured a front-page article attacking the DS for its coarse methods.[42] According to *Pravda*, the DS violated the principle of cooperation, whereby controversial questions were solved by agreement between Democrats and

Communists, as well as trampling on all principles of judicial independence, sacrificing them to the interests of the "Populist wing" of their party. *Pravda* maligned the Democrats' recall of Daxner as an attempt to bring unrest into Slovak public life, an effort that brought joy only to antistate elements. Ominously, the article mentioned that the Daxner affair was no longer a matter of relations between Communists and Democrats, but of broad state interest.

On May 23, the government met, discussed the recall of Daxner, and resolved to ask the SNR presidium to halt the execution of its decision and submit the matter for resolution at the next meeting of the government.[43] *Pravda*, in its May 25 issue, reported on the government's decision, including a column by parliamentary and SNR representative Ladislav Holdoš entitled "Dangerous Steps."[44] Holdoš accused the DS of making the protection of the separatist and fascist Tiso its topmost political goal and condemned the April Agreement as an immoral fellowship that created an "Agrarian-Populist coalition." He went on to praise Daxner for fulfilling his function in accord with the political-moral principles of the national-liberation struggle and in a nonpartisan manner. Holdoš charged the DS with trying to incite Slovakia with an act of provocation against the government, and welcomed the government's request that the SNR presidium halt its recall of Daxner. In a charge that would now become a major part of the Communists' rhetorical and political arsenal, and one with ramifications for Slovakia's autonomy, Holdoš accused the Democrats of misusing the SNR presidium for their own personal and partisan policy. Continuing its attack, on May 28 *Pravda* ran a front-page article on the squall over Daxner, claiming that the DS had not had the courage to vote for clemency in the SNR presidium, so were now attacking Daxner to make up for it (a rather accurate analysis one must admit).[45]

Despite pressure from a number of directions, the Democrats in the SNR now refused to back down. On May 24, Lettrich rejected Daxner's complaint in writing as unacceptable.[46] That week, Široký and others met with leading Democrats, urging them to rescind the recall of Daxner, but to no avail.[47] Meanwhile, Ursíny, who as deputy prime minister was the leading Democrat in the government, tried to convince Prime Minister Gottwald to accept a compromise—the SNR would permit Daxner to stay on and handle a few more cases, those of the Nazi Germans rather than of the Slovaks, then resign.[48] This approach to the crisis had the benefit of avoiding the thorny situation of having an SNR decision overturned in Prague, something that would embarrass the SNR and harm Czech-Slovak relations. Moreover, it would allow Daxner's resignation to be presented as voluntary and dissociated from the Tiso trial. Ursíny tried to sell this idea to Lettrich, but without success. When Ursíny's efforts fell through, Gottwald brought before the government, at its June 3 meeting, his own proposal: that the government annul the recall of Daxner as illegal and void.

During the June 3 meeting, ministers rehashed all the old arguments about the matter.[49] A number of speakers attacked the SNR's decision as a violation of judicial independence. According to Czechoslovakia's constitution, judges can be removed only in the event of a reorganization of the judiciary, or on the basis of findings in disciplinary proceedings against them. Neither of these conditions obtained in Daxner's situation. At issue was whether the SNR presidium had the authority to recall a judge without government approval. In the Democrats' estimation, the retribution legislation in Slovakia that gave the SNR presidium the authority to appoint and recall judges was sufficient to justify Daxner's recall.[50] According to everyone else, the constitutionally enshrined principles of judicial independence and immunity of judges from removal on political grounds,[51] though a carryover from the prewar constitution that had already faced a number of ad hoc modifications after the war, trumped postwar legislation in Slovakia. Apart from constitutional questions, which Drtina admitted were ambiguous and open to multiple legal interpretations, both sides of the debate accused the other of acting from political motives. Široký accused the Democrats of seeking Daxner's removal because they did not like the way the trials of Tiso and Mach turned out; the Democrat Pietor, while not making any direct accusations, reported that in Slovakia it was suspected that this affair was being driven by a desire to see the DS ejected from the government.

It did not bode well for the Democrats' position that the Czech Populists sided with the rest of the government at this meeting. While defenses of judicial independence coming from the mouths of Communists and left-wing Social Democrats like Fierlinger should be taken with more than a grain of salt, the Czech Populists had a track record of defending constitutional principles, including the independence of judges from political pressure. When Gottwald called the vote, his proposal passed with all but the Democrats voting for it. The government resolved to annul the recall of Daxner on the grounds that such recall violated the constitutional principle against the removal of judges for political reasons, noting that such decision was within the government's authority, based on the constitution and the Third Prague Agreement.[52] Gottwald was authorized to inform Daxner and the SNR presidium of the decision.

On June 13, the government received Lettrich's written response to its resolution, dated June 9.[53] According to Lettrich, the SNR presidium regarded the government's decision as "manifestly illegal, and therefore invalid and legally not in force." He argued that the government's action had no support in Czechoslovak law nor in any of the three Prague Agreements. Rather, the retribution decree of the SNR, a valid legal order, gives the SNR the exclusive authority to appoint and recall judges. According to Lettrich, as an extraordinary court with a limited term of existence, Slovakia's National Court did not fall under the constitution's stipulations regarding the judiciary.[54] Lettrich expressed the hope that the government would correct its error, revise its decision, and in the future consult the SNR presidium for information about the regulations valid in Slovakia.

The government met on June 13 to consider Lettrich's statement. Ministers from the left wing of the political spectrum condemned Lettrich's action in the strongest of terms.[55] It was "an unprecedented document" (Gottwald), a "gross provocation" (Július Ďuriš, minister of agriculture, KSS) and "document of resistance" (Zdeněk Nejedlý, minister of social welfare, KSČ). If allowed to stand, it would mean "total anarchy," as a Slovak organ would be setting itself up as the final arbiter in matters that it itself defined (Zdeněk Fierlinger, deputy prime minister, Social Democratic Party). Foreign Minister Jan Masaryk called it "extremely dangerous." Speaker after speaker drew parallels with the events of 1938 and 1939 that destroyed the interwar Czechoslovak Republic. Fierlinger asserted that the government cannot retreat over this issue, lest its authority disappear and it end up at the edge of a precipice as in 1938. Ďuriš claimed that not every "Slovak national organ" is a genuine national organ; in the past, for example, organs designated as such had served Hitler. The Communist Jaromír Dolanský (minister of finance) stated that, in this post-Munich period, it was impossible to get away with such a resistance against the government in Prague. Gottwald compared the actions of Lettrich or the SNR presidium to those in the wake of the Munich Agreement, when the HSĽS initiated a series of ultimata to the government that led to the events of October 6, 1938, and March 14, 1939. According to Gottwald, the spirit of Munich was speaking from the grave through Lettrich's letter. He declared, "If these gentlemen think they can act like Sidor,[56] Tiso, Tuka and Ďurčanský, they are greatly mistaken, because it is not 1938 or 1939, but 1947, and it seems that these gentlemen in Slovakia have forgotten this." Several speakers leveled veiled threats at Lettrich and the SNR. Kopecký proclaimed, in the name of the KSČ, that "its patience is at an end and its restraint is exhausted." He later noted that if developments continued as such the government would not be afraid to introduce into Slovakia a special government committee. Some speakers called for an investigation into who exactly was behind the letter, warning those responsible that the government would draw the appropriate consequences from their refusal to recognize its authority. Others noted how the moderation and restraint shown by the Communists thus far throughout the crisis over Daxner had only encouraged the DS to be more belligerent. Though the discussion at the meeting was clearly paving the way for a new diminution of the authority of Slovakia's national organs, several speakers professed that Lettrich's views were not those of the Slovaks, but rather of the Populist faction within the DS.

Discussion at the meeting was dominated by the Communists and left-wing Social Democrats. The Nationalist Socialists said little, and the Czech Populists stuck mainly to repeating their opposition to the removal of judges for political reasons. Significantly, the Democrats in the government offered little defense of Lettrich's action. By their own admission, they had been unaware of the letter. Mikuláš Franek, the minister for unification of laws, openly expressed his disagreement with parts of Lettrich's letter and his conviction that the government could not yield on this matter. Ursíny, twice when asked if he agreed with Lettrich's letter, refused to give a clear and direct answer. When it came time to vote on Gottwald's proposal, he was similarly evasive. Those present resolved, with an overwhelming majority by show of hands, to authorize Minister of Justice Drtina to implement the government resolution of June 3, which annulled Daxner's recall by the SNR, as well as to launch an investigation into the details behind Lettrich's letter. Gottwald announced that the proposal passed, mentioning that Ursíny had voted for it. A debate then broke out over whether or not Ursíny had indeed voted for the proposal, with Ursíny denying it but others present claiming that he had.

The meeting of June 17 demonstrated a number of things. First, that the Communists meant business in their dealings with the DS and were firmly resolved to see that no Democratic controlled Slovak organ would be able to act autonomously on issues that mattered to them. Second, the non-Communist Czech parties, while not sharing the Communists' vehemence in attacking the Democrats, nevertheless closed ranks with the leftist parties over the Daxner crisis. A genuine devotion to judicial independence, coupled with a suspicion of Slovak nationalism and a fear to cross the Communists on an issue they were pushing so hard, accounts largely for their position. Third, the Democrats' words and deeds made it clear that there was profound opposition within the party to Lettrich's hard line over the Daxner affair, and to his failure to consult with his colleagues in the government before sending the protest letter.

Meanwhile, concurrent with the government's session of June 17, the SNR presidium was meeting in Bratislava.[57] The two Communists present insisted that the presidium respond favorably to the government's decision to annul Daxner's recall. The three Democrats resisted, though Polák was ready to support the government if, and only if, the government admitted that it took its decision on political grounds instead of justifying itself with legal arguments. Lettrich stood by his protest letter, claiming the government's attempt to override a decision of the SNR warranted an unprecedented response. Šmidke argued that what was really unprecedented was the Democrats' deciding on an important issue without Communist agreement. After a long and circular argument, those present learned of the government's resolution to carry out the reinstatement of Daxner (or, more precisely, the annulment of his recall). With that, the presidium resolved to put off discussion of the matter until the government officially informed them of its decision.

As it turned out, the matter passed out of the hands of the SNR altogether. Drtina notified Commissioner of Justice Štefánik of the government's resolution, and Daxner remained in his post. The Daxner affair was settled via intervention from Prague. The Democrats' attempt to punish Daxner for his treatment of them and his dubious handling of the Mach case, as well as to mollify angry Catholics upset with the Tiso verdict, ended as a failure, if not a fiasco.

While some Catholics may have appreciated Democratic efforts in this respect (if they could overlook the party's earlier failure to deliver an SNR vote for clemency), the price the DS paid was high. The Daxner case resulted in a further weakening of the authority of the Slovak national organs, where the DS had some influence, in favor of the government in Prague, where they did not. It also exposed some of the disharmony within the DS, with

Lettrich at odds with his party's chief representatives in Prague. Moreover, it further exposed the DS's impotence—the party that had won a landslide in the 1946 parliamentary elections in Slovakia was helpless to remove a judge who treated it in a hostile and belligerent manner.[58] Finally, it handed the Communists another weapon in their newly commissioned campaign against the Democrats in the wake of the Tiso trial.

From late spring to late summer 1947, two issues dominated the Communists' relationship with Catholics and Democrats—education and security. Regarding education, the KSS sought to achieve passage of the new Czechoslovak school law, which would be a big blow to the Catholic Church and further expose the DS's impotence. Regarding security, the Communists tried to implicate leading Catholics in the DS in an alleged antistate conspiracy, hoping to drive a wedge between key factions in the DS and keep the Democrats in a defensive paralysis.

As we have seen, education was a contentious issue in post-1945 Czechoslovakia, and one about which the Catholic Church cared deeply. In the fall of 1946, a commission set up by the Ministry of Education began its work on the latest draft of the school law, which was ready for public discussion by early March.[59] The conflict of opinion over the draft centered on two issues: whether Czechoslovakia's education should be a state monopoly and whether a so-called uniform system should be implemented. The latter issue, which concerned how soon or late in their academic career children should receive a specialized education (e.g., academic, vocational), reflected to some extent class divisions in Czechoslovakia, with politicians and pedagogues on the left favoring a common (uniform) education for students for as long as possible and politicians and pedagogues of so-called bourgeois orientation favoring earlier differentiation of students into career tracks. The question of a uniform school system did not break down along lines of religious allegiance, however. Although many Democrats opposed the uniform system and tended to line up against the Communists on this aspect of educational reform, this issue did not capture the Catholic Church's interest the way the state monopoly on education did. Indeed, Archbishop Josef Beran of Prague, at a large rally sponsored by Catholic organizations in defense of parochial schools in Prague on May 13, 1947, stressed that they were not opposed to a uniform school system if it allowed for reasonable differentiation, but were decidedly against the state monopoly of education.[60] And the Slovak bishops, in their pastoral letter of June 2, 1947, made the point that they were not against the uniform school system in form, but rather due to its content.[61] The other issue, the state monopoly of education, was highly charged with religious significance, along with a related issue—the place of religious instruction in the curriculum.

The new draft of the school law was much discussed and debated across Czechoslovakia through the spring and summer of 1947. Supporters and opponents of the law organized rallies, passed resolutions, and peppered newspapers and scholarly and professional journals with arguments pro and con. The Communists numbered among the strongest and most vociferous supporters of the law. On May 13, the KSS's Central Committee resolved that "the central committee considers it as necessary . . . to secure the acceptance of the new school law on the principle of a uniform state education."[62] Communist dominated or influenced organizations mobilized their forces on behalf of the law. Most notable in this respect was the Union of Educational and Cultural Workers, a part of the Communist led Revolutionary Trade Union Movement. A number of teachers' organizations also held rallies for the new law.

The Communist press threw itself energetically into the campaign for the new law. Communist authors argued that teachers supported the law, as it gave them legal security and decent pay unavailable at parochial schools. Teachers would no longer be subordinated to control by church authorities and would be protected from being turned into "downtrodden and obedient" servants of the priests.[63] The Slovak people, too, favored the state monopoly, according to Communist authors. Their experience with it over the past two years taught them that it improved the quality of education, unburdened them of having to support parochial schools, and promoted national unity instead of narrow religious intolerance.[64] Even Catholic priests, according to the Communists, would be happy with a state monopoly on education. Catholic schools were a lot of trouble for them, and, since the state schools already made provision for religious education, parochial schools were not only burdensome but superfluous.[65] The Communist press alleged that clerical support for the petition drive on behalf of parochial schools, launched in the fall of 1946 by Bishop Čársky's Catholic Educational Council, did not find an enthusiastic response among Slovak priests.[66] The DS, of course, was often targeted in these polemics over education. *Pravda* pointed out, for instance, that Lettrich was commissioner of education during the Slovak National Uprising and had signed the decree nationalizing education in Slovakia, and that opposition to a state monopoly of education was a violation of the Košice Program, to which all of Czechoslovakia's political parties were theoretically committed.[67]

Opponents of the school law likewise mobilized in word and deed. On June 2, Slovakia's bishops, in conference at Nitra, issued a pastoral letter on the school question.[68] The bishops presented a number of arguments against the state education monopoly—it violated the rights and obligations of the church to found and maintain schools; it was contrary to the will of most Slovaks and hence undemocratic; it violated religious freedom by depriving parents of the option of providing their children with a parochial education. In a positive sense, according to the bishops, the legalization of parochial schools would strengthen morality among youth and bring a healthy competition into the school system. The bishops concluded by reminding Catholics that they were bound by conscience to use all legally allowable means to see that the law was changed and urged them to ask their parliamentary representatives to opposed the law as it stood.

Also in early June, *Katolícke noviny* published a report issued by the Catholic Educational Council from its meeting of May 2, criticizing the school law.[69] The report reiterated the bishops' basic objections to the law, adding a number of further points. The council argued that the new law sanctioned the state's appropriation of property acquired by the church from private donations and interfered with the church's right to have property for its religious, social, and cultural goals, a violation of the principles of the Atlantic Charter and the Four Freedoms.[70] Further, the law failed to include legal protection against antireligious and antichurch teaching in the schools, a departure from the school law in the interwar republic. The report devoted much attention to refuting the claims that the proposed law guaranteed religious education within the state-run schools. By making religion classes optional and restricting their place in the curriculum mainly to the lower grades, by introducing nonconfessional (i.e., "atheistic") education for nonbelieving students, and by subordinating religion classes to the overall goals of the state and its nonreligious mission, the schools established by the new law hardly replaced Catholic schools. Rather, the law constituted the "most audacious and wide-ranging attack on the Christian spirit" of the nation in its history and were an effort to legally establish the system of dialectical materialism in the schools. The report objected to the request that nonrural children begin kindergarten at age three, an indication of the tendency of the school to take the place of the mother in child development, and to the exclusion of single-sex schools from the system despite pedagogical evidence, including from the Soviet Union, of their efficacy. If the new law passed, according to the Catholic Educational Council, it would mean the unleashing of a *Kulturkampf.*

Through the summer of 1947, press polemics over the school law intensified. Koza, as usual, led the charge for Catholics.[71] In a series of columns in *Katolícke noviny*, he tossed some additional contentions into the debate—for example, a parochial education was not some privilege that Slovak Catholics sought from the state, but something that, as taxpayers, was rightfully theirs; the fact that religion still had a place in the curriculum was only a temporary expedient for the state, which would soon push it to the side and then out the door; and religion classes were taught at times of day when the pupils were tired or hungry. In July, polemics between Koza and the Communists took to the low road. Koza's column featured several horror stories of alleged incidents in state schools. Alongside stories of teachers ridiculing pupils for questioning the theory of evolution or teaching them that their parents had them out of self-interest rather than love and thus were owed nothing from them, Koza cited a case from Hungary where a male teacher compelled middle-school girls to strip naked in physical education class.[72] *Nové slovo* countered by citing the case of a Catholic priest caught in sexual indiscretions with fourteen-year-old girls; in reply, Koza argued the priest was violating the church's beliefs, while the teacher was implementing those of the state schools.[73]

While the Catholic bishops, associations, and press were the most energetic forces in Slovakia in opposition to the new school law, the same can be said for Catholic institutions in the Czech lands. In fact, education was one of the few issues where Czech and Slovak Catholics readily stood side by side. Czech bishops issued pastoral letters opposing the state monopoly of education in Slovakia.[74] Czech Catholic organizations held rallies in defense of parochial schools, at which Slovak representatives took part. Prague's Archbishop Beran called the nationalization of schools in Slovakia a "great mistake." The Czechoslovak People's Party led all members of the government in speaking out against the state monopoly of education.[75]

Though it did not match the effort and energy put into the debate over education by Czech and Slovak Catholic institutions, the DS also joined in the efforts to thwart the new law. At its meeting of May 19, the DS's presidium unanimously voted against the proposed new school law and declared itself in support of parochial and other private schools.[76] *Nové prúdy* ran articles through the summer of 1947 opposing the proposed law. One article noted that the proposed system of education required teachers to adapt themselves to the political perspective of the government and brought ruptures into the relationships between teachers and religious-believing parents and children.[77] Another drew heavily from the teachings of Pope Pius XI, including his teaching that it was unjust for the state to force parents to send their children to state schools.[78]

The controversy over the school law presented both opportunities and pitfalls for the DS. On the one hand, it gave Democrats an opportunity to regain credit with Catholic voters upset over the party's failures regarding Tiso and Daxner. It helped that Slovakia's major Protestant body, the Evangelical (Lutheran) Church, also supported parochial schools.[79] At the same time, however, the DS was committed to the legacy of the Slovak National Uprising, which included nationalized education as one of its features. Thus, while raising Catholic hopes that it would champion their cause, the party leaders had to be careful not to give Communists more reason to accuse them of abandoning the Uprising, the enterprise which brought the DS the progressive credentials necessary for participating in Slovak political life in the first place. Moreover, the DS had to face the fact that there was relatively little apparent opposition by teachers in Slovakia, including Democratic ones, over the present system and the new law. Finally, a total defeat on the school question could further expose Democratic impotence and increase Catholic disillusionment with the party.

At discussions in May, the Czechoslovak government was unable to reach an agreement over the proposed law, so it set up a commission of five ministers to seek compromise over the most contentious issues, above all the question of state monopoly. Composed of a National Socialist (Minister of Education Stránský), a Social Democrat (Fierlinger), a Slovak Communist (Široký), a Czech Communist academic (Nejedlý), and a Czech Catholic (Hála), the commission could reach no agreement and soon referred the matter back to the government, which in the fall of 1947 turned it back over to the commission, which subsequently failed to meet. While the political left was pressing for a quick acceptance of the law, the non-Marxist parties were apparently inclined to wait for the ratification of Czechoslovakia's new constitution, if not for new parliamentary elections.[80]

Less focused than the education question, and far more dangerous for the Catholic Church and the DS, was the matter of state security in Slovakia.

The summer of 1947 saw a marked intensification of Communist efforts to present Slovakia as infested with antistate elements, an infestation supposedly made possible by the alleged connection of the Catholic wing of the DS and the Catholic hierarchy and clergy with underground elements at home and Tisoite activists abroad. At a press conference on May 30, Gottwald told a group of Slovak journalists touring the Czech lands that "the Populist separatist movement, linked with the names Ďurčanský, Sidor and others, has nestled itself inside the DS," masking its goals and ambitions with Catholicism and seeking positions from which it can thwart the consolidation of the republic.[81] According to the prime minister, "It has become routine in Slovakia to say 'Catholic' and think 'Populist,' to say 'Catholic rights' and think 'the rights of Populist separatists.'" Gottwald went on to say that, unlike the Czech clergy, who developed a positive attitude toward the republic, the Slovak clergy maintained a negative standpoint. According to Gottwald, "the chief blame here falls on the Slovak episcopate, not on simple parish priests, or at least not on the majority of them." *Čas*, in a front-page headline article, responded that it was rather the Communists who were equating Catholic with Populist and branding basic calls for Catholic rights as separatist or even antistate. *Katolícke noviny* objected to Gottwald's attempt to divide Catholics by focusing blame on the bishops, asserting that in Slovakia, bishops, priests, and laity stood together.

The next move in the Communist offensive came within the Czechoslovak National Front, in conjunction with the controversy over Daxner. On June 11, the National Front met to discuss the security situation in Slovakia, an issue vigorously pressed by the Communists. At the meeting, Slovak Communists presented a detailed report, produced with the help of the state's security organs, which depicted developments in Slovakia as gravely threatening.[82] The report argued that the April Agreement had enabled enemies of the Republic to hold important political, administrative, and economic positions throughout Slovakia and that, consequently, government intervention against this danger was imperative. The leftist parties hoped that the National Front would resolve to carry out a purge of the DS and various organs and institutions across Slovakia. Interior Minister Nosek, after colorfully and dramatically portraying underground activity in Slovakia, remarked that "there is only one solution: the DS must resign from everything that April 6, 1946, that is, the pact with the Populists, signifies."[83] The National Socialists and Czech Populists, however, responded tepidly to the Communist allegations, while

Lettrich condemned the report as the exaggerated work of panicmongers and defeatists. Ursíny accused the Communists of unleashing a campaign against the DS because they were not satisfied with the results of the May 1946 elections. Ultimately, the NF resolved to set up a special multiparty commission to investigate the charges and make recommendations of measures for ridding Slovakia of allegedly reactionary, fascist, and subversive elements. The NF also resolved to oppose claims at that time in the foreign press that the Communists were preparing a coup in Czechoslovakia based on speculation that they were trying to drive the DS from the government.

Such speculation was not without foundation, given events elsewhere in Eastern Europe in the first half of 1947. Increased Communist aggression reflected worsening relations between the United States and the Soviet Union and a growing chill in the cold war across Europe. It was during this period that a number of key milestones on the road to a bipolar Europe were passed—in March, the United States, with the Truman Doctrine, signaled its determination to keep Communism out of Greece and Turkey; in May, Communists were excluded from the governments of France and Italy; in early June, the American secretary of state announced the Marshall Plan for economic recovery in Europe. Meanwhile, Communist assaults on non-Communists in Poland, Romania, Bulgaria, and elsewhere in Eastern Europe, already under way from the time of the Soviet occupation in 1944, grew in quantity and quality. In Hungary, the country watched most closely by Slovaks, Soviet attempts to uncover an "antistate conspiracy" led to the arrest of Béla Kovács, the popular general secretary of the Smallholders Party, in early 1947. During interrogation, the Soviets alleged that Kovács implicated his fellow Smallholder Ferenc Nagy, Hungary's prime minister, who in early June was forced out of office and into foreign exile.[84]

Events in Hungary led to speculation among Slovaks that the Communists were planning a similar maneuver in Slovakia (as indeed they were). Such speculations made their way into the foreign and DS press and were heard among the Slovak population.[85] Like the Democrats, the Smallholders had defeated the Communists soundly in the postwar parliamentary elections (57 percent to 17 percent),[86] and thus stood as an impediment to Communist control. As the Hungarian crisis was developing, Czechoslovakia's Communists took steps aimed at implicating the Democrats in a similar conspiracy. In spring 1947, a "Slovak department" emerged in the Prague Headquarters of the security police, composed entirely of Communists.[87] Meeting in mid-

May, the KSČ's Central Committee decided to force a purge of the DS. Nosek was instructed to draw up a list of alleged Populist sympathizers associated with the DS, and the Communists would follow with demands that the DS remove them.[88] If it did not comply, the Communists considered either driving the DS out of the government, or fomenting a political crisis in Slovakia by having the Communist members resign from the Board of Commissioners.[89] While the Communists would indeed resort to this latter maneuver later in the fall, for now their focus was on forcing a purge of the DS, and of other organs and institutions in Slovakia, including those belonging to or affiliated with the Catholic Church.

Communist concerns about key personnel in the Catholic Church can be found in an undated report from late spring or summer of 1947, almost certainly written by Straka.[90] In the first part of a two-part report, entitled "The Roots of the Evil," the author itemizes all the institutions in Slovakia where he claims Catholics are engaged in antistate activity.[91] Among other things, the report argued that *Katolícke noviny*'s editorial staff was composed of fascists and collaborators and was trying to drive voters into the DS. The Central Catholic Chancellery (ÚKK) was branded as a center of espionage for émigrés, with agents throughout Slovakia's schools. A large proportion of high school teachers were allegedly fascist and educated their students in that spirit, as did allegedly pro-Hungarian and fascist oriented clergy. The formerly Catholic dormitory Svoradov and the Catholic Women's Union made the list,[92] as did the Bishops' Council, where all of Slovakia's bishops were accused of being staunchly antistate (except for Gojdič, Hopko, and Lazík).[93] These Catholic efforts to undermine the Republic, according to the report, had support from within the DS from a number of leading Catholics, including Cvinček, Kempný, and Bugár. Part 2 of the report suggested a number of personnel changes for Catholic institutions. It proposed several candidates for the office of bishop, men who were evidently more willing to accommodate the KSS. It warned against accepting any bishop from a religious order and stressed that Bishop Buzalka must be removed because he was poisoning students at the seminary in Bratislava. The report also called for a purge at *Katolícke noviny*, insisting on the removal of the entire editorial board, and especially Koza-Matejov. The ÚKK also needed a purge, including a new director. The report stressed the need to get reliable people in place as rectors and professors at all seminaries and included a number of suggestions as to who needed to go and who their replacements should be. Vojtaššák's seminary at Spiš was regarded as particularly antistate. Some suggestions were made for removals of personnel at gymnasia and dormitories and at the Women's Union. The report also mentioned the circle of "fascist priests" connected with the Košice periodical *Verbum* and the need to bring that journal "under control." The report concluded by identifying Čarnogurský and Obtulovič as the main inspirations behind all this evil. They allegedly terrorized the bishops and had lobbied them hard on behalf of the April Agreement. The report charged Čarnogurský of having ties with the émigré Sidor and labeled Obtulovič as an "acidic demon" whose office and apartment were the venues for secret fascist meetings under the veil of Catholicism.

While privately the KSS was considering what personnel changes it desired within Slovakia's Catholic institutional structure, publicly it focused its efforts on the DS. The special commission set up by the National Front at its June 11 meeting to consider a purge in Slovakia did not begin its work until September, but in the meantime Slovak Communists and Democrats sparred over the extent of the threat to national security in Slovakia and the degree of Democratic responsibility for it. Communist speakers and writers called for a purge of the DS and accused it of behaving like an opposition party, violating the government's foundational document, the Košice Program, and minimizing the danger of reaction in Slovakia.[94] Democratic leaders defended themselves against these charges and counterattacked. Lettrich voiced support for a purge of public life in Slovakia, *provided* it was nonpartisan and just.[95] In an interview of June 24, the DS chairman noted that Slovakia was no different than anywhere else in Europe in having remnants of reaction and that these were without influence and would disappear over time.[96] He noted that "reaction" was a vague term and often misused. Democrats also accused the KSS of misusing trade unions and resistance organizations. *Nové prúdy* published an article by the Democrat Fraštacký, vice-chairman of the Board of Commissioners, in which he lamented that the resistance and trade union organizations were, in their letters, telegrams, and delegations, serving the interests of a single political party.[97] Blaming this situation on organizational leaders who acted against the interests and desires of their general membership, he noted that these organizations were squandering the great moral capital that they had built up in Slovakia. Fraštacký accused the Communists of artificially invoking a political crisis, thereby damaging the Republic's reputation and impeding reconstruction. He defended the DS's outreach to former Populist rank and file as a means of reconciling that element to the Republic, and noted that the KSS too courted former Populists.[98]

Through the summer of 1947, the Communists used popular rallies and meetings as venues from which to attack the Democrats and their church allies. On July 6, the third annual All-Slavic Day was celebrated at Devín.[99] Slovakia's bishops declined to take part in this Communist dominated and controlled event, holding their own celebration in Nitra. The honored speaker at Devín was Prime Minister Gottwald, who called for a general purge of subversives from Slovakia's political life. Though he did not identify the Democrats or the Catholic hierarchy by name, his remark that the enemy "had penetrated to significant places in the political life of Slovakia, in the state administration and the economy, and that they were even misusing religious titles and tribunes for their dark machinations" left little doubt about whom he was talking.

On August 18 and 19, the Union of Slovak Partisans held a Slovakia-wide conference at the Reduta hall in Bratislava.[100] The Communist dominated organization called for a purge of Slovakia's political and public life, even naming names of figures who had to go. If the authorities did not carry out the purge by September 20, the Partisans threatened to carry it out themselves, and they sent an ultimatum to that effect to the SNR and Board of Commissioners. The Partisans also made another equally ominous demand—that Partisan units be allowed to rearm in order to help the Republic combat the so-called Banderovci, a right-wing Ukrainian militia from the wartime whose remnants were still active in parts of Slovakia.[101] The Democrats, with good reason, were suspicious of this request, suspecting that the real reason for rearming the Partisans was to intimidate the DS. *Čas* wrote on August 23 that the Banderovci threat was exaggerated and something that the Czechoslovak army and police forces could deal with. The Partisans would be better used in civil reconstruction than in such military mopping-up operations.[102] On September 16, however, the government approved the call-up of 3,630 Partisan reservists and members of the Union of Soldiers of the Slovak National Uprising for monthly training exercises.[103] Democratic suspicions were confirmed by the behavior of some of the Partisans. In Brezno nad Hronom, for example, Partisan units refused to give up their arms until several Democrats were removed from the local national committee, and there was even talk of a march on Bratislava to force the acceptance of Partisan demands.[104]

Before examining the fruits of Communist efforts to intimidate the DS, saddle it with the charge of unreliability, and inflict it with a crippling purge, a couple of developments from the summer of 1947 are worth considering for the light they shed on the religious question in Slovakia at the time. In the village of Tvrdomestice, near Topoľčany, some local children claimed to have seen an apparition of the Virgin Mary on May 27. On the twenty-seventh day of the subsequent months, large numbers of Slovaks congregated at the site in anticipation of further miracles. On June 27, for example, over 80,000 people showed up.[105] For the leftist press, large-scale congregations of Catholics in strongly Catholic regions were dangerous demonstrations of pro-Tiso sentiment and intolerance toward non-Catholics. There was no evidence, however, that the large numbers of Slovaks drawn to Tvrdomestice were seeking to make a political or confessional statement. As is often the case with Marian apparitions, Slovakia's church hierarchy reacted coolly.[106] In an article of July 27, appearing on the eve of the next anticipated influx of pilgrims to Tvrdomestice, *Katolícke noviny* editor Justín Štibraný asserted that, while there was no proof of the veracity of the apparitions, there were many reasons to argue for restraint. He noted that the children only recognized the apparition as Mary after they had returned home and spoke with others. Miracles alleged to have occurred in conjunction with the apparitions either did not have the character of miracles, were untrue, were unworthy of Mary, or, in the case of alleged solar phenomena, not confirmed by consistent and uniform testimony. Štibraný also noted that thousands of Slovaks missed obligatory Sunday Mass in order to visit the apparition site on Sundays, and that local hawkers were making a good profit selling to visitors food, drinks, and pious paraphernalia, such as signed photographs of the children ("a shameful waste of money that could be better spent on one's family or other praiseworthy goals"). The article concluded by urging Slovaks not to go to Tvrdomestice, but to wait and see if the apparitions turn out to be legitimate. In the meantime, they should be content with pilgrimages to sites recognized by the church, or with worship at their own parish church. That the editor of a newspaper closely associated with the Catholic bishops would write such an article makes it clear that it was spontaneous peasant piety, not Catholic ecclesial or political leaders, that was the engine driving the events at Tvrdomestice.

More popular were the mainstream pilgrimages to places like Marienka, a Catholic shrine not far from Bratislava. Organized by the ÚKK, as many as 30,000 to 40,000 Catholics participated in these periodic expressions of piety, long a popular part of devotional life in Slovakia. The pilgrimage from Bratislava to Marienka in late spring 1947 included large numbers of university students, marching behind a cross carried in legs of two hundred meters by various Catholic leaders, including Koza and Čarnogurský. Although Communists accused the church of organizing these as political manifestations, they remained predominately devotional in character.[107]

Communist policy, meanwhile, was driven by an intensifying global rift between East and West. This manifested itself in a number of ways, including a greater stress on class division and conflict in KSS propaganda. Communist attempts to play the class card culminated in August 1947, with the demands by the Marxist parties for a "millionaires' tax"—that is, an extraordinary tax on property exceeding one million crowns, to be used to cover grain subsidies.[108] While the tax initiative was designed as a republic-wide assault on the so-called bourgeois parties, particular efforts were made to harmonize Communist policy with Christianity. In Slovakia, this can be seen in a pair of articles appearing in late summer in major Communist periodicals. One, by K. Koržinský, appeared in the August 29 issue of *Nové slovo*, a weekly geared toward Communist intellectuals, and was entitled "Christ and the Communists." The other, written by Straka, appeared on page one of *Pravda* on September 14, under the title in large headlines of "Woe to You Who Are Rich" ("*Beda vám, boháčom!*"). The articles, though sharing much in common, represent two distinct Communist approaches to presenting the relationship between Communism and Christianity for a Slovak audience

Koržinský's article professed to be an examination of the great similarities between the teachings of socialism and those of Jesus Christ.[109] Jesus taught love of neighbor; socialism teaches freedom from exploitation. Jesus taught against storing up earthly treasures; socialism teaches the equal distribution of property. Jesus condemned avarice and taught to do unto others as you would have others do unto you; socialism advocates a just wage. Jesus offered rest to those who came to him; socialism advocates just rest periods for workers. Jesus called people to care for the sick; socialism advocates free health care. The author sums up, "From this comparison, we see that the teachings of socialists and communists about the coexistence of human society not only do not oppose the teaching of Jesus Christ, but on the contrary fully agree with it and complement it." Koržinský demonstrated the link between Jesus and Stalin: "The teaching of Jesus Christ is the basis of modern sociology. Marx and Engels processed it scientifically and introduced it into practical life. Jesus Christ proclaimed his teaching according to idealistic methods, which Marx, Engels, Lenin and Stalin processed scientifically and introduced into practical life on the basis of materialistic methods." The Christian Church, the article went on to argue, distanced itself from the purity of Jesus' teaching as it gained worldly wealth and power after Emperor Constantine became its patron. The wealthy ruling classes misused religion to exploit the people, teaching them to humbly suffer in this life and await liberation in the next. It was this Christianity, not the pure teaching of Jesus, that socialists and communists disparaged as the opiate of humanity (Marx) or a type of spiritual brandy (Lenin). As an example of the wrong kind of Christianity, the author cited the two greatest Catholic social encyclicals, Pope Leo XIII's *Rerum novarum* (1891) and Pope Pius XI's *Quadragesimo anno* (1931). By teaching that private property was a natural right, that social equality was an impossibility, that social classes should cooperate and fulfill their respective roles in society responsibly, and that the state should not encumber private property, the Catholic popes were departing from the teaching of Christ.

While the article in *Nové slovo* was clearly an anti-Catholic effort to use Jesus Christ as a club with which to beat the church, Straka's article in *Pravda* took a different approach. Here, the author tried to show that wealth redistribution policies such as the millionaires' tax and land reform were in harmony with the church's tradition and with Catholic papal teaching.[110] According to Straka, Jesus Christ, Christianity, and the Communists all agreed that the rich should bear the heavy brunt of the tax burden. Straka rattled off a litany of scriptural accounts of Jesus' less than sanguine view of the rich—the several times that he spoke unambiguously against the unjust use of property and wealth; his statement "Woe to you who are rich" from his Sermon on the Plain (Luke 6:24); his call to the rich young man to sell all he owned and give it to the poor; his claim that it would be easier for a camel to pass through the eye of a needle than for a rich man to get into heaven; his parable juxtaposing the rich man and Lazarus to the detriment of the former's eternal fate. According to Straka, Jesus Christ would certainly support a tax on millionaires, on the principle that property should serve the general good of society and not only some elect and privileged rich men and profiteers.

For the same reason, Christianity was for a land reform that would parcel out large estates to the needy. In making his case that Christianity supported property redistribution, Straka quoted Pius XII, who in a recent speech to members of the organization Catholic Action, said, "The Church is against estates being accumulated in the hands of several rich men while wide layers of people are drowning in poverty. A more just distribution of wealth is a social task whose fulfillment it is necessary to strive for." Straka argued that the present distribution of property in Slovakia was unjust and in need of urgent reform, even if this impinged on the church itself. "Our goal must be that the greatest number of people have the opportunity for a share in property," he concluded. Social justice and Christian love demanded it.

Straka's approach, in trying to demonstrate that the church itself taught the redistribution of property and even citing the current pope to support his position, differed sharply from Koržinský, who presented the church and popes as antitheses of Jesus' teaching. A good deal of the difference in approach is explained by the different nature of the periodicals and of the authors. Straka was a Catholic priest seeking to win Catholics over to Communism and writing in a daily newspaper geared toward the party's rank and file, among which were certainly a number of Catholics; Koržinský was presenting a Marxist critique of institutionalized Christianity in a weekly for other Communist intellectuals.

It was precisely at the height of agitation over the millionaires' tax that Communist efforts to crush the DS bore their ripest fruit. On September 14, Slovakia's Commissioner of the Interior Ferjenčík announced the uncovering of an antistate conspiracy. As the affair developed, the police implicated a number of Democrats, including major figures from that party's Catholic wing. Most prominently among these were Kempný and Bugár, general secretaries and parliamentary representatives for the DS, along with Staško, also a member of parliament.

Attacks on these three Catholic Democrats began immediately after the May 1946 elections. The KSS, with assistance from Communists within the police, began accumulating evidence against them, as well as against other Democratic members of parliament.[111] The intent was to establish links between Catholic Democrats and Ďurčanský and use the issue to split the DS.[112] According to a note from a Communist meeting in Ružomberok of June 6, where Ladislav Holdoš presented KSS policy to local Communist members, the KSS planned to expose the DS's "anti-state activity and dissolve the party as such on the basis of this evidence."[113] Toward this end, a case was to be made that leading Democrats, or members of the DS's Catholic wing, were guilty of fascism and enmity toward the Czechoslovak Republic and they were to be "arrested and tried by the people's courts, which would see that they don't present an obstacle to us in the future." Holdoš also mentioned the goal of getting members of the Bishops' Council locked up for their "fascist work" during the election campaign. Though this Communist wish list was easier proclaimed than accomplished, it is another indication of the direction the party was headed in the aftermath of its electoral defeat. While the KSS would have to wait until after the Communist takeover of Czechoslovakia in February 1948 before it could dissolve the DS and begin arresting bishops, it could and did go after leading Catholic Democrats almost at once.

After a summer of clandestinely collecting material, with the help of the Communist dominated Sixth Department of the State Security services, Holdoš put together an exposé on Kempný, Bugár, and company in the fall of 1946. The KSS's Central Committee resolved, on December 2, to deliver the exposé to all political parties with the aim of the political isolation of the DS within the National Front.[114] At the same time, the Central Committee resolved that "Comrade Nosek [Czechoslovakia's interior minister] have the security service examine the KSS's objections and report on them to the government."[115]

The KSS presented its case against Kempný, Bugár, and Staško directly to the DS on November 28, 1946, in a letter to the Democratic deputy chairman of the Board of Commissioners, Fraštacký.[116] Regarding Kempný, the KSS charged that he was an activist in the Populist student movement before the war, that he maintained close ties with those who helped destroy Czechoslovakia in 1938–39 (including Tiso), that he received a top position in the economic life of the Slovak state (as secretary-in-chief of the Union of Timber Production), from which he cooperated with German firms in the export of wood to Nazi Germany. Kempný was accused of having no ties with the wartime resistance and eschewing participation in the Slovak National Uprising. Most damningly, the Communists accused him of being one of Ďurčanský's agents in Slovakia and presented his earlier work toward creating a Catholic political party and ultimately concluding the April Agreement as done in accord with the plans of the Slovak emigration. The KSS letter similarly charged

Bugár with Populist sympathies, with using his position in the economy of the Slovak state (as director of a company specializing in the movement of freight) to serve German interests, and with having no ties to the wartime resistance. Staško was charged with carrying out intelligence and propaganda work on behalf of the Slovak state while a student in France in 1939. He allegedly betrayed a number of Slovaks who worked in the resistance, participated indirectly in the deportation of Slovak Jews by finding non-Jewish replacement labor for Slovak employers, and, like Kempný, remained in Slovakia after the war to carry out Ďurčanský's orders. The KSS demanded that the DS remove all three allegedly compromised individuals from their positions in the party leadership and parliament.[117]

The Communist charges appear to be a mixture of truth, half-truths, exaggeration, and fabrication. Normal professional and economic activity of the sort carried out by Slovaks of all political persuasions from 1939 to 1945 was depicted as high-level collaboration with Nazi Germany. Casual, or unsubstantiated, associations were portrayed as close, conspiratorial ties. Political activity carried out completely separately from, or even in opposition to, Ďurčanský's wishes was presented as missions carried out at his command.[118]

The Communists based their efforts to associate Kempný with Ďurčanský on the yet publicly unknown memoirs of one Jozef Kosorín, a young Populist activist whose papers were seized by the police in 1946. In his notes, Kosorín mentioned that he and a number of other young Populists met regularly during the final months of the war in private apartments to discuss social and political problems.[119] Kempný attended these get-togethers, and even hosted a few. Sometimes Ďurčanský attended. On January 15, 1947, the leftist press began publishing articles based on Kosorín's memoirs, but without mentioning him by name. An article in the January 15 issue of *Hlas práce* prompted Kosorín to write its author, Ján Čaplovič, to protest against the distortion of his memoirs.[120] A series of articles in *Nové slovo* by Husák, under the pen-name Historicus, included Kempný among the so-called black opposition that met regularly with Ďurčanský.[121] Husák noted the subversive nature of the matters discussed at the meetings, drawing on Kosorín's notes, to show that Ďurčanský was making plans for keeping up the struggle for the Slovak state in emigration, in cooperation with collaborators in Slovakia.[122]

In the face of the KSS's letter to Fraštacký and the press attacks, Lettrich asked Kempný to write a letter defending himself. In a letter to Lettrich dated March 1, Kempný denied a number of the Communist charges. Regarding Ďurčanský, Kempný wrote, "I did not maintain nor do I maintain any regular contacts with a group of Populist agents; I am not executing the orders of any such group, nor the orders of the anti-state underground, nor of Dr. Ďurčanský, but rather those of my Catholic, democratic, and civic conscience."[123]

Kempný also defended himself in the press. On February 4, he wrote an article in *Čas* entitled "About my 'Underground' Activity" in response to Čaplovič's attack in *Hlas práce*. Kempný denied any part in the Piešťany Congress of January 15, 1945, a gathering of young supporters of the Populist movement who were critical of the regime's policies of the time. The KSS had been trying to pin this charge on Kempný since the elections and had the police in Piešťany seeking, without success, to substantiate the charges.[124] He also denied being in close contact with Ďurčanský. As Kempný explained, he had met with Ďurčanský on three or four occasions in the winter of 1944–45, as part of a larger group of people critical of the policies of the Slovak regime at the time. These meetings included a representative of the International Red Cross from Switzerland, and there was no discussion of any sort of future political mission.[125] Ďurčanský, in Kempný's view, was reluctant to raise such issues in the presence of a foreigner, and of people like Kempný, who were not in his circle.

In spring 1947, the KSS intensified its assault on Kempný along a number of fronts. By June the KSS press was openly citing Kosorín to implicate Kempný in Ďurčanský's plans for advancing Populist goals in Slovakia. Husák recounted Kosorín's account of Ďurčanský's strategy, expressed at one of the meetings, whereby some supporters of the Slovak state would go into emigration while others would try to acquire influential positions back in Slovakia.[126] According to Husák, Kempný and his associates represented Ďurčanský's fifth column in Slovakia. From this perspective, Kempný's efforts during the election campaign to draw former Populist supporters into the Democratic camp took on a sinister dimension. For example, when Kempný wrote in *Čas* on May 9, 1946, that "everyone should work in his own place" for Slovak Catholic interests, Husák saw the application of Ďurčanský's master plan, which was not simply an appeal to Slovak Catholics to elect the party that most closely represented their views and interests.[127] Kempný's efforts to found a Catholic party in fall and winter 1944–45 and conclusion of the April Agreement were only more evidence that Kempný was working in tandem with Ďurčanský.

As they did with Kosorín's notes, the KSS also tried to twist a deposition given by Čarnogurský during his time in prison in the summer of 1946 into a noose around Kempný's neck. Čarnogurský's testimony that Kempný "enjoyed the trust of official Catholic circles and of that part of the Slovak generation that declared itself for Catholicism and laid claim to political representation and the advancement of national interests," that Kempný could best defend the interests of this group within the DS leadership, and that he cooperated closely with Slovak Catholic activists and was seen as one of "their men" in the DS leadership could only mean that Kempný was the agent of dark forces tied to the emigration.[128]

Although Kosorín's notes made it clear that Kempný had met with a group of Populist activists, including Ďurčanský, on a number of occasions and even hosted some of the meetings, it gave no evidence he was serving as Ďurčanský's agent.[129] The Communists overlooked the fact that most Slovak Catholic activists who had chosen to remain in Slovakia did so in an effort to build political futures for themselves within the restored Czechoslovak Republic and opted to place their hopes in the DS and Czechoslovakia's quasi-democratic system, not in the delusions of a quixotic émigré. Instead, in the KSS's view, nonexistent or tenuous links became close bonds, and normal political activity was conspiracy. Communist rhetoric contained a blanket condemnation of any ex-Populists working for the DS as subversives linked to the underground and the emigration.

The KSS took its campaign against Kempný to parliament and to the National Front. Communists in parliament raised objections against the fitness of Kempný, Bugár, and Staško to hold parliamentary office and asked parliament that their seats be revoked.[130] While avoiding such a drastic step, the parliament's verification committee requested information on the three representatives. At the June 11 meeting of the National Front, the Communists made Kempný and associates the chief targets of their attacks on the DS, with Nosek using Čarnogurský's testimony to paint a suspicious portrait of Kempný. Lettrich came to the defense of Kempný and other Democratic parliamentarians at the meeting.[131] Communist intentions can be seen in a draft proposal they produced at this time on antistate activity in Slovakia.[132] The Communists proposed that a number of important Democrats, mainly activists of the Catholic wing, be excluded from public positions as carriers of subversive, antistate tendencies. They also proposed that the Interior Ministry take measures against Čarnogurský and his circle for allegedly working to subvert political life in Slovakia in connection with the underground, and asked the DS to abrogate the April Agreement and annul its consequences. They also called for exploring the possibility of recall of "several compromised members of the Bishops' Council in Slovakia" and for appealing to priests in Slovakia to refrain from interfering in political life and especially from misusing religious positions, institutions, and ceremonies for political goals.

The summer of 1947 also saw several police provocations against Kempný and Bugár, namely suspicious persons seeking private meetings with them. In late July, Bugár refused to meet with a visitor to his law office named Križan and reported the incident to the police.[133] In late August, he asked police commissioner Jozef Ilčík not to send provocateurs to him. Kempný also had a suspicious visitor, in early August, one that would come back to haunt him.[134]

While Kempný was the prime focus of KSS attacks, Staško came in for his share of abuse as well. Like Kempný, he was seen as a close collaborator with Ďurčanský, and it did not help that Kosorín's memoirs identified him as the organizer of the meetings of the "black opposition" in late 1944 and early 1945.[135] The June 7 issue of *Nové slovo* included an article by Rašla that highlighted the propaganda and intelligence work that Staško did for the Slovak state while a student in France in 1939.[136] Bugár, on the other hand, was rarely attacked in the Communist press, most likely because he was not implicated in any meetings with Ďurčanský by Kosorín's memoirs. Nevertheless, as stated earlier, he did have to deal with attempted provocations, and the KSS was seeking information on him and demanding his removal from party and parliamentary office.[137]

By summer 1947, the DS leadership was acutely aware that their party was under siege like never before.[138] Party circulars warned DS members to beware of provocations and to turn in any suspicious mail they might receive, particularly antistate printed matter from abroad, to the police at once.[139] Local DS secretariats were also asked to document members' participation in the Slovak National Uprising or pro-Czechoslovak underground during the war.[140]

In late summer and early autumn 1947, the growing political crisis in Slovakia, and in Czechoslovakia as a whole, reached a new level of tension. Attempting to deflect attention from a bad harvest, for which the Communist led Ministry of Agriculture was taking the blame, Czechoslovakia's Communists raised their demand for a millionaires' tax, and the KSS in particular intensified its attacks on the Democratic led commissions of Food and Agriculture for the problems of shortages of goods and rises in prices. This was also the time that three prominent Czech leaders received mail bombs in an apparent assassination attempt.[141] At the founding conference of the Cominform in Szklarska Poręba, Poland, Czechoslovak Communist delegate Rudolf Slánský reported on September 26 that "our first priority task is now to strike at reaction in Slovakia."[142] In his October 2 account to the KSČ leadership about the Cominform conference, Slánský laid out a series of tasks that faced his party with respect to Czechoslovakia's domestic policies. Among other things, the Communists were to use the antistate conspiracy in Slovakia to strike a final blow against the DS, as part of a broader Communist assault on "reactionaries" and "antistate groups." This assault was already under way before the Cominform conference, when the government on September 16 allowed the arming of Partisans for use against the Banderovci, and Slovakia's wartime resistance organizations assembled for a conference in Bratislava scheduled to coincide with the September 20 deadline of the ultimatum given by the Union of Slovak Partisans a month earlier, demanding a purge of Slovak public and political life. Slovakia was clearly in the throes of a crisis.

It was amidst this increasingly tense atmosphere that what turned out to be the greatest assault to date on the DS's Catholic wing began. On September 16, the commissioner of the interior issued an official report on the uncovering of an antistate conspiracy in Slovakia. The report alleged that a collection of underground groups were plotting to restore the Slovak state, spreading pro-Tiso and antirepublic literature, organizing terrorist activity and sabotage, forming armed units, cooperating with the Banderovci, and preparing assassination attempts against political opponents, including President Beneš.[143] Eighty people were arrested, whom police identified as connected with the so-called Žilina group, named for its center of operations.[144] The conspiracy, long infiltrated and watched by the police, was a third-rate operation with no participation by anyone of political importance. Nevertheless, at once the Communists ratcheted up their already long-standing efforts to implicate top Catholic Democrats in antistate activity.

The Communist assault came energetically across a broad front. On September 15, the Central Committee of the KSS met and took steps to organize a Slovakia-wide movement to purge the DS and Slovak organs of alleged "enemies of the people and the Republic," to engage the Communist press in the action, and to work in cooperation with resistance, trade union, and farmers organizations.[145] In practice, this meant that these organizations produced resolutions demanding an immediate purge of Slovak public life, declarations that delegations from these organizations presented to the Board of Commissioners and the Slovak National Front between September 19 and 22.[146] In addition, the Slovak Partisan organizations held a conference in Bratislava on September 21 and a rally in front of the Slovak National Theatre the next day. Both venues featured a series of speakers, with the non-Democrats present concentrating their attacks on the DS. While a number of issues, all with an anti-Democratic edge, dominated the agenda at these meetings and rallies, charges of the DS's "misuse" of religion and harboring of Populists within its Catholic wing dominated. The resolution of the Partisan conference of September 21, for example, demanded among other things a purge of all those who misused the religious feeling of Slovakia's people for Populist ends and rejected "the agreements of political parties, according to which the adherents of some religion are favored."[147] This attack, in essence, was on the affirmative action policy for Slovak Catholics that was the cornerstone of the April Agreement. At the rally on September 22, in another example, the speaker for the Union of Slovak Women warned that the clergy must not misuse religion for political goals.[148]

Communist pressure on the DS was relentless. At a series of meetings of its Central Committee in late September and October, the KSS resolved to use leaflets, radio broadcasts, a factory congress, and mass rallies against the conspirators and their alleged protectors in the DS. The party further resolved to use the investigation of the conspiracy to either force the DS out of the government, compel it to accept certain conditions for remaining in the government, or even bring about the dissolution of the party itself.[149] The KSS also planned ways to increase Communist influence in Slovakia's judicial apparatus. Communist leaflets depicted the antistate conspiracy as the fruit of the April Agreement, which "evoked and strengthened religious incitement, religious intolerance, the misuse of the religious feeling of the people for matters that have as little in common with religion as water with fire."[150]

Meanwhile, the DS defended itself in a number of ways—denying involvement in the antistate conspiracy, charging the Communists with exaggerating it, and noting that a number of Communist Party members themselves had been implicated. On September 15, its presidium met and announced that it took a "fundamentally positive" position toward the purge but protested that the action was being misused for partisan political goals.[151] The presidium rejected the "tendentious and malicious" reports in some periodicals that tried to connect the conspiracy with members or policies of the DS. The party appealed to its members to be on guard and avoid provocations. The DS press continued in the ensuing days to deny that the DS had anything to do with the conspiracy and to protest the political misuse of the affair.[152] In a headline article of September 19, *Čas* took exception to "how the whole affair of the conspiracy was developed and manipulated" on the part of the state security forces. In an editorial on September 25, Lichner noted that the "political desperados" behind the conspiracy are largely insignificant and unknown people. On September 28, Peter Podhorský accused the Communists as resembling the Nazi Goebbels in their propaganda, noting how the Communists turn an accusation against one Democratic secretary into an implication of the entire DS, or the antistate activity of several priests into the attitude of the entire Slovak clergy. A long and prominent article in *Čas*'s October 5 edition alleged that the Communists were fomenting political unrest in Slovakia because they had lost the election. The article featured the Communist Holdoš's address of June 6, 1946, to a party meeting in Ružomberok, quoting him as saying, "The leadership of the KSČ has worked out a precise plan, containing fifteen points for the breaking up of the DS, this fascist-Populist camp, and for the seizure of power into our hands. In the DS we must under every circumstance demonstrate anti-state activity and on the basis of this evidence dissolve it!" The author went on to elaborate a long list of Communist policies and tactics used against the DS, among other things their dominance of Partisan and trade union organizations, which they mobilized to threaten the Democrats; their influence in and misuse of the security forces; and their opposition to autonomy for Slovakia, which necessitated that they put Slovakia in as negative a light as possible regarding antistate activity there.[153]

In defending their party, Democrats also went on the offensive. *Čas* parried Communist charges that the arrest of some minor DS functionaries implicated the party in the conspiracy, pointing out that some KSS members were arrested as well.[154] In this vein, *Čas* began running a series of minibiographies of minor Communist functionaries with shady political pasts, mainly former Hlinka Guardists.[155] The KSS responded by defending those "little people" who were members of the HSL'S, Hlinka Guard, or Hlinka Youth during the war. According to Friš, such people were often only formal members of such organizations, or youth who in a time of confusion succumbed to a propagandistic press. In turn, these nominal Populists redeemed themselves by joining the antifascist struggle, participating in the Slovak National Uprising, and working diligently for the postwar reconstruction of the Republic.[156] In a statement both designed to appeal to ex-Populist small fry and threaten the DS, Friš wrote, "To drive away, to express disgust at, to become indignant at, to vilify, to castigate these little people would be nonsensical and worthy of punishment."

While the Communists and their allies continued to raise a ruckus against the Democrats, behind the scenes the state security police carried out a succession of interrogations and further arrests based on them. Two detainees in particular proved to be crucial to the case that state security, or more precisely, those Communists working within it, wanted to make against leading Democrats. One of these, Rudolf Komandera, was an agent of émigrés who had made two trips to Slovakia in an effort to make links with whomever he thought might be sympathetic to the émigré cause. Komandera made attempts, to no avail, to establish ties with Kempný and Bugár. Nevertheless, his testimony gave police what they were looking for—a way to link the names of Kempný and Bugár with the bona fide enemies of the Republic. Things were going from bad to worse for the Democrats, as the fifteen-month-long Communist campaign to use Kempný and Bugár to discredit the DS bore fruit with an indictment. On September 29, the authorities requested that the National Assembly strip the two of their immunity so they could be arrested.[157] The parliamentary immunity committee took up the case, and Kempný and Bugár prepared for it a common letter of defense, sent also to Minister of Justice Drtina.[158] In it, they denied the accusations and pointed to the campaign against them since May 1946, noting, "In the first place this matter is not about us, but about democracy," as the Communists were using them in pursuit of the "liquidation of democratic forms of life in the ČSR and of everything that is non-Communist."[159]

On October 15, the immunity committee voted in favor of stripping Kempný and Bugár of their immunity and handing them over to the Provincial Court.[160] The next day, the National Assembly approved the recommendation, adding the stipulation that the men be handed over to the Ministry of Justice—that is, not to the security police.[161] That same day, Kempný and Bugár turned themselves in at the Palace of Justice in Bratislava, and they ended up in court prison awaiting interrogation.[162] Before the vote, Fedor Hodža spoke on behalf of the DS, expressing his party's trust in Kempný and Bugár's character, sincere Czechoslovak patriotism, and innocence.[163] Hodža declared, "This is not only a purge of public life, it is political pressure against the Democratic Party." The vote showed the KSČ, KSS, Social Democratic Party, and most of the National Socialist Party voting to hand over Kempný and Bugár, with the DS and Czech Populists and a few National Socialists abstaining.[164] However, this Communist victory was tempered by the stipulation that Kempný and Bugár be surrendered to the Ministry of Justice, not to the security police as the Communists had hoped.[165]

Why did the Democratic representatives in Parliament abstain rather than vote against handing over Kempný and Bugár? One can suspect a couple of reasons—divisions within the DS itself over Kempný and Bugár's innocence and a fear of provoking the Communists and others by taking a blatant stand on behalf of suspected conspirators. It was likely that the KSS would stir up anti-DS unrest in Slovakia should the Democrats come out too strongly for Kempný and Bugár.

While Kempný and Bugár's arrest was based on the shaky testimony of the key witness Komandera, another crucial witness led to the fall of an even more highly placed Democratic leader—Jan Ursíny. Oto Obuch, a person of dubious political past, was temporarily employed in the office of Ursíny. Because Obuch was a genuine member of the antistate resistance, his testimony provided the Communists in state security with a bonanza—a link between a very high-ranking Democrat and a conspirator. Obuch had worked in the Ministry of Propaganda during the war, and after the war he found employment at the Prague headquarters of the Czechoslovak film industry.[166] In December 1945, he was released on account of his service to the Slovak state.[167] Seeking employment, he was hired by Ursíny as a clerk dealing with press affairs in the office of the deputy prime minister. In 1946, Obuch established links with the Slovak underground through the mediation of a Catholic priest, Father František Mitúch, and began sending weekly reports on the political and economic situation in Czechoslovakia to Ďurčanský abroad. Obuch acquired much of this information from working in Ursíny's office. While most of it was simply extracts from the press, he did manage to get hold of some significant documents, such as the notes of the Czechoslovak government meeting that discussed Tiso's request for clemency (which explains why this information became known among Slovak émigrés shortly after the meeting took place). In the wave of arrests of "antistate conspirators" in September 1947, Obuch was imprisoned and interrogated. Because he worked in Ursíny's office, the security police sought to use him as a means of implicating Ursíny. The police had long been following Ursíny's activity, at least since the time of the April Agreement, but had found no evidence of antistate activity. Now they had their hands on a genuine conspirator who provided the link that could precipitate Ursíny's downfall.

Police agents arrested Obuch on September 23; on September 25 they searched his desk, with Ursíny's permission. On the night of September 25, the security services secretly and without authorization searched Ursíny's office, and the next day searched it again (though not his desk) with Gottwald's authorization, interrogating several of the employees. Nothing was found that could certify that Ursíny knew of Obuch's underground activity or affiliation with Ďurčanský, or that Ursíny had any special dealings or relationship with Obuch beyond normal professional interaction. Obuch, however, under police interrogation and in testimony that changed many times, gave the impression that Ursíny knew of his ties with the emigration but still nonetheless gave him access to official and confidential documents.

Pressure, meanwhile, was mounting on Ursíny. The leftist press implied that Obuch's misdeeds implicated the DS. *Pravda*'s headline article on Obuch's arrest regarded his case as the "ruinous consequences of the DS's April Agreement" and asserted that "it is clear that the political leadership of the DS made it possible for enemies of the Republic to penetrate into the highest places of the state apparatus and public life, where they have access to the most confidential state documents."[168] The DS's presidium denounced the press campaign and unanimously resolved to place its "full and unconditional trust" in Ursíny.[169] Behind the scenes, though, the pressure on Ursíny only grew worse. He was summoned to the Interior Ministry in Prague, where Nosek informed him that Obuch had accused him of sharing with him some military secrets regarding the Jáchymov uranium mines. Ursíny then met with Gottwald, who repeated the accusation and asked Ursíny to resign. Lettrich and Ursíny then turned to President Beneš, who agreed to meet with them, separately. According to Ursíny, Beneš was eager to see his resignation, noting that, while he believed that Ursíny had nothing to do with the Obuch affair, "it was a political mistake that you had this man in your office, and political mistakes are corrected politically."[170] Lettrich tried, to no avail, to get Beneš's support for a plan whereby Ursíny would remain in the government but on vacation until the affair was settled. He and Ursíny then sought assurances from Gottwald that, if Ursíny were to resign, Gottwald would set up a government commission to investigate the affair and presumably clear Ursíny's name. With Gottwald's agreement to this, Ursíny resigned on October 30.

Thus, by the end of October 1947, the Communists had engineered the fall of three of the architects of the April Agreement, one of them the top-ranking Democrat in the government and the other two in important leadership positions in the DS acquired as fruits of that agreement. Without any direct evidence, the police had managed to entangle leading Democrats in a conspiracy against the state. A number of historians of this period have noted the illegal means used by the Communist dominated police organs in their efforts to build a case against leading Catholic Democrats.[171] We find coerced testimonies, dubious witnesses, and stories changed repeatedly to reflect police needs—in a nutshell, the same methods used by Communist police at this time across Eastern Europe. Barnovský sums up the Slovak situation best: "Truth here was interwoven with half-truth and fabrication and put forth as evidence." Even today it is not easy to distinguish "political activity from criminal activity, provocateurs from genuine adversaries of the ČSR [Czechoslovak Republic], truth from lies."[172]

The Catholic Church in Slovakia more or less laid low during the period of the antistate conspiracy. While a few priests were implicated in the conspiracy, the Communist press concentrated its attacks on the DS far more so than on the Catholic clergy. *Katolícke noviny* responded to the uncovering of the conspiracy with apprehension. On September 21, the Catholic weekly printed the official note on the conspiracy of Slovakia's Interior Commission, followed by its own commentary.[173] The newspaper stated that it would take a reserved stance toward the conspiracy, pointing to the dubious "uncoverings" in neighboring countries, and in particular to that of the so-called Kolakovič affair a year and a half earlier in Slovakia. A week later, Koza presented his own take on the conspiracy.[174] He downplayed the affair, noting the meager and apparently harmless amount of weapons and other purportedly dangerous materials found (three revolvers, a "deaf-and-dumb" radio transmitter, and other trifles). Nevertheless, he saw the affair as ominous for Catholics, boding ill for Slovak and Catholic interests. Koza also commented on the actions of Slovak Catholics during the Second World War. According to Koza, they saved what they could: "They saved the nation and Slovakia from being torn apart. They preserved peace, order, and thousands of lives. They saved economically what was possible. They sought to reduce to a minimum the exploitation of Slovakia by the Germans, and with their own bodies they concealed the uprising being prepared and systematically sabotaged German goals and demands." Koza went on to note that this defensive political action by Slovaks often entailed a certain cooperation with the Germans, for which Slovak Catholics were now being condemned. It was rare indeed to hear in the postwar Czechoslovak media such a forthright defense of Slovak wartime collaboration, and it is no surprise that this was the last such column that Koza published in *Katolícke noviny*. In the October 26 issue, he announced that he was nervously exhausted and would be going away for a while to recuperate. He warned his readers against falling prey to provocations, noting that any alleged confidential or secret messages they may receive purporting to be from *Katolícke noviny*, the ÚKK, Church leaders, politicians, members of religious orders, or any illicit organizations or movements should be ignored or reported to the police. According to Koza, "Today, even seemingly trivial things can cause great unpleasantness for you."[175] He went on to reiterate what had long been his position on Catholics and politics in Slovakia—that is, that Catholic interests had primacy and any alliances by Catholics with any political parties should be merely tactical, based on and conditional upon the degree to which such alliances were a boon or a bane to Slovak and Catholic interests. With the DS now entangled in a horrible mess, Koza declared, "So don't bind yourself to any political groups or parties. It is best if you remain outside politics, free, without obligation. And then, when necessary, Catholics can throw their weight where the Slovak and Catholic interest demands." After this column, Catholicism's most engaging and provocative journalist in Slovakia would not grace the pages of *Katolícke noviny*, as Slovakia reeled from one crisis to another, culminating in the Communist takeover of February 1948.

Regarding the issue of antistate conspiracy, Slovakia did have a genuine underground, and no one was denying that. But while everyone agreed that an underground existed, what was disputed was its strength, its pervasiveness, and its connection with the DS, the Catholic Church, and the émigrés. The Democrats, in the far more accurate assessment, regarded the underground as the work of a relatively small number of fanatics and political adventurers and whichever Slovaks they could mislead onto their quixotic quest to restore the Tiso state. These individuals and groups had sporadic ties with each other and tenuous links with Populist émigrés. The Communists, on the other hand, saw a relatively large conspiracy, closely linked to foreign émigré centers, especially Ďurčanský's, with a web of conspirators throughout

Slovakia, including in all echelons of the DS, and finding sympathy among Slovakia's Roman Catholic priests and bishops. It was this question of linkage that was key as Communists sought to implicate leading Catholic Democrats in the underground and use this link to bring down the DS, as well as harm the Catholic hierarchy. With the leftist press keeping up its incessant attacks on the DS, the "antistate conspiracy" would hound the DS all the way until the Communist takeover of 1948 and beyond.

By mid-autumn 1947, the Democrats were in a serious crisis. Not only had they been unable to translate their extraordinary electoral victory into commensurate influence in Slovakia, but the Communists had successfully embroiled them in a situation that threatened to divide, decapitate, or even destroy the party. That the KSS and its allies identified the Catholic presence in the DS leadership as that party's most vulnerable point called the April Agreement itself into question. Henceforth, the DS had to remain in damage-control mode and fight for its survival as Czechoslovakia entered what would later become its final few months before the state's definitive takeover by the Communists.

5

CONTINUING CRISIS

From the October Putsch to the February Coup

LATE autumn and winter 1947–48 were bookended by two attempted Communist coups—the first in Slovakia in late October, the second in Prague in late February. Between these two events, the DS experienced a decline of its authority in Slovakia, intensifying internal strife, and the abrogation of the April Agreement. It had to face Communist challenges on the question of the land reform and repeated attacks on DS-run commissions, in particular food and agriculture. It continued having to deal with the implication of some of its leaders in the antistate conspiracy and sparred with the Communists over security questions. It also held its long-awaited party congress. As Communist aggression intensified across Czechoslovakia, the DS drew closer than ever to the Czech nonleftist parties and cooperated with them during the crisis that culminated in the Communist takeover. During that crisis, Czechoslovakia's Communists outmaneuvered the so-called bourgeois parties, including the DS. It drew leftist Democrats and sundry disgruntled elements from that and other parties into its camp. A faction split off from the DS which cooperated with the Communists during the February coup, with the rest of the party being destroyed. Slovakia's Catholic Church during this time remained largely on the sidelines, trying to play it safe and saying little during these turbulent final months of "pre-February" Czechoslovakia. The KSS, meanwhile, continued to try to woo Catholics away from the DS while attacking that party for allegedly harboring Populist sympathizers, especially among its leading Catholics.

In a series of monthly meetings beginning September 29, the KSS's Central Committee laid out the ends and plotted the means for a major putsch against the Democrats.[1] The goal of their campaign was "to change the entire political structure of Slovakia, that is, the composition of the Board of Commissioners and other organs of people's power." The KSS hoped ultimately to bring about either the DS's expulsion from the government, its dissolution, or its continuation in the government only under certain conditions.[2] It also hoped to change the composition of the Board of Commissioners to the Democrats' disadvantage—forcing the Democrats out of key positions, bringing representatives of Communist controlled or influenced mass trade union and resistance organizations onto the board, and including representatives of Slovakia's smaller parties as a way to dilute Democratic influence. In pursuit of these goals, the KSS resolved to intensify popular pressure on the DS over the issues of state security (above all, the antistate conspiracy) and critical shortages of foodstuffs and consumer goods (problems that could be blamed on the DS since Democrats held the Commissions of Food and Agriculture). Democrats were to be assaulted at commemorations of Czechoslovak independence on October 28, at peasant rallies, in the Communist press, in interviews on Radio Prague, and in brochures produced and distributed by the party. October 30 and 31 (Thursday and Friday, respectively) would represent the climax of the Communist plot—a Congress of Factory and Employees Councils would be held on Thursday, where the tone of the event and content of its resolutions would be decidedly anti-DS, while on Friday the Communist members of the Board of Commissioners would resign and force a recomposition of that organ to the KSS's advantage.

The Congress of Factory Councils was a textbook example of Communist mobilization of a social organization for political purposes, a tactic used by Communists wherever they sought political power. Communists were instructed to take the initiative at local factory council meetings in calling for a congress, and the Central Committee set up a high-level committee to direct the action.[3] The party instructed its district secretariats on how to influence the selection of delegates to the congress. It also determined the basic program for the congress, including the slogans to be used, and worked to coordinate it with the activities of peasant and resistance groups, as well as with the Slovak Trade Union Council. By coordinating the activities of social organizations infiltrated and dominated by Communists, the KSS hoped to contribute to a prerevolutionary atmosphere in Slovakia and thus set the stage for the putsch of October 31.

On October 30, trade union representatives met in Bratislava for the Congress of Factory and Employees Councils, the event coming off according to plan and fulfilling its function in the larger Communist directed scheme. Over 1,800 delegates attended, who issued a declaration in line with Communist wishes.[4] The declaration contained a long list of complaints about the situation in food supply and agriculture, which it connected to the security situation by claiming that "several components of the National Front [i.e., the Democrats] are directly in league with antistate elements and making it possible for them to occupy key positions," from which they can undermine the economy in Slovakia. After the usual Communist denunciations of "capitalist exploiters" and "reactionary intrigues" against the trade union movement, the declaration threatened that "our patience is at an end. It is time to say clearly and emphatically: Enough!" Asserting that Slovakia was in a "deep political crisis," the declaration depicted the Board of Commissioners as "an arena of tenacious struggle between the forces of progress and reaction," a struggle that was exhausting its energies and making it impossible to solve the pressing problems facing the Slovak people. It accused a part of the Board of Commissioners (namely, the Democratic part) of defending "big-time profiteers, embezzlers, large-scale landowners, and conspirators," concluding that "Reconstruction of the Board of Commissioners is unavoidable!" The declaration demanded the resignation of the present board and reconstitution of one to include "the broadest concentration of all pro-state, democratic, and anti-fascist forces of the Slovak nation," code for the inclusion of Communist dominated worker, peasant, and resistance organizations. The declaration ended its demands by calling for an immediate convocation of the Slovak National Front, where the representatives of such organizations, along with party leaders, would discuss the composition of a new board.

The declaration of the Factory and Employee Councils suited Communist needs most fittingly, hardly surprising since the KSS played a central role in organizing the congress. The congress reflected Communist aims in several ways. It connected the issues of security and supply, presenting the case to Slovaks that their lack of basic goods was a result of the DS's cooperation with antistate elements. It raised the issue of political participation of mass organizations, giving Communists a means of influence they could not gain at the ballot box. Finally, it concentrated its demands on the Board of Commissioners, the venue for the impending Communist putsch. The congress's call for a new board served, as intended, as the pretext for the KSS to make its move.

The next day, October 31, Husák reported to the SNR's presidium that seven of the fifteen members of the Board of Commissioners had resigned, which "in accordance with parliamentary custom I regard as the resignation of the whole Board."[5] Among the alleged resignees Husák included the Democrat Filo and the nonpartisan Ferjenčík. The same day, the KSS organized a meeting of the Slovak National Front to include Communists, representatives from the tiny party Social Democracy in Slovakia and the Party of Freedom,[6] along with representatives of the trade union and resistance organizations. Among them were delegates from the Slovak Trade Union Council, which earlier that day had informed the Board of Commissioners of the declaration of the Congress of Factory Councils and announced that it would call meetings in factories across Slovakia for November 5 if its demands were not met.[7] The meeting resolved to accept the resignations and authorized Husák to begin talks on reconstituting the board.

That evening the DS, whose members were not present at the meeting, issued reports denying both that any Democrats had resigned and, given the absence of the DS from the proceedings, that the meeting called by Husák was indeed a meeting of the Slovak National Front. In the DS's view, the board remained in place, and the Front had yet to meet. The next day, the Democratic commissioners issued a statement denying that any of them had resigned and blaming the KSS for intentionally provoking a crisis by its actions.[8] The statement made reference to Communist abuses of state power and unjust attacks on Democratic commissioners.

The five Communist commissioners responded with a statement of their own, entitled "Why We Left and What Sort of Board of Commissioners Should Run Slovakia."[9] The Communists blamed the April Agreement for the crisis in Slovakia—namely, that because of its obligations to the past the DS was unable to support a genuine cleansing of Slovakia of antistate elements and spent more time and energy defending violators of state regulations involving supply of goods than in implementing them. Such actions, according to the statement, paralyzed the board, prompting its Communist members to ratify the Congress of Factory Councils' call for resignation and ask the Democrats to do the same.

The crisis set off by the resignations lasted nearly three weeks. At first, the DS acted as though the Board of Commissioners continued to function and refrained from meetings to deal with its restructuring.[10] On November 3, however, Democrats joined in a long and torturous series of negotiations, involving a number of governing and political institutions and covering a range of issues where DS and KSS stood at loggerheads. During the period of crisis, both sides attempted some degree of popular mobilization, with the Communists holding various rallies and meetings of workers and peasants, and the DS staging several rallies across Slovakia on November 16.[11] On November 3, the Slovak National Front began a series of meetings to address the crisis. Meanwhile, the Czechoslovak National Front in Prague tried to meet to take up the issue, but Communist insistence that delegates of trade union, Partisan, and peasant organizations take part met stiff resistance from National Socialist, Czechoslovak People's, and Democratic party representatives, making it impossible for the meeting to proceed.[12] The next day, the KSČ proposed at a government meeting that the government be empowered to solve the crisis in Slovakia, but National Socialist and Czech Populist ministers protested against this violation of the Third Prague Agreement.[13] However, the government did agree to send Gottwald to Bratislava to broker a compromise. From November 8 through 10, his visit did manage to achieve some mutual concessions and partial agreements but fell short of ending the deadlock. Upon leaving Slovakia, Gottwald announced that he would submit a proposal to the government on how to solve the crisis, concluding, "It's unfortunate that we couldn't solve this problem here, that we'll have to solve it in Prague!"[14] Finally, on November 18, the Czechoslovak National Front, after two days of turbulent discussions, engineered a compromise solution, accepted by the government and the relevant agents in Slovakia by November 19.

The points of contention between the KSS and DS during the crisis were numerous.[15] At least five issues figured prominently in discussions:

Who would hold the Commission of the Interior? The KSS did not want the post to go to a Democrat, while the DS wanted to keep it out of Communist possession. In the end, both sides agreed to retain the nonpartisan specialist Ferjenčík, whose work had pleased the Communists to a considerable degree.

Who would hold the Commission of Justice? The Communists very much wanted this position, while the DS hoped to keep it in Democratic hands. Ultimately, it was agreed that the post go to a nonpartisan specialist "who had the trust of the resistance groups," namely Andrej Buza.

Should representatives of Slovakia's two smaller parties be represented on the board? The KSS supported the inclusion of both the Party of Freedom and the Social Democracy in Slovakia party on the board, hoping thereby to dilute DS influence. The DS was open to accepting representatives from the smaller parties, but only if it would not leave the Democrats short of an absolute majority on the board. As the winner of 62 percent of the vote in the parliamentary elections, the Democrats were loath to allot most of the board's seats to non-Democrats. Nevertheless, in the end the DS had to make a big concession and admit to the board a representative from each of Slovakia's smaller parties, at the expense of DS positions, thereby reducing the Democratic share of seats to well below absolute majority.

Should representatives of mass social organizations be represented on the board? For the KSS, this was a welcome measure that would effectively give the Communists dominance on the board through the inclusion of organizations they dominated or heavily influenced. For this reason, the Democrats vehemently opposed this Communist proposal, and the Czech National Socialists and Czech Populists backed them up. Consequently, the most the Communists could get here was an agreement that the board have greater cooperation with such organizations in the future.

Which party should hold the Commissions of Agriculture and Food? The KSS for months had been targeting the Democratic trustees Kvetko and Filo, hoping to use a bad harvest and shortage of basic goods in Slovakia to dislodge these Democrats from their positions on the board and replace them with Communists. The DS dug its heels in hard over these positions and refused to budge until the very end, when a compromise was worked out whereby the Democrats kept the two commissions but replaced the particular commissioners.[16]

The final compromise that settled the crisis can be seen as a defeat for the Democrats, albeit not a total one. Before the KSS precipitated the crisis, the DS held nine of the board's fifteen seats, with the KSS holding five and a nonpartisan expert, Ferjenčík, holding one. Now the DS held only six of fifteen seats, losing one seat each to the Party of Freedom, Social Democratic Party, and the nonpartisan expert Buza. Along with losing its absolute majority, the Democrats lost the important Commission of Justice. On the credit side, the DS managed to keep the most highly contested commissions out of Communist hands and keep mass organizations from official representation on the board.

Even before the crisis, the KSS had more influence on the board than its electoral showing warranted. With nearly two-thirds of Slovakia's vote, the Democrats should have held both the board's chairmanship and the Commission of the Interior. The Communists, however, by charging that the DS's margin of victory came from the votes of disgruntled ex-Populists bought off by the April Agreement, and threatening to mobilize mass organizations against the Democrats, were able to keep those key positions out of Democratic hands. The crisis of October 31, which would have been hard to pull off if the board had had a Democratic chairman and head of police, was a fruit of this Communist policy.

As Democratic writers pointed out, the KSS was trying to achieve via political maneuvering what it could not achieve at the ballot box.[17] They noted, for example, that Husák's fingerprints were all over the Congress of Factory Councils.[18] The Communists, as usual, countered that such events represented the genuine views of the Slovak population, which had supposedly moved in the KSS's direction since the May 1946 elections.[19] Communists tried to put a nationalist face on the crisis, accusing the DS of colluding with "Czech reaction" in opposing a place for the trade union and Partisan representatives on the board. The KSS presented this as Czech interference in Slovak affairs.[20] *Pravda* likewise accused the DS of intentionally prolonging the political crisis so as to increase opportunities for Czech intervention.[21] Of course, these charges are absurd, given the fact that it was precisely the Communists who from the beginning wanted to give Prague the power to solve the Slovak crisis, while the Czech National Socialist Party voted with the DS in giving the Slovaks more time to work things out on their own.[22] The Communists themselves catered to "Czech reaction" through appeals to Czech unity.[23] For example, Gottwald and the Communists pressed for a reinterpretation of the Third Prague Agreement that would allow the Czechoslovak government to solve this and similar crises in Slovakia, while the National Socialists and Populists supported the Democrats in rejecting such an aggrandizement of central authority. In the end, the Third Prague Agreement was somewhat modified through a binding governmental agreement on the interpretation of Article II, paragraph 2, whereby the Slovak National Council's presidium would have seven days to replace a commissioner in whom the government expressed its lack of confidence. If the government did not approve of said replacement, it would appoint a new commissioner itself.[24]

Particularly significant for our purposes is the place of the April Agreement in the crisis. From the start, the Communists made it a central part of their assault on the Democrats. In a letter of November 9, addressed to Gottwald as prime minister, the KSS demanded that the DS "publicly revoke all its obligations toward Populist elements following from the April Pact."[25] On November 9, in the thick of the crisis, the DS's presidium met to discuss the April Agreement and called on the party's Executive Committee to declare the agreement as inoperative and nonbinding.[26] On November 22, in the aftermath of the crisis, the DS's Executive Committee met and did just that, designating the April Agreement as "a provisional inner party measure of the post-war period . . . that has been overcome by developments and hence no longer suitable for the inner life of the party."[27]

The DS was clearly responding to demands that it clean its house of Populist sympathizers. Along with the abrogation of the April Agreement, the DS resolved to recall several of its secretaries who had fulfilled official functions in the wartime republic.[28] How Catholics responded to this step by the DS away from its prior commitments, themselves not always honored, is hard to gauge. To soften the impact, for example, Lettrich insisted for moral reasons on the continuation in practice of some sort of proportionality toward Catholics.[29] It was also clear that the DS was taking desperate measures in an effort to survive an assault by the Communists and needed to show a determination to break with past policy in order to stave off further attacks.

The Catholic Church in Slovakia, as discerned from its chief press organ and a pastoral letter by its bishops, tried to ride out the fall crises and keep a safe distance from the antistate conspiracy and attempted coup on the Board of Commissioners. In their pastoral letter of October 26, Slovakia's bishops repeated their oft-made assurances that the church had a positive relation to the Czechoslovakia Republic, citing Romans 13:1, where St. Paul instructs Christians to be subject to the governing authorities, and urged Catholics not to take part in any antistate activity.[30] At the same time, the bishops expressed the hope that the investigations into the conspiracy be carried out in a correct and just manner, and noted their belief that the wave of political trials was harming the consolidation of the nation and state.

While the bishop's pastoral letter did not touch specifically on politics, a couple of articles in *Katolícke noviny* sought, implicitly, to foster a Catholic distance toward the DS. In the October 26 issue, Koza-Matejov, as previously noted, informed his readers that he was taking some time off due to nervous exhaustion.[31] (This stepping aside of the most combative champion of Slovak

Catholic interests in the Slovak media could itself be read as an effort by the church to stay aloof from the turbulent events of that autumn.) In his farewell address, Koza advised his readers, among other things, to avoid provocations, to maintain Catholic unity, to cooperate with Czech Catholics on religious, cultural, and educational issues, and to be model citizens. Most significant, he advised them "not to tie themselves to any political groups or parties. It is best when you stay outside of politics, free, unattached. And then, when it becomes necessary, Catholics will put their weight where Slovak and Catholic interests demand." A week later, *Katolícke noviny* ran a column in Koza's usual spot expressing similar sentiments, "Catholics in Politics" by Jozef Pravda.[32] In stressing the necessity for Catholics to apply their principles in politics and public life in general, he noted, "The Catholic Church does not make a partisan politics, but gives guidelines to Catholics for their public and political life. And Catholics are bound in conscience to act according to these guidelines. Above all in elections." He went on to claim that the Catholic Church and its institutions "remain aloof from partisan politics. Catholics can pursue partisan politics as individuals, but not Catholicism as a whole. The effort by Catholicism to see Christian and moral principles realized in public, cultural, social, and economic life is not a partisan policy. These are truths which the church cannot give up, because it would thereby stop fulfilling its mission." These articles served as assurances by Slovakia's leading Catholic organ that Catholics were not a danger to the state, that they nonetheless were dissatisfied with much about their current situation, and that they were not putting all, or even most, of their eggs in the DS basket.

As Slovakia was reeling from the autumn crises, and as an uncertain future loomed on the horizon, it is difficult to find much of anything on the pages of *Katolícke noviny* that could be construed as assertive, combative, or controversial. With Koza gone, the DS on the defensive, and the church anxious about the course of investigations into antistate conspirators, the Catholic press ignored or tiptoed around Slovakia's pressing issues. For weeks, *Katolícke noviny* appears to have studiously avoided publishing anything that might needlessly antagonize its enemies. For instance, a column in January on the sixtieth birthday of the Slovak Catholic writer Ignác Grebáč-Orlov covered his life story only up to 1935. The last significant article in *Katolícke noviny* before the Communist coup was in the February 22, 1948, issue, in which the paper responded to those Slovaks who reproached it for not being oppositional enough.[33] The author noted that the paper must take into account the circumstances of the time, where there were limits on what one could express and where one had to navigate as though on ice. He also reproached those who called for a more aggressive Catholic press, stating that mocking one's enemies is never heroic nor Catholic, and that reason, not just feeling, is needed for defending Catholic and human values.

Like the Catholic Church and press, the DS had plenty to worry about during and after Slovakia's fall crises of 1947. From the time of the outbreak of the antistate conspiracy, through the Communist putsch, and beyond, the DS not only had to deal with a number of assaults from without but considerable tensions within. Some Democrats thought the party was behaving too timidly in defending itself against Communist strong-arming. Others thought the DS could do more to dissociate itself from those members implicated in the conspiracy. Still others tried to utilize the discontent of Catholics in various intrigues aimed at changing the course of DS policy, or even taking over or splitting the party.

The DS setback during the Board of Commissioners crisis did not play well with the party's rank and file in staunchly Catholic regions like the one around Topoľčany. A DS situation report from that region notes that the party membership was considerably unsettled by recent developments and, along with much of the local population, regarded the new composition of the Board of Commissioners to be a total defeat of the DS.[34] The report noted that the DS was being sharply criticized on every side. Discontent also surfaced in the upper echelons of the party. Michal Zibrín, a Democratic member of parliament, wrote an angry letter to Lettrich on December 8, complaining of recent personnel changes in the Commission of Justice that represented a decisive strengthening of Communist influence over that department.[35] Zibrín had harsh words for Lettrich and other DS leaders for not facing up to this threat to Slovakia's judicial administration and taking steps to thwart it. Zibrín also criticized Lettrich for the party's apparent disinterest in Kempný and Bugár, passing no resolution on their behalf. He also noted that this and other failures to express sufficient concern that its arrested members be treated in accordance with legal norms was gaining for the DS the reputation that it did not defend its own people. Zibrín appended to his letter a report outlining the legal and judicial irregularities and abuses allegedly committed by the Communist dominated police—holding people without charge; holding and interrogating witnesses and accused in police prisons in cases where the law stipulated they be handed over to the courts; using brutal methods of interrogation.

Discontent also surfaced on the left wing of the party. Polák, the DS leader closest to the Partisans, began to distance himself from Lettrich and press for a comprehensive purge of the party.[36] Ševčík, like Polák a veteran of the Slovak National Uprising and a former Commissioner for the Post Office and Telegraph, wrote a letter to the DS leadership on November 5 in which he demanded that the party distance itself from the conspiracy and change its leadership and policy alike.[37] Ševčík's criticism had a Catholic twist—he called on the party to revoke the April Agreement, which he himself had signed, and reproached the DS for not expressing the views of sincere Democrats, especially Catholic ones, who were true to the Republic.[38]

Along with Polák and Ševčík, another prominent Democrat on the party's left, Minister of Transportation Ivan Pietor, began to agitate for a purge, with the aim of using the DS's problems to marginalize Lettrich and Ursíny, take over the DS, and move it in a direction more amenable to the Communists.[39] Shortly after the antistate conspiracy was announced, and backed by a circle of supporters, Pietor presented himself as someone concerned with protecting Catholic interests. He met with Archbishop Kmet'ko, while his political adviser Vilinskij met with Slovak bishops Nécsey and Škrábik, hoping to convince them that changes in the DS would benefit the Catholic Church in Slovakia and its adherents.[40] According to the Vilinskij, the bishops were willing to accept changes in the DS, including an abrogation of the April Agreement, provided that Catholics were treated justly by the DS and that young Catholics unburdened by the past received their share of new positions opened up after a purge. Pietor, as part of his efforts to court the Catholic hierarchy, also promised to defend Kempný to the hilt.

In early November, Pietor met separately with Gottwald and Beneš, hoping to win their support.[41] Though we know little of the content of these talks, it is clear that Pietor did not succeed in gaining any serious support from either the prime minister or the president. Meanwhile, Pietor pressed his case at DS meetings.[42] On November 6, he called for a purge of the party, a move backed by Polák, agreed to by Ursíny, and reluctantly accepted by Lettrich after sharp argument. A measure of this reluctance can be seen in the fact that a three-member purge commission was established in the DS, composed of Lettrich, Cvinček, and Polák, only one of whom was an avid supporter of the idea. Ševčík, however, was later added. The fruits of the commission were meager—a recall of the handful of Democratic secretaries who had held functions in the HSĽS in the past. These steps were part of the same Democratic effort to protect its reputation that saw the abrogation of the April Agreement on November 22. Pietor's intrigues, however, ultimately failed, as he won over neither the Communists, the Czech non-Communist parties, Slovakia's bishops, Beneš, nor enough of the DS leadership to make a difference.

Communist disinterest in working with Pietor to move the DS to the left can be explained by the Communist approach to the DS during this time of crisis. By late 1947, the KSS, like all other parties in Czechoslovakia, had to take into account the next round of parliamentary elections, sure to be slated for 1948. Communists hoped to strengthen their position in Slovakia in advance of the elections, or even engineer a decisive grab for power statewide.[43] With these considerations in mind, they reinvigorated their old policy of wooing Catholics away from the DS. Alongside the usual charges against the DS (sabotaging of the land reform to the benefit of magnates, even German and Hungarian ones; defending wholesalers and black marketeers; being responsible for supply problems; and defending and harboring antistate conspirators),[44] the Catholic question figured prominently. The Communists hoped both to exacerbate tensions within the DS between Catholics and Protestants and to neutralize the Catholic bishops and clergy.

The KSS believed that the time was ripe to exploit Catholic disaffection with the DS. The abrogation of the April Agreement on November 22, the growing cooperation between the DS and the Czechoslovak National Socialist Party, and the overall sense that the DS could not deliver on its promise to represent Catholic interests all served as indicators that Communists could revisit the Catholic question with greater success than in the past. The KSS was also aware that, according to a memo from Široký to Gottwald of November 12, certain Catholic circles had reproached the KSS for talking only with Lettrich during the fall crisis surrounding the Board of Commissioners.[45]

On January 9, 1948, the KSS's Central Committee met to discuss relations with Catholics.[46] After a report on the matter by Novomeský, the party resolved to open talks with church representatives in an effort to convince the Bishops' Council and Catholic clergy to remain neutral in the upcoming elections. Novomeský himself was even dispatched to sound out Bishop Čársky on the matter.[47] The Central Committee also resolved to enlist Communist press organs in the campaign to court Catholics and support their disaffection with the DS and to be more accommodating to the Catholic Church on the question of land reform—for example, by postponing the redistribution of Catholic lands until the fall. Finally, the Communists agreed not to oppose any new Catholic political party that might emerge from a split in the DS.

As the DS prepared for its upcoming party congress, *Nové slovo* analyzed the DS's "Catholic problem."[48] According to *Nové slovo*, the Populists in the DS were in a bind—they had been unable to achieve anything politically from the DS, but at the same time were in no position to establish a new party based on their version of political Catholicism. As a result, they would stay in the DS, but not do much on its behalf. The Agrarian wing of the DS, at the same time, needed the Catholics mainly as a counterweight to the Communists, so the Democrats could more effectively defend their wealthier members from confiscatory socialist policies. This analysis served the Communist purposes of presenting the DS as using Catholics for its own ends and reminding Catholics that the DS had accomplished little for them. The Communist press also liked to point out how the DS was increasingly turning to the Czech bourgeois parties for support. This the Communists portrayed not only as a coalescing of Czechoslovakia's non-Communist parties on an anti-Communist platform, but also as the DS selling out Slovak national interests to ally with Czech anti-Slovaks in defense of class interests.[49] *Nové slovo*, for example, lampooned this marriage of convenience in a cartoon in its February 7 issue.[50] It depicted, quite unattractively, a male National Socialist giving a flower to a female Populist, a symbol of their engagement to marry. The two are holding papers that read "Anti Slovak Program" and "Anti-Czech Program," respectively. In the background stand the happy fathers of the engaged couple, a wealthy German and Hungarian drawn to look like pigs.

Both the Catholic Church and the DS noticed Communist efforts to reach out to Catholics while attacking the DS. *Katolícke noviny* noted, "In recent months we are not being attacked by those resistance organization periodicals which previously attacked us with indiscriminate means."[51] *Čas*, at the same time, made it clear that the DS knew what the Communists were up to. On February 5, the DS organ noted that the Communists were appealing to both the Catholic and the Lutheran-Agrarian camps of the DS in an effort to set them against one another.[52] To Catholics, Communists noted that the DS had abrogated the April Agreement and argued that the party was Lutheran dominated, Czechoslovak and Agrarian in orientation, and that it had abandoned the victims of the crackdown on antistate conspirators, while drawing close to the anti-Catholic, anti-Slovak Czechoslovak National Socialist Party. To the Lutheran-Agrarian camp, Communists pointed to alleged Populist and émigré influence in the party.

One means the KSS hoped to use to split the DS along confessional lines was the question of a fifth Slovak political party—one catering to Catholics disaffected with the DS. Here the point man for the Communists was the Catholic Democrat Jozef Kysely̌. As noted earlier, the KSS's Central Committee, at its meeting of January 9, 1948, resolved not to oppose a new political party that might emerge with the splitting of the DS.[53] This was not a contingency plan for some imaginary development. In December 1947, some Catholics in the DS were actively trying to set up their own party. The leader of these efforts was Kyselý, a Democrat who served as the lord mayor of Bratislava as well as representative to the Slovak National Council.[54] Certain suspicious circumstances surrounded Kyselý. In September 1947, he was the target of a whispering campaign fostered in the Communist press, alleging his participation in the antistate conspiracy. His arrest followed. After being held for eleven days by the security police, he was released. During this time, the DS asked him to resign his position for the sake of the party, but he refused. Once free, Kyselý began criticizing the DS leadership. In December, he began organizing a circle of Catholics disgruntled with the DS, and in January he presented his demands to Lettrich, ostensibly on behalf of the "young Catholic intelligentsia." The DS presidium responded by expelling Kyselý from the party on January 23, the eve of the party congress.

In its official report on Kyselý's expulsion, the DS's general secretariat proclaimed that Kyselý "violated, in an egregious manner, party orders, above all by engaging in discussions with the leading representatives of the KSS regarding the founding of a new political party in Slovakia."[55] The Communists immediately rushed to Kyselý's defense, calling the DS's charges against him "fabricated and mendacious," and publishing his public response to his expulsion, as well as an interview with him on the affair.[56] Kyselý noted that he had joined the DS shortly after liberation, but came to see that the party was not pursuing a policy in accord with the "mentality of our people" but rather one out of step with the thinking of the times. He accused the DS leadership of enriching a few families and individuals, of offering promises rather than deeds, and of religious intolerance, among other things. For these reasons, Kyselý gathered young Catholic intelligentsia around himself and presented their demands to Lettrich, asking especially for "proportionate representation of progressive and young Catholics in the party leadership and a diminution of the influence of three Lutheran families."[57] He also called for a socioeconomic policy that was further to the left. For these reasons, the DS's presidium voted to expel him from the party. Regarding his efforts to found a new political party, Kyselý claimed that he was sounding this out among *all* political parties represented in the National Front, not just the Communists, as new parties needed broad National Front approval. The party would be unequivocally pro-republic, socially and economically progressive, and defend the interests of the Catholic community. Alleging a strong dissatisfaction among Catholics in the DS, Kyselý claimed that he already had found much support for the new party and that its appearance was imminent.

Kyselý's efforts, and Communist support for them, indicate the challenges facing the DS at the time with respect to its relations with Catholics. Other related problems included the continuing fallout from the antistate conspiracy and Catholic disaffection over the abrogation of the April Agreement and Democratic rapprochement with the Czechoslovak National Socialist Party. In this context, the DS sought to reach out to Catholics at its long-awaited and several times postponed party congress, held on January 24 and 25 in Bratislava.

The Democrats' party conference included a number of features meant, directly or indirectly, to mollify Catholics. First, speeches and programmatic statements stressed the party's essential commitment to a Christian worldview and Christian ideals.[58] Second, Lettrich's keynote address explicated the Democrats' dilemma.[59] He walked his audience through Slovakia's recent past, citing the origins of the April Agreement, the Tiso trial, the Daxner affair, the antistate conspiracy, and the crisis over the Board of Commissioners. Lettrich noted how the Communists were using these events (all connected in some way with Catholics in the DS, one might add) to undermine the Democrats and gain for themselves an influence that they could not win in competitive elections. Lettrich addressed in detail some issues of pressing concern to Catholics. With respect to the April Agreement, he noted how it often made the DS the brunt of political attacks, with the party's enemies ascribing even the antistate conspiracy to it. For these reasons, the DS's Executive Committee had resolved on November 22 that the agreement was "overcome by developments" and should be abrogated. According to Lettrich, "It is necessary to understand this decision as follows, that the principles of the agreement on the just representation of Catholic members in various positions has become an inseparable part of internal policy and tactics, so that these principles are and will be adhered to even without a formal agreement. Therefore, this is not a question of violating or renouncing a given promise, as our political enemies would like to argue. On the contrary, it is a matter of the obligations taken on becoming a pledge of honor by the party without regard for the present or future political constellation."

Lettrich also addressed the alleged involvement of several leading Democrats in the antistate conspiracy, noting that the DS would not take definitive measures against implicated Democratic parliamentary representatives due to the lack of sufficient evidence. Lettrich pointed out that all the DS had to go on were incomplete investigations by the security organs and inaccessible judicial examinations. The DS could only wait for reliable data before making a decision. As Lettrich's speech showed, by abrogating the April Agreement but pledging to keep it in principle, and by electing neither to defend nor condemn Kempný and Bugár, the DS leadership was walking the tightrope between, on the one hand, alienating Catholics and, on the other, provoking the party's Lutherans as well as its leftists.

The DS program also contained some elements meant to woo Catholics.[60] The congress's cultural commission resolved that "we are for a harmonious coexistence of state and church and for the support of the churches and their religious mission both morally and materially," and that "we call for the churches to be given the possibility to realize their educational, cultural, social, and charitable missions in public life." The commission also came out in defense of church-affiliated religious organizations and institutions, which the DS pledged to support with all its forces. It recommended that the dissolution of the Catholic and Lutheran young organizations be revoked. Regarding education, the commission recognized that "the churches have the right to establish schools. This is their duty and mission." It also called for religion to "again take first place among the required subjects" in Slovak schools. All of these resolutions could be identified with the prevailing view of Slovakia's Catholics, as well as many Lutherans, on these matters of church and state. In a final sop to Catholics, the DS elected Mikuláš Franek, a Catholic, as general secretary.[61] Lettrich was reelected as party chairman. The Congress placed a heavy premium on party unity. Both the party program and party speakers stressed harmony between Catholics and Lutherans.[62] Billed as a "working congress," it tried to avoid conflict as much as possible. When a delegate from Bratislava, for instance, asked why Kyselý was not present, the DS read its official position on his expulsion from the party of the day before.[63] It appears that little controversy ensued. The Communist press ascribed this to the DS's Agrarian-Lutheran wing's stacking the delegations to the congress in their favor.[64]

Apart from its congress, the DS gave other indications in late 1947 and early 1948 that it was concerned with its image among Catholics. Front-page headlines from *Čas* from mid-February read: "The DS Calls for Church Schools Alongside State Ones" and "DS Represents the Interests of the Clergy."[65] Education remained a battleground issue where the Democrats needed to convince Catholics of their good will. *Čas* argued that "the right to have their own schools should not be denied to any of the churches recognized by the state," something which "fully corresponds to the spirit of genuine democratic principles."[66] Slovakia's Catholic bishops themselves at this time were less assertive than the DS on this issue. A pastoral letter of October 26 lamented only that religious education and the teaching of virtues was being neglected in the schools.[67] *Nové slovo*, meanwhile, accused the Ministry of Education of dragging its feet with Slovakia's draft school law, buried for over a year in a ministry commission.[68]

Another church-related issue that received public play at this time was land reform. The Catholic Church was very interested in this issue, and two Slovak bishops visited Husák as chairman of the Board of Commissioners on February 11 to complain about recent proposed revisions of land reform policies.[69] In the name of the Bishops' Council, they complained that the revision was done without their consultation and in conflict with the so-called modus vivendi, the working relationship between the Vatican and Czechoslovakia dating from 1928. The bishops claimed that in their understanding the reform was to proceed benevolently and in agreement with the Vatican. They asked that church property and parish benefices be given legal exemption, or at least that the government be empowered to grant exceptions to "small-scale church property." The Slovak Bishops' Council also sent a protest to Minister of Agriculture Ďuriš against current and planned seizures of church property.[70] *Čas* took up the church's cause in a column on February 4, in which the author argued that such church property supported orphanages, poorer parishes, seminaries, and shrines.[71] He argued that church property was being well managed, in accordance with modern methods, and claimed that confiscated land was not being given only to Slovakia's peasants, but rather to Slovak immigrants from Hungary or to collective farms. He furthermore noted that such policies could only damage Czechoslovakia's relations with the Vatican and called for negotiations between the government, the Vatican, and church circles in Czechoslovakia. An article in *Pravda* defended the Communist position.[72] It argued that confiscations of church property flowed naturally from the principle "the land belongs to those who work it," and that the church needed to give up the vestiges of its feudal privileges. The author also noted that land issues in Czechoslovakia were the domain of elected officials and were a matter in which the Vatican does not have a right to interfere. Not only did the modus vivendi not give the Vatican this right, but the Vatican itself failed to keep up its own end of the deal when it allowed the Catholic Church in Hungarian occupied Southern Slovakia to come under Hungarian ecclesiastical jurisdiction during World War II.[73]

Apart from conflicts over education and land reform, Communists on the one hand and Catholics and Democrats on the other sparred over a number of issues. Government expectations that people work on Sundays and holy days as part of the reconstruction effort continued to draw condemnation from Slovakia's Catholic bishops.[74] The Communist press, misunderstanding the intricacies of the Catholic liturgical calendar, incorrectly accused the Catholic Church in Slovakia of moving the commemoration of the feast of St. Joseph from March 19 to April 14, the eve of the anniversary of the verdict and death sentence against Tiso.[75] The Communists kept up a steady buzz of criticism of the DS for its alleged protection of Kempný, Bugár, and other so-called antistate conspirators. Democratic commissioners continued to be targets of criticism over problems related to agriculture and food supply.

The DS, in many ways still reeling from the events of autumn 1947, began to fight back, on certain fronts, more vigorously. The DS drew closer to the Czech non-Communist parties, the National Socialists, and the Czech Populists. Democrats also became more aggressive in raising the issue of Communist abuse of the security forces. Already at a DS rally in Bratislava on November 16, Lettrich condemned the misuse of security forces for political ends and "brutally forced confessions."[76] For this, Lettrich was attacked at the next meeting of the Czechoslovak National Front for calumniating the state police.[77] On December 19, Democratic representatives in parliament and the SNR presented a number of accusations against the police, in particular the Seventh Department, and called for the establishment of a special committee to investigate the charges.[78] Among other things, the Democrats charged the police with politically motivated forced confessions, inflicting on the interrogated broken teeth, loss of hearing, and beatings that drew blood.[79] Communist members of the SNR demonstratively walked out of that organ's plenary session after the Democrats presented their charges.[80] Both *Čas* and *Nové prúdy* were confiscated for reporting on the event.[81] Commissioner of the Interior Ferjenčík issued a declaration in parliament denying the charges, and claimed that spot inspections by him and others, including the Democrat Fraštacký, uncovered no abuses.[82]

Democratic voices, writing in *Nové prúdy*, also began to be heard raising a topic that was previously pretty much taboo in the postwar period—Communist collaboration with Nazis and Fascists in the early years of the Second World War. Articles in the Democratic aligned journal questioned the Communists' patriotism and antifascist credentials. An article on November 9 mentioned how Communists did not go into opposition after October 6, 1938, when Populists gained control of Slovakia.[83] In line with the Soviet Union's August 1939 pact with Germany, Communists in Slovakia were more likely to sabotage illegal activity than assist in it. They were in the Hlinka Guard, not the underground. Even when this policy shifted after Hitler's attack on the Soviet Union in June 1941, Slovakia's Communists considered fighting for "another republic than the Czechoslovak one," a veiled reference to Slovak Communist dreams of a Soviet Slovakia. The article also noted the good relations between Czechoslovakia's Communists and those of Hungary, implying a lack of patriotism on the part of the native Communists. Subsequent articles continued to allude to the manifest Communist lack of resistance and even friendliness with Hitler's Germany between the time of the Munich Agreement and the Nazi invasion of the Soviet Union.[84]

The press was also a venue for some telling discussions at this time about the relationship between communism, capitalism, and Christianity. In late November 1947, *Katolícke noviny* ran a front-page opinion column critical of capitalism, accusing it of misusing capital in exploitative ways, opposing just regulation of economic life by church or state, and leading to anarchy in production, unemployment, and poverty.[85] The author noted that popes Leo XIII and Pius XI had condemned that system in major social encyclicals and claimed that capitalism was founded on unlimited egoism and a childish optimism. The article also expressed an extremely negative view of the rich and positive view of the poor, citing saints Ambrose and Thomas Aquinas, the Old Testament (Sirach 31:3–6) and the Gospels, where Jesus Christ says, "Woe to you who are rich!" (Luke 6:24) and "Blessed are the poor in spirit" (Matthew 5:3). The article ended with a litany of all that Catholic clergy had done historically for the poor, including giving aid to poor students and the impoverished elderly. Interestingly, *Katolícke noviny* eschewed any condemnation of Communism, though such was an integral part of the same Catholic social teaching that criticized capitalism. *Čas*, a fortnight later, ran a front-page editorial entitled "Christianity and Communism" that presented Catholic teaching more fully.[86] The article opened by describing the similarities between Christianity and Communism. Both allegedly opposed the exploitation of man by man, the unjust distribution of property, and using people as a means to gain material and political advantages. Both were for a just social order, where one had the right to the fruits of one's labor. Both defended the dignity of the socially weak. The author reminded readers that Catholic teaching did not oppose the nationalization of industry or state intervention in the economy on behalf of the common good, citing the teaching of *Rerum novarum* and *Quadragesimo anno* that property had a social function, with property rights not being absolute. The article then went on to describe fundamental differences between Christianity and Communism. Christians opposed the nationalization of all means of production and believed that a social order should be based on the laws of God. The article ended by noting how Communists in neighboring countries had retreated from their support for freedom of religious conviction. In this article, it is noteworthy how the Democratic author gave Communists the benefit of the doubt when it came to their alleged concern for justice and dignity. Finally, on Christmas Day, 1947, Straka published an article in *Nové slovo* in which he examined the prospects for a synthesis of Christianity and Communism.[87] He noted how Christianity many times sought accommodation with any regime that respected the fundamental rights of Christianity and its members. He argued that capitalism, being based on radical materialism, was not something that Christians could defend. Like Communism, Christianity was devoted to the solution of material and social problems, standing on the side of the oppressed and exploited. Christian social teaching was founded on the equality of all people and their natural right to happiness and well-being, and it taught that wealth and property had a social function. As Jesus Christ said, "The worker deserves his wages" (Luke 10:7). As he had been doing since he joined up with the Communists several years earlier, Straka was pushing the idea that Catholics had nothing to fear from, and good reason to cooperate with, the Communists.

The interrelationship between Communism and Catholicism in Slovakia would undergo a change in February 1948 that would fundamentally alter it for the next four decades. Over of period of just thirteen days, Czechoslovakia would experience a governmental crisis that resulted ultimately in a Communist takeover of the Republic, the destruction of the DS, and the establishment of a Communist regime under which Catholics would have to find their place whether they wanted to or not.

Developments in Czechoslovakia had been on a trajectory toward such a crisis since at least the autumn of 1947. On the one hand, the Communists realized that they could not count on taking power in Czechoslovakia on the basis of parliamentary elections. They had lost big in Slovakia back in May 1946, and there was no guarantee that they would carry the day in the next elections either. Nor was it a safe bet that the KSČ would repeat its victory in the Czech lands, though many Communists were optimistic.[88] It was likely that, whatever the electoral outcome, the DS, National Socialist Party, and People's Party in combination would be enough to obstruct Communist ambitions for total control of the republic, especially if the Social Democratic Party continued on the line set by its party congress of November 1947, when the pro-Communist Fierlinger was replaced as party chairman by the more independent-minded Bohumil Laušman, a move clearly intended to distance the Social Democrats from the Communists.[89] A weakening of their electoral position could threaten Communist control over the handling of the antistate conspiracy. Indeed, Slovak Communists were already concerned that Commissioner of Justice Buza could not be trusted to satisfy Communist desires in this respect. The worst scenario for the Communists would be a repeat of what happened in France and Italy in May 1947—that is, the other parties would drop the Communists from the coalition and govern without them.

At the same time, Czechoslovakia's Communists had reason to be confident that they could gain power without having to risk elections. In Slovakia, the DS seemed vulnerable. It had been weakened by the antistate conspiracy and ensuing crises of fall 1947; it had disappointed its Catholic base by revoking the April Agreement; and it was fraught with divisions between left and right, and Lutherans and Catholics, fault lines that in themselves were not enough to split the party but which could be exploited in a time of crisis. The fall crises had shown that the DS would back down in the face of mass pressure from Communist dominated organizations.

After its partial success in fall 1947, the KSS was eager to follow through with the destruction of the DS. At the end of 1947, the KSS set out its goals and means—to isolate "reaction" and force it out of the NF by mobilizing the masses and using their pressure to back Communist positions and actions in the government, the National Front, and the Board of Commissioners, and to intensify efforts to destroy the DS from within.[90] The Communists also anticipated an attempt by the rightist parties to evoke a government crisis that would lead to a "government of experts," a maneuver used with success back in 1920 to effectively isolate the Left from governing authority.[91] In the second half of February 1948, all of these plans and anticipations bore fruit.

First, the Communists decided to use two pending issues—reform of the salaries of state and public employees and revision of the land reform—to mobilize the Communist dominated mass organizations. On February 10, the government failed to approve a proposal by the Communists and the Communist led Central Council of Trade Unions to raise the pay of state employees, prompting the latter organization two days later to call a Congress of Factory and Employee Councils for February 22 in Prague.[92] Also on February 12, Parliament's agricultural committee voted not to discuss a Communist proposal to revise the law on ownership of farmland, which in turn led the Communists to call a Congress of Farmers' Commissions to Prague for February 28. Thus, using political and legislative setbacks as a pretext, the Communists organized two successive weekends of mass agitation in the capital city.[93]

No sooner were their plans set in motion than a third issue, state security, came to a boiling point. On February 13, Nationalist Socialist, Czech Populist, and Democratic ministers took a stand against the transfer of eight district leaders of the Corps of National Security in Prague by a lieutenant-commander of the police working under Interior Minister Nosek. Coming after months of intense conflict between the Communists and the other parties over the question of Communist misuse of the police for partisan purposes, the transfers were clearly aimed at strengthening Communist control over Prague's police units and nothing less than a provocation.

Security as an issue of conflict had been brewing for some time now in both Slovakia and in the Czech lands. On September 10, 1947, when parcel bombs were discovered addressed to ministers Masaryk, Drtina, and Petr

Zenkl, the Ministry of the Interior assigned to each minister in the government a bodyguard, who submitted regular reports on that minister.[94] In November the security forces sought to implicate leading National Socialists in the so-called Most affair, in conjunction with an alleged British spy hiding in the region around the northern Bohemian town of Most.[95] As it became evident that the Most affair was a Communist inspired provocation, the Justice Ministry asked the security police to hand over two of its officers involved in the provocation, Müller and Kroupa, for prosecution. The Communists, of course, backed the security police, and the issue provoked bitter conflict at the government meeting of February 13, setting the stage for further conflict. It was at this point that the Social Democrats and National Socialists raised a protest against the transfer of the eight district police commanders in Prague, decreed the day before.[96] In a stormy meeting, a majority of ministers resolved, against Communist opposition, that "the government order the Interior Minister to cease and desist from carrying out, and to rescind, the order of the lieutenant-commander of the Corps of National Security." The government also agreed unanimously to inquire into complaints about state security and the Ministry of Justice and to report on it by February 24.

When the government met again on February 17, Zenkl asked at the outset whether Nosek had rescinded the decree, as the government had ordered on February 13.[97] When Gottwald made it clear that this had not been done, and that he had no intention in seeing that it be done, the meeting became in effect paralyzed, ultimately being adjourned until February 20. In the meeting's aftermath, actors on all sides began maneuvering for the impending showdown. The presidiums of the KSČ and KSS met to agree on a common policy.[98] Over the next several days, the Communist press attacked the alleged intransigence of the National Socialist, Czech Populist, and Democratic ministers, arguing that their behavior was an unconstitutional attempt to intervene in the affairs of the Interior Ministry and to effect a coup by forcing the fall of the government and its replacement by a "government of experts" that would prepare nondemocratic elections.[99] On February 19, the KSS's central committee entrusted several KSS leaders to establish links with oppositional forces within the DS and urge them to oppose that party's leadership over the Nosek affair.[100] This move took to a new level the Communist attempt to split the DS from within.

As it became obvious that the Communists had no interest in budging over the Nosek affair, the National Socialists, Czech Populists, and Democrats began discussing their next move—resignation from the government. The National Socialist Zenkl held talks with ministers from both other parties to that end.[101] The three parties were holding to their position on the Nosek affair no less tenaciously than the Communists. Talks within the National Front broke down over the issue on February 18, and the ministers of the three parties refused to show up for a meeting of the government's presidium that same evening.[102]

In preparation for the next scheduled meeting of the government, called by Gottwald for February 20, preparations intensified on all sides. On February 18, Gottwald and Nosek lobbied Beneš, warning him not to appoint a government of experts.[103] On February 19, Soviet Deputy Foreign Minister Valerian Zorin arrived in Prague, where he informed Gottwald that Moscow favored a putsch against those parties standing in the Communists' way.[104] The same day, American Ambassador Laurence Steinhardt promised moral and diplomatic support for the non-Communist parties.[105] With Zorin's backing, the Communists decided on a forceful solution to the impasse, and the next day the three opposing parties presented them with a handy opportunity to bring things to a head.

On February 20, the government met at 10:00 A.M. The National Socialist, Czech Populist, and Democratic ministers, upon learning that Nosek had refused to rescind the order, refused to attend. At 11:30 A.M., Zenkl informed Beneš that the ministers had decided to resign, and that afternoon they submitted their resignation letters to Beneš and Gottwald. As the Democratic ministers noted in their letter, the ministers were resigning on account of Communist misuse of the security forces and the government's unwillingness to address the issue satisfactorily.[106]

This maneuver by Czechoslovakia's three non-Marxist parties has long been examined and criticized, and further analysis need not detain us here.[107] Suffice to say that the action contained a number of problems. First, not enough ministers resigned (twelve of twenty-six). The failure to get the Social Democrats on board for the move meant that the resigning ministers were in the minority when the Social Democratic Party responded to these resignations by staying in the government. Second, the ministers made their move in the hopes that Beneš would respond by naming a caretaker government of experts and calling new elections. In fact, Beneš was not sure how to respond and ultimately ratified Gottwald's approach to the crisis. Third, there was not sufficiently solid support for the resignations within the DS. In fact, on February 19, the DS presidium met to consider the issue and voted against resignation by a vote of seven to three.[108] Thus, when the Democratic ministers joined with their National Socialist and Czech Populist colleagues and resigned, they were bucking the prevailing view of the party leadership. Finally, the resignations gave the Communists cause to mobilize the social organizations in their camp, bringing enormous pressure on Beneš and the non-Marxist parties.

What ensued was the sort of prerevolutionary situation in which Communists characteristically thrive.[109] It soon became clear that the Social Democrats had no intention to resign, though they also resolved to ask Beneš not to accept the resignations, hoping that something could be worked out within the existing political party constellation. The Communists, with Gottwald in the lead, proposed that the crisis be solved by replacing the resigned ministers with members of the left wings of those ministers' parties. Already by February 21, Gottwald got pledges from a number of such potential appointees, the National Socialists Emanuel Šlechta and Alois Neuman, the Populists Alois Petr and Josef Plojhar, the Democrat Ševčík, and Vavro Šrobár, nominally with the Party of Freedom. To give some muscle to their proposal, and pressure President Beneš to go along with it, the Communists initiated popular and organizational mobilization to a more intense degree than ever before. Police units, Partisan units, and workers militias were mobilized across the country. Communist sympathizers in the military, most notably Minister of Defense Ludvík Svoboda, saw that the army remained neutral during the crisis. Communist controlled trade unions scheduled a one-hour general strike for February 24. Mass rallies for Gottwald and his proposed solution to the crisis took place on Wenceslas Square in Prague and across Czechoslovakia, outnumbering rallies in support of the resigning ministers. As a tool of mobilization and influence throughout the land, Gottwald called for the creation of so-called action committees, bodies which could make local decisions during the crisis at the various levels of state administration, as well as in offices, factories, universities, political parties, and other organizations or places of employment. Communists were instructed to ensure that their party dominated these committees and used them on behalf of the party's aims. With Beneš wavering and the non-Marxist parties trying to convince him to resist Gottwald's proposed solution, the Communists engineered the creation of a central action committee of the Czechoslovak National Front, an ad hoc organization that served as the body overseeing the revolutionary situation. The Communists implemented a series of repressive measures against anyone whom the Communists regarded as a rival. The police took more severe action against the offending parties. They lost their supplies of newsprint; they were forbidden to stage rallies; their ministers were prevented from entering their offices; and those whom the Communists found displeasing were released from their public functions, or even arrested. Democrats and Czech Populists disgruntled with their own leaderships or even sympathetic to the Communists founded their own action committees, effectively creating alternative party leaderships willing to cooperate closely with Gottwald. On February 24, millions took part in a one-hour protest strike on behalf of Communist aims, and the Communists reiterated to Beneš their refusal to negotiate with the three parties and demand that he name a new government along the lines proposed by Gottwald. Thousands of resolutions engineered by the Communists poured into the President's Castle from across Czechoslovakia. Communists also exerted pressure on the Social Democrats, as Gottwald informed them that if they wanted to be included in his new government, they had better agree to support his proposal at once, which they did along with purging those leading Social Democrats who opposed that decision. On February 25, a quarter of a million people assembled in Wenceslaus Square in a Communist inspired demonstration to await Beneš's decision on the matter. At 4:30 that afternoon, Beneš caved in to the pressure and agreed with Gottwald's proposal to form a new government. It would consist of twenty-five members; thirteen Communists, nine members of non-Communist parties, and three members without party affiliation. The non-Communists in the government were all figures whom the Communists deemed amenable. At this point, little stood in the way of a complete Communist takeover of the state and installation of a Communist regime.

During these five days of crisis, events ran roughly parallel in Slovakia and the Czech lands. The DS's presidium met to discuss the crisis, and its first order of business was how to handle the resignation of DS ministers, a move that the party's presidium had voted against on February 19. Now, after some debate in which Polák questioned the maneuver, the presidium resolved to support unanimously the resignations and expressed its full trust in the ministers.[110] The DS also resolved to appeal for calm from Slovakia's population and affirmed that the DS had by no means abandoned its policy of cooperation in the spirit of the National Front, an organization to which it reaffirmed its membership.

The KSS's Central Committee, meanwhile, met on February 21 and decided on its course of action, which included the arming of Partisan groups and workers' militias, the establishment of action committees, including a central one in the Slovak National Front, the expulsion of Democrats from the Board of Commissioners, and the initiation of talks with disgruntled oppositional elements in the DS.[111] Partisan groups and factory militias, along with the security forces, mobilized on behalf of Gottwald and the Communists.[112] Across Slovakia Communists, but also members of the other parties, organized action committees over the next several days in offices, factories, and other venues of political, economic, and professional life, thereby creating an alternative administration to the state's.[113] Soon they existed in half of the districts in Slovakia. The Communists also held a rally that evening in support of Gottwald at the Reduta, where Husák declared that the resignation by the DS ministers in Prague was tantamount to a resignation by the DS commissioners in Bratislava.[114] In line with this view, Husák, as chairman of the Board of Commissioners, sent a letter to each Democrat on the board, informing them that he considered them as resigned, owing to the fact that their colleagues in Prague had left the government, and because the DS's campaign against the security organs was in violation of the board's programmatic statement.[115]

The Democratic commissioners soon responded with a letter of their own, protesting against Husák's assumptions and action.[116] Calling his views transparent and naive, they accused him of acting unconstitutionally on the grounds that by no means should the chairman of the board unilaterally decide who is and is not a member. Rather, this should have been discussed by the entire board and approved by the presidium of the Slovak National Council and the government. The Democratic commissioners affirmed that they had under no circumstances broken with the board's official program and informed Husák that they continued to regard themselves as members of the board.

On February 23, the DS held a meeting for its functionaries from across Slovakia.[117] Lettrich, addressing those present, accused the Communists of trying to foment a crisis on the Board of Commissioners in an illegal and unconstitutional manner. He expressed his conviction that Beneš would not give in to Communist demands and called on Democrats to resist Communist efforts to split the DS. He also instructed Democrats not to join action committees. Cvinček, for his part, appealed for harmony between Catholics and Protestants in this time of crisis.

Lettrich's appeals were already past effect. Democrats across Slovakia, in an atmosphere of confusion and uncertainty, joined action committees. Communists were without a doubt carrying out a putsch in Slovakia. On Sunday, *Čas*'s publisher was closed, thereby ending the run of the DS's chief newspaper with that day's issue.[118] The next day, on Husák's orders, Communist members of the Board of Commissioners were installed by the police in the functions and offices of those commissions headed by Democrats.[119] Armed trade unionists along with Partisan units took over the DS's central headquarters in Bratislava. City Hall was also taken over by an action committee set up for that purpose, and telephone and telegraph ties with Prague were cut. The Slovak station of Czechoslovak Radio was taken over by Communists, with the knowledge and agreement of Commissioner of Information, Jozef Lukačovič, a Democrat and Catholic priest who was sympathetic to the Communists.[120] By Tuesday, February 24, DS rallies were banned, Ursíny indicted,[121] and Lichner's secretary arrested.[122] In all, 173 people were arrested and 334 fired from their positions as the DS bore the brunt of Communist aggression.[123]

On February 25, despite assurances that he gave to Beneš and other Democratic leaders the evening before that he would not give in to Gottwald's demands, Beneš relented.[124] The Communists meanwhile had been paving the path toward a new regime. In Slovakia, they courted a number of leading Democrats during the crisis, prompting them to establish an Action Committee of the Democratic Party to serve as a replacement leadership for the DS as the rest of the party crumbled. On February 25, Polák, Jozef Mjartan, and Lukačovič announced the formation of such a committee and began to speak in the name of the DS. Ševčík had already agreed to serve in Gottwald's replacement government, and, once Beneš accepted it on February 25, joined it as state secretary in the Ministry of National Defense.[125] Meanwhile, the other leaders of the DS Action Committee joined the new Action Committee of the Slovak National Front, established on the evening of February 25.[126] Headed by the Communist Široký, it authorized Husák to begin talks on forming a new Board of Commissioners. The committee began taking control over the action committees across Slovakia, purging them of former Democrats deemed unamenable to the new order.[127] Next came changes in the Slovak National Council. Lettrich resigned as chairman on February 26 and fled into emigration. The next day he was replaced by the Communist Šmidke. The Board of Commissioners also continued to undergo a purge. Ferjenčík resigned as commissioner of the interior, replaced by the Communist Daniel Okáli, and Buza was dismissed as commissioner of justice.[128] By March 6, a new Board of Commissioners was in place. Of its fourteen members, eight were Communists, including the chairman Husák, two represented the DS's Action Committee (Lukačovič and Mjartan), the rest representing smaller parties, trade unions, and Partisan organizations. By March 23, the new Slovak National Council was named, consisting of one hundred members, with the previous non-Communist membership purged and replaced by representatives willing to give their full support to the new Communist regime and its program.[129]

The Communist takeover in Slovakia reflected similar developments across the rest of the republic. Gottwald's new government represented a big gain in Communist influence. Twelve of its twenty-four members were Communist; the rest consisted of members of other parties and organizations whom the Communists regarded as collaborators. Only five members came from Slovakia, down from six in the previous government. Beside three Slovak Communists and Šrobár of the Party of Freedom sat Ševčík, representing the DS opposition. Parliament likewise was reconstructed, with a number of leading Democrats dropped from its ranks. These included Lettrich, Ursíny, Bugár, Kempný, Staško, Cvinček, Fraštacký, Hodža, Kvetko, Lichner, and Pietor.[130] Other non-Communist parliamentarians had to promise to cooperate with Parliament's newly formed action committee and with the new Gottwald government. Beneš approved the changes, staying on as president until his resignation on May 4. On March 11, Parliament, or more precisely, all 241 members present (of a total of 300), unanimously accepted the new government. Czechoslovakia now entered the next phase of its history, one with significant implications both for Slovakia and for the Catholic Church there.

Catholic Democrats figured in the crisis that brought down the regime in a number of ways. Those loyal to the DS and the postwar regime, with its limited pluralism and civil liberties, fell along with the DS. Some had already been on their way out as accused conspirators, like Kempný, Bugár, and Staško. Others, like Cvinček, had fastened their hopes on the April Agreement, and even after its abrogation had continued to support the Catholic alliance with the DS. Consistent in that stand up to the end, Cvinček's political career ended when the DS disintegrated. We see him at one of the DS's last official gatherings, appealing for Catholic-Lutheran cooperation. On the other end of the spectrum are those Catholic Democrats who were more than happy to cooperate with Communists. They responded to the crisis by maneuvering themselves into positions in the new regime. Ševčík gained a ministerial position. Lukačovič, in alliance Democrats like Polák and Mjartan, obtained a seat on the Board of Commissioners. Among the opposition leaders within the DS, only Pietor remained marginalized. Kyselý stepped into the position he had been aspiring to since the fall of 1947, of self-appointed spokesman for Slovak Catholics disgruntled with the DS and open to cooperation with the Communists. On February 25, he spoke on Czechoslovak Radio, appealing to all progressive Catholics in the DS and outside it to fully support the new government and Board of Commissioners.[131] He called on Democrats to abandon their party leaders who have led them "into a rut and to catastrophe," to seize control of the party from its "agro-confessional" leadership, and to help build a new DS, one that would support the government and its program of reconstruction.[132] "In particular, I appeal to those Catholics who were most greatly deceived by this perfidious policy. I feel called to stand at the head of this movement and cement together all those who think honestly with respect to the nation, state, and church," Kyselý proclaimed. He praised the Košice Program for, among other things, its "clear and undeniable provision for a guarantee of religious freedom and the undisturbed development of the church" and noted that Gottwald was the author of such a Catholic friendly program. He went on to assure Catholics that the new government would in no way threaten Catholicism in Slovakia.

February 25 meant the end of the DS. The action committee of the DS opposition eventually renamed itself, at the Communists' behest, the Party of Slovak Revival (Strana slovenskej obrody). The Catholic bishops, who remained on the sidelines during the crisis, had to accommodate themselves to a new political situation for the fourth time in ten years. The KSS was now dominant in Slovakia and only collaborators remained. The April Agreement, on which Catholics had placed their hopes, was now more than defunct, and voices like those of Koza-Matejov would be silenced for decades. Catholic activists charged with antistate conspiracy would be prosecuted, and the church lost any hope of making its position felt on issues such as education or land reform. In its March 6 issue, *Katolícke noviny* resignedly noted that all that happens is in accordance with God's will and that Catholics should take a sincere, positive, and loyal attitude to the nation and state and give all due respect to the authorities.[133] Jesus Christ's command to "render unto Caesar," St. Paul's admonition in Romans 13:1 that "every person be subject to the governing authorities," and Pope Leo XIII's teaching on the obligation to recognize and accept the state in the interest of the common good all served as bases for this appeal to Catholic cooperation. With respect to Catholics in public life, the future belonged to men like Straka and Lukačovič, priests ready to cooperate with the new regime. Other Catholics would experience a considerably troubled period for the church as Slovakia endured four decades of Communist dictatorship.

The interaction between Catholics, Communists, and Democrats from 1945 to 1948 in Slovakia provides some telling insights into the way these various players sought to maneuver through a critical period of transition. While some of the developments of the time are particular to the situation in Slovakia, others have implications for the relationship between Communists and their opponents, especially Catholics, more broadly speaking. Because Slovakia was one of the few places in Europe that combined a heavily Catholic society, a state strongly influenced by the Communists, and a relatively pluralistic political situation, it provides an especially appropriate venue for examining these interactions.

First, religion played an enormous role during this period, in the sense that nearly every important development or issue in Slovakia in the years immediately following the Second World War had a strong religious dimension. Both major political parties in Slovakia devoted considerable attention to courting Catholics and keeping them out of their rival's camp. The issues of education, land reform, and policy toward the Magyar minority were all closely connected with religion, as the Catholic Church sought to defend parochial education, church-owned land, and the rights of minorities to worship in their native languages, among other things. The retribution trials, and especially the trial of Jozef Tiso, mixed religion, politics, and nationalism as Slovakia's new leadership dealt controversially with that country's recent past. The Slovak underground harkened back to the nationalism and Catholicism of the wartime Slovak Republic in its efforts to undermine the new people's democratic regime. The Democratic Party's alliance with Catholics in the April Agreement made it easier for the Communists to induce Prague to cut back on Slovakia's autonomy, playing on Czech fears of Slovak Catholicism and nationalism of the sort manifested during the war. And Communist attempts to cripple the DS centered on alleged conspirators among the Catholic activists in leading roles in that party.

Second, each of the major players investigated herein pursued goals that were, if not contradictory, at least very difficult to achieve simultaneously. The Communists, for instance, sought to weaken the Roman Catholic Church, depriving it of as much influence—social, political, economic, cultural—as possible, while at the same time presenting themselves as friends of Slovakia's Catholic population. While pushing down the church with one hand, the Communists were reaching out to Catholics with the other. In seeking to weaken the church, the KSS adamantly supported the elimination of parochial education, the takeover of Catholic and other confessional-based dormitories, the appropriation of church-owned land as a component of Czechoslovakia's land reform, the shutting down of a number of Catholic organizations and periodicals, and the prosecution of collaborationist clergy, above all Slovakia's former president, Father Jozef Tiso. At the same time, Communists packaged some of these policies in ways meant to appeal to Catholics. Take education, for example. While Communists championed a state monopoly of the school system, thereby eliminating parochial schools, they also insisted that Christian catechism classes be taught in the schools. Furthermore, they presented the nationalization of education as a means of "unburdening" Slovakia's clergy from the responsibility of managing parish schools. Politically, Communists encouraged Catholics to found their own independent Catholic party, a way to keep them out of the hands of the Democrats. When this failed, the KSS targeted those Catholics who had made a pact with the DS in the April Agreement of 1946, seeing them as the Democrats' Achilles' heel and using them as evidence that the DS was harboring supporters of the now outlawed Populist Party and its wartime regime. But even while using the DS's Catholic wing as a club with which to beat the Democrats, Communist rhetoric remained largely Catholic friendly. For instance, Communist leaders and writers were careful to distinguish between Catholic and Populist—most Catholics were not categorically denounced as Populists; rather, only a devious minority seeking to misuse the religious feelings of the Slovak population to mislead them into dangerous and reactionary political adventurism was attacked by the KSS. The rest of Slovakia's Catholics, including most priests, were praised as patriotic Slovaks who supported the Slovak National Uprising and were loyal to Czechoslovakia's new people's democracy.

Even Catholics who had been in the Populist movement, if they were common people and not political activists or intellectuals, were regarded as victims rather than perpetrators of the wartime events. On some occasions the KSS even sought to set Tiso in opposition to the Catholic Church. For example, the Slovak Communist press attacked him in December 1945 because, in deporting Slovakia's Jews to Nazi death camps, he was obeying Adolf Hitler rather than Pope Pius XII, an opponent of the deportations. Communist propaganda aimed at Catholics was aided considerably by Jozef Straka, the most prominent Roman Catholic priest in the Communists' service at this time, and at times the rhetoric coming from Straka could reach ridiculous proportions, as when he wrote that the Communist Party has always supported the fulfillment of the mission of the Roman Catholic Church. It is hard to gauge how much success the Communists had in their propaganda. They certainly did not win enough Catholic support to prevent a landslide DS electoral victory, though such rhetoric may have helped disarm Slovakia's Catholics and make them less adamant in resisting Communist encroachments.

Thus, an in-depth investigation into postwar Slovakia reminds us of something obscured by the highly publicized persecutions of Catholic leaders in the early Communist period in East Central Europe, such as Alojz Stepinac in Yugoslavia, József Mindszenty in Hungary, and Josef Beran in Czechoslovakia—that in the immediate postwar years, Communists endeavored to assure Catholics that they had little to fear from Communists and even tried to win them over to their side. This policy can be observed not just in Slovakia but elsewhere across the region. Commenting on Hungary between 1945 and 1948, Peter Kenez notes that the Communists "again and again emphasized that they were not against religion and even attempted to win the allegiance of at least some believers."[134]

Just as the Communist Party, the Catholic Church also had some difficult navigating to do, as it too pursued joint goals that were hard to reconcile. The church wanted to defend what it saw as its rights and prerogatives (for example, parochial schools, Catholic dormitories, Catholic organizations and periodicals, Church lands, etc.) without appearing to be hostile or disloyal to the new regime or associated with its now-criminalized predecessor. In defending the church's interests, Catholic bishops collectively sent memoranda on occasion to the appropriate government leaders and bodies. The Catholic press, chiefly *Katolícke noviny*, parried attacks from the left and presented a Catholic viewpoint on the pressing issues of the day, sometimes with surprising brashness, but often exercising due caution. There were limits to Catholic activism, however. These became clear in the summer of 1945 when the bishops tried to organize a petition drive on behalf of parochial schools. This led to an immediate crackdown by the police, including searches and seizures of episcopal and parish offices, followed by a denunciation of the bishops by both the KSS and the DS. After this experience, the Catholic leadership in Slovakia refrained from trying to mobilize the broad masses of the Slovak Catholic population on behalf of a Catholic cause. Rather, Catholics looked for a political party to champion their interests.

Catholic responses to the postwar situation in Slovakia were diverse. We see everything from Catholic clergy cooperating in antistate demonstrations and activities (the village priest who helped initiate the Piešťany demonstrations), to priests siding wholeheartedly with and serving the KSS (Straka), to priests seeking a unique Catholic "third way" that was as leery of the West as of the East (Kolakovič). We also see attempts to organize an independent Catholic party. However, despite these diverse responses, the Catholic hierarchy and population overwhelmingly chose to reconcile themselves with the new regime and align themselves with the Democratic Party. The April Agreement, however, brought danger and ultimately disillusionment. Having supported the Tiso regime during the Second World War, the church was in a position that left it exposed to Communist attacks. Moreover, while the April Agreement brought more political positions and influence to Slovakia's Catholics, it was unable to deliver them the right to maintain parochial schools, nor did it spare Tiso from the hangman's noose. By 1947, Catholics were increasingly disillusioned with the DS, while the Democrats saw the April Agreement as an albatross around their necks.

The case of Straka provides a telling indication of the church's dilemma. Afraid to bring the wrath of the Communists down upon themselves, Slovakia's bishops tolerated the antics of a Catholic priest who in his writings and activities zealously supported the KSS and its policies. Only when Straka went so far as to claim his own bishop approved of his activities do we see a public statement, and a rather perfunctory one at that, by a Slovak bishop dissociating himself from Straka's actions. Straka's case also reminds us that, along with the well-known reluctance of church leaders to constrain clergy on the radical right from collaborating with Nazis and fascists during the war,[135] there were also cases of a reluctance to restrain clergy on the radical left who worked with the Communists in the postwar period. Even in the context of a multiparty regime, absent a Soviet military occupation, and in a region where a party allied with Catholics won 62 percent of the vote, the bishops were afraid to silence a priest who enthusiastically and openly collaborated with the Communists.

Of all the difficulty in maneuvering, no one in postwar Slovakia had it worse than the Democrats. On the one hand, they sought to win the support of Slovakia's Catholics, while at the same time staying true to the heritage of the Slovak National Uprising. This latter association was crucial for the party. First, it was the party's raison d'être, the DS having been founded during the war in opposition to the Tiso regime. Second, participation in the resistance provided a crucial pedigree for participation in Czechoslovakia's postwar politics. Third, the DS contained a faction of Partisan activists whose concern it was to keep the DS on the progressive path. Outreach to Slovakia's Catholics brought the Democrats' continuing association with the Slovak National Uprising into question, gave Communists cause to question their very right to participate in the government, and provoked concern among the DS left. By including in top positions in the party some Catholics who had served rather than resisted the Tiso regime, the April Agreement exposed the DS to enormous pressure, manifested in Communist attacks on leading Catholic Democratic activists, the failed attempts to obtain clemency for Tiso and the resignation of Daxner, the implication of some leading Democrats, including Ursiny himself, in the "antistate conspiracy," and growing tensions within the party over the April Agreement.

Viewed from a broader geographical and historical perspective, 1945 to 1948 in Slovakia represented the Communist Party's attempt to subvert the results of the parliamentary elections of May 1946, an election it lost largely due to the Catholic vote, and assume mastery of Slovakia by undermining the Democratic Party by attacking the Catholic wing. Unable to triumph at the ballot box, Slovakia's Communists employed a host of strategies and tactics to this end. These included conscious attempts to sow discord within the DS (or what the Communists called "internal differentiation"), efforts to use the Tiso trial to discredit the Democrats in both the eyes of Slovakia's Catholics and Czechoslovakia's other political parties, a trumped-up antistate conspiracy investigation, and an attempt at a putsch. Communists used their strong position in the state security services and in various social organizations, especially trade unions and Partisan and other resistance organizations, to pressure and persecute the DS. They cooperated with non-Communist Czech parties to scale back the autonomy that Slovakia had received at the end of the war. Though these measures gained much of their character, in particular their close connection with religious issues, on account of their Slovak context, they represent the sort of things Communists were doing elsewhere in Europe where they wanted power but were unable to achieve it through the ballot box. Hungary, where the Communists won 17 percent to the Smallholders' 57 percent in the elections of November 1945, represented a similar case in certain respects.

During the period between Slovakia's liberation from the Third Reich and its incorporation into the Soviet bloc, Slovakia had more democracy and more political pluralism than it would at any time between 1938 and 1989. Each of the major players in Slovakia discussed herein brought with it a legacy, and in some cases a burden, from the wartime period. The interaction of Catholics, Communists, and Democrats set the tone and shaped the contours of political developments in Slovakia in this period. Democrats wanted Catholic support but suffered from the vulnerabilities that such support brought with it. Communists brazenly sought to court Catholics while weakening the church and assaulting the DS for the pro-Catholic April Agreement. Catholics responded to the new situation in a number of ways, but above all they tried to survive a dangerous period by hitching their wagon to the DS. Freed from Hitler, the Catholics and Democrats hoped to keep Slovakia, and Czechoslovakia, out of the hands of Stalin and his allies. However, the Communists triumphed. With the February coup of 1948, the DS was essentially destroyed, and the Catholic Church had to endure four decades of some of the most extensive repression it would face anywhere in the world.

NOTES

Preface

1. Among the works that treat the 1945–48 period in Czechoslovakia are Bradley F. Abrams, *The Struggle for the Soul of the Nation: Czech Culture and the Rise of Communism*, Harvard Cold War Studies Book Series (Lanham, Md.: Rowman and Littlefield, 2004); Karel Kaplan, *The Short March: The Communist Takeover in Czechoslovakia, 1945–1948* (London: C. Hurst, 1987); Josef Korbel, *The Communist Subversion of Czechoslovakia, 1938–1948: The Failure of Coexistence* (Princeton, NJ: Princeton University Press, 1959); Korbel, *Twentieth-Century Czechoslovakia: The Meaning of Its History* (New York: Columbia University Press, 1977); Vladimir V. Kusin, "Czechoslovakia," in *Communist Power in Europe 1944–1949*, ed. Martin McCauley (London: MacMillan Press, 1977), 73–94; Igor Lukes, "The Czech Road to Communism," in *The Establishment of Communist Regimes in Eastern Europe, 1944–1949*, ed. Norman Naimark and Leonid Gibianskii (Boulder, Colo.: Westview Press, 1997), 243–65; Radomír Luža, "Czechoslovakia between Democracy and Communism, 1945–1948," in *A History of the Czechoslovak Republic, 1918–1948*, ed. Victor S. Mamatey and Radomír Luža (Princeton, NJ: Princeton University Press, 1973), 387–415; Martin R. Myant, *Socialism and Democracy in Czechoslovakia, 1945–1948* (Cambridge: Cambridge University Press, 1981); Hubert Ripka, *Czechoslovakia Enslaved: The Story of the Communist Coup d'état* (London: Gollancz, 1950); Dana Adams Schmidt, *Anatomy of a Satellite* (Boston: Little, Brown, 1952); Pavel Tigrid, "The Prague Coup of 1948: The Elegant Takeover," in *The Anatomy of Communist Takeovers*, ed. Thomas T. Hammond (New Haven, CT: Yale University Press, 1975), 399–432; and Paul E. Zinner, *Communist Strategy and Tactics in Czechoslovakia, 1918–1948* (New York: Praeger, 1963).

2. See Jan Rychlík, *Češi a Slováci ve 20. století; Česko-slovenské vztahy 1945–1992* (Bratislava: Academic Elektronic Press, 1998) for the most thorough coverage of Czech-Slovak relations during this period.

3. George Weigel made this point in a review of *The Columbia History of Eastern Europe in the Twentieth Century*, the index of which lists nine entries for King Zog of Albania but only one for Pope John Paul II.

4. According to the 1930 census, 71.61 percent of Slovakia's inhabitants identified themselves as Roman Catholics, and an additional 6.42 percent identified themselves as Greek (or Eastern Rite) Catholics. This means 78.03 percent of Slovakia's popula-

tion identified itself as Catholic. By 1950, the percentages had changed little, and even increased. In that census, 76.20 percent of Slovaks identified themselves as Roman Catholics, and 6.55 percent as Greek Catholics, for an overall Catholic proportion of 82.75 percent. The remainder of Slovakia's population was largely Protestant. Lutherans comprised 12.02 percent of the population according to the 1930 census, and 12.88 percent in 1950; for Calvinists, the proportions were 4.38 percent and 3.25 percent respectively. Thus, in the 1950 census, 98.88 percent of Slovakia's inhabitants identified themselves as Catholic or Protestant Christians. This data, to be sure, includes not only practicing believers but also those who belong to a particular confession only nominally; Jan Pešek and Michal Barnovský, *Štátna moc a cirkvi na Slovensku, 1948–1953* (Bratislava: Veda, 1997), 13.

5. Hlinková Slovenská Ľudová Strana.

6. The term "church" in the context of this study will refer to the Roman Catholic Church, though I realize that in other contexts it can mean all of Christianity, or any or all of its Eastern or Protestant churches.

7. In the First Czechoslovak Republic's most recent parliamentary elections, of 1925, 1929, and 1935, the HSĽS drew 34.3 percent, 28.27 percent, and 30.1 percent of Slovakia's vote; the Communist Party of Slovakia never drew more than 14 percent in any of these three elections. Moreover, while the HSĽS received nearly all its support from ethnic Slovaks, the Communists received considerable support from non-Slovaks, above all the Hungarian minority; for the data, and a discussion of these elections, see James Ramon Felak, *"At the Price of the Republic": Hlinka's Slovak People's Party, 1929–1938* (Pittsburgh: University of Pittsburgh Press, 1994).

8. The successor states of the Habsburg Empire presented a broad spectrum of situations in the immediate postwar years. On the one extreme was Yugoslavia, where, owing to the success of Jozef Broz Tito's Partisans, the Communists were firmly in control by war's end. In Poland and Romania, Communists, aided by the occupying Soviet Red Army, pushed hard and early for dominance and kept non-Communist forces on the defensive right from the start. In Hungary, the Communists moved somewhat more slowly but succeeded in crippling effective opposition by mid-1947. At the other extreme was Czechoslovakia, which enjoyed a limited though, by the standards of the neighborhood, considerable political pluralism up to the Communist coup of February 1948. Austria, like Germany, was divided into American, English, British, and Soviet zones of occupation.

9. Two excellent surveys of this period have been produced by Slovak historians, namely Michal Barnovský, *Na ceste k monopolu moci: Mocenskopolitické zápasy na Slovensku v rokoch 1945–1948* (Bratislava: Archa, 1993) and Róbert Letz, *Slovensko v rokoch 1945–1948 na ceste ku komunistickej totalite* (Bratislava: Ústredie Slovenskej Kresťanskej Inteligencie, 1994).

10. The most thorough study to date of Catholicism in Slovakia during this period is Ivan A. Petranský's *Štát a katolícka cirkev na Slovensku 1945–1946* (Nitra: Garmond, 2001), though it treats only the first year of the postwar period, ending its coverage with the parliamentary elections of May 1946. Václav Vaško's *Neumlčená; kronika katolické*

církve v Československu po druhé světové válce, vol. 1 (Prague: Zvon, 1990), provides the most thorough coverage of Catholicism in the Czech lands during this period, with some coverage of Slovakia as well.

11. Ján Ursíny, *Z môjho života* (Martin: Matica Slovenská, 2000); Pavol Čarnogurský, *Svedok čias* (Bratislava: USPO, 1997).

12. Karel Kaplan, *Dva retribuční procesy: Komentované dokumenty, 1946–1947* (Prague: Ústav Pro Soudobé Dějiny ČSAV, 1992); František Vnuk, *Dokumenty o postavení katolíckej cirkvi na Slovensku v rokoch, 1945–1948* (Martin: Matica Slovenská, 1998).

13. Jozef Jablonický, *Podoby násilia* (Bratislava: Kalligram, 2000); Štefan Šutaj, *Maďarská menšina na Slovensku v rokoch, 1945–1948* (Bratislava: Veda, 1993).

Chapter 1: Setting the Stage

1. On September 29, 1938, Great Britain, France, Germany, and Italy compacted the Munich Agreement, which required Czechoslovakia to cede large portions of its border territories to Germany, ostensibly on account of the desire for national self-determination of the ethnic German population living in the border regions of Bohemia and Moravia. In the wake of the Munich Agreement, on October 6, Slovak nationalists demanded and received autonomy for Slovakia in the Žilina Agreement, with the First Czechoslovak Republic soon replaced by a federal Czecho-Slovakia. On March 14, 1939, autonomous Slovakia's leadership, at Adolf Hitler's insistence, declared independence, and the next day Germany's armies occupied what remained of the Czech lands, which were incorporated into the German Reich as the Protectorate of Bohemia and Moravia.

2. Joseph Rothschild, *East Central Europe between the Two World Wars* (Seattle: University of Washington Press, 1974), 94.

3. *Komunistická strana Československa.*

4. *Demokratická strana.*

5. *Komunistická strana Slovenska.*

6. See Ľubomír Lipták, *Politické strany na Slovensku, 1860–1989* (Bratislava: Archa, 1992), 303–4, for data on the number of votes attained by each competing party in Slovakia's four interwar parliamentary elections.

7. Kaplan, *Short March*, 38–39.

8. Peter Ratkoš, Jozef Butvín, Miroslav Kropilák, and Marta Varíková, eds., *Z prameňov našich dejín* (Bratislava: Slovenské Pedagogické Nakladateľstvo, 1974), 315.

9. Jan Rychlík, *Češi a Slováci ve 20. století. Česko-slovenské vztahy, 1945–1992* (Bratislava: Academic Elektronic Press, 1998), 15.

10. Štefan Šutaj, *Maďarská menšina na Slovensku v rokoch, 1945–1948* (Bratislava: Veda, 1993), 196.

11. Victor S. Mamatey and Radomír Luža, eds., *A History of the Czechoslovak Republic, 1918–1948* (Princeton, N.J.: Princeton University Press, 1973), 404.

12. The Prague Agreements were dated, respectively, June 2, 1945; April 11, 1946; and June 28, 1946. The First Prague Agreement made it clear that Czechoslovakia would be set up on an asymmetrical basis, namely that Slovakia would retain its own national organs while the Czech lands would be under central administration. Slovak organs

would share competence with central organs in various realms, administrative, financial, economic, and social, deemed of statewide significance. According to the agreement, presidential decrees pertaining to common affairs needed the approval of the Slovak National Council, and Slovakia's Board of Commissioners held executive power in Slovakia. The Second Prague Agreement transferred to the Czechoslovak president certain powers hitherto held by the Slovak National Council—for example, to grant clemency and to appoint college professors and certain judges. It also assigned some legislative competence over Slovakia to the yet to be elected National Assembly. The Third Prague Agreement was the most drastic, clearly subordinating Slovakia's Board of Commissioners to the government in Prague; see Rychlík, *Češi a Slováci ve 20. století,* 29, 37–39, 45–50, for a thorough discussion of these agreements.

13. Mamatey and Luža, *History*, 366.

14. Though the DS drew support from a diversity of elements in Slovakia, its core leadership was largely composed of Lutherans of the former Agrarian party. This was particularly true of the DS's two most important figures at this time, Lettrich and Ursíny. A Protestant intelligentsia, with heavy intermarriage, had long constituted a disproportionately large part of Slovakia's elite. Traditionally having much closer ties to the Czechs than did Slovak Catholics, Slovakia's Protestants prospered during the First Republic, taking advantage of their connections with Prague and their leading role in the Slovak branch of the Agrarian Party. For instance, when the central government appointed representatives for the Slovaks to the National Assembly in 1918, half of them were Protestants, though Protestants made up less than 17 percent of the ethnic Slovak population. The reverse situation obtained under the wartime Slovak Republic, when Protestants held only five seats in a Diet of eighty. After 1945, Slovakia's Protestants reasserted themselves through their dominance of the DS, which gave the party the reputation in the eyes of many Catholics of being a Protestant institution; see Václav L. Beneš, "Czechoslovak Democracy and Its Problems," in *A History of the Czechoslovak Republic, 1918–1948*, ed. Victor S. Mamatey and Radomír Luža (Princeton, N.J.: Princeton University Press, 1973), 57, 77–78; Lipták, *Politické strany*, 257; and Jörg K. Hoensch, "The Slovak Republic, 1938–1939," in Mamatey and Luža, *History*, 278n.

15. For a discussion of some of the problems between the Catholic Church and the regime of the First Czechoslovak Republic, see Teodorik J. Zúbek, "Katolícka cirkev na Slovensku v rokoch, 1918–1948," in I. Kružliak and J. Okál, *Svedectvo jednej generácie* (Cambridge: Dobra Kniha, 1990), 133–35, 145–49; Beneš, "Czechoslovak Democracy," in Mamatey and Luža, *History*, 83; and Felak, *"At the Price,"* 20–23.

16. Moreover, religious identification was stronger in Slovakia. In the censuses of 1921, 1930, and 1950, only 0.23 percent, 0.51 percent, and 0.26 percent of Slovakia's inhabitants identified themselves as being without religious affiliation; the corresponding proportions for Czechoslovakia as a whole are 5.32 percent, 5.8 percent, and 4.18 percent, respectively; see Karel Kaplan, *Stát a církev v Československu, 1948–1953* (Brno: Doplněk, 1993), 5.

17. For a discussion of the nationalization of education, see Owen Johnson, *Slovakia 1918–1938: Education and the Making of a Nation* (Boulder, CO: East European Monographs, 1985), 318–19, and Zúbek, "Katolícka cirkev," 146–47.

18. Slovak Protestants had closer ties to Czech political leaders in Prague than did Slovak Catholics; moreover, Slovak Protestants had long been socially and economically better off than Catholics, and played a disproportionately large role in the Slovak national movement of the nineteenth century. On account of these and other factors, Slovak Protestants received the lion's share of positions in Slovakia and left Catholics feeling aggrieved and discriminated against; see Beneš, "Czechoslovak Democracy," 77–78, for a discussion of this issue.

19. The party later incorporated the name of its illustrious leader into its title, calling itself Hlinka's Slovak People's Party.

20. See Zúbek, "Katolícka cirkev," 147–49 for a discussion of the modus vivendi.

21. Petranský, *Štát a katolícka cirkev*, 25–33; Yeshayahu Jelinek, *The Parish Republic: Hlinka's Slovak People's Party 1939–1945* (Boulder, Colo.: East European Quarterly, 1976), 52; Ivan Kamenec, *Slovenský štát (1939–1945)* (Prague: Anomal, 1992), 34.

22. See Jelinek, *Parish Republic*, 109–11; John S. Conway, "The Churches, the Slovak State and the Jews 1939–1945," *Slavonic and East European Review* 52, no. 126 (January 1974), 89; Petranský, *Štát a katolícka cirkev*, 32.

23. Zúbek, "Katolícka cirkev," 151–52; Jelinek, *Parish Republic*, 111.

24. Relations between church and state were not completely rosy, however. The Vatican, for example, was lukewarm at best in its relation to the new Slovak regime, with which it neither concluded a concordat nor appointed a diplomatic representative at the level of nuncio. Rome also protested the regime's discriminatory and lethal policy toward Jews on a number of occasions, in particularly the passing of racially based anti-Semitic legislation in fall 1940 (the so-called Jewish Codex) and the deportation of tens of thousands of Slovakia's Jews to Nazi death camps beginning in spring 1942. Slovakia's bishops also registered protests against the regime's policy toward Jews, most notably pastoral letters opposing the deportations in spring of 1942 and 1943. See Ivan Kamenec, Vilém Prečan, and Stanislav Škorvánek, eds., *Vatikán a Slovenská Republika (1939–1945): Dokumenty* (Bratislava: Slovak Academic Press, 1992), for the texts of repeated Vatican interventions with the Slovak government on behalf of Slovakia's Jews.

25. By contrast, Czech Catholicism emerged from the Nazi occupation and war with significant moral capital. Vaško notes that nearly five hundred Czech priests were imprisoned by the Nazis, and more than seventy lost their lives. (Kaplan puts the figures at more than five hundred priests imprisoned, one-fifth of whom were killed.) The Vatican helped enhance the reputation of Czech Catholicism by appointing several former prisoners of Nazi concentration camps and well-known supporters of the Czech resistance as bishops at the end of the war. Like most Czechs, the church leadership was overtly patriotic during the immediate postwar period. In contrast to Slovakia, where patriotic tendencies could be associated with sympathy for the Tiso regime, Czech patriotism was universally regarded as wholeheartedly pro-Republic; see Václav Vaško, "Církevněpolitické poměry v Československu, 1945–1949," *Střední Evropa* 59 (April 1996): 85; and Kaplan, *Stát a církev*, 12.

26. See Slovenský Národný Archív (hereafter referred to as SNA), Fond Úrad Predsedníctva Slovenskej Národnej Rady (hereafter referred to as ÚP SNR), Carton 1A, Folder 21/45, Folio 41; and Fond Ústredný Výbor Komunistickej Strany Slovenska (here-

after referred to as ÚV KSS), Carton 2157, Folder GT 248, Bundle 1, Folios, 1–8 for the Catholic bishops' complaints to the Slovak authorities about these and other grievances.

27. Vnuk, *Dokumenty*, 59–61.

28. SNA, Fond Ústredný Akčný Výbor Slovenského Národného Frontu (hereafter referred to as ÚAV SNF), Carton 2, Folder "Církevn školy."

29. Vnuk, *Dokumenty*, 60; see Petranský, *Štát a katolícka cirkev*, 139–41, 153–54, for examples of this unrest.

30. SNA, ÚAV SNF, Carton 2, Folder "Církevné školy," letter of May 29, 1945, from Škrábik to Kmet'ko.

31. Vilém Prečan, "Úloha katolické hierarchie na Slovensku před Únorem 1948," in Bohumil Černý, ed., *Církve v našich dějinách* (Prague: Orbis, 1960), 192.

32. Petranský, *Štát a katolícka cirkev*, 146.

33. For these documents, see SNA, ÚV KSS, Carton 2159, Folder GT-255, Bundle 4, Folios 1–9 and Bundle 3, Folio 11, respectively.

34. Jaroslav Červinka, "Príspevok k histórii bojov o jednotnú a štátnu školu v Československu v rokoch, 1945–1948," in Ondrej Baláž, ed., *Rozvoj spoločnosti a vychova* (Bratislava, 1977), 32–33.

35. *Slovenský národný front.*

36. *Pravda*, July 20, 1945, no. 121, p.1.

37. SNA, ÚV KSS, Carton 2159, Folder GT-255, Bundle 4, Folios 1–9.

38. *Pravda*, July 20, 1945, no. 121, p.1.; "Populist," or *L'udák* in Slovak, was the term for members of the HSL'S.

39. SNA, ÚAV SNF, Carton 2, Folder "Církevn školy."

40. *Pravda*, July 20, 1945, no. 121.

41. *Pravda*, July 20, 1945, no. 121; *Čas*, July 20, 1945, no. 73.

42. SNA, ÚV KSS, Carton 2157, Folder GT-248, Bundle 4, Folios 2–5.

43. *Katolícke noviny*, March 3, 1946, no. 9, p. 2.

44. *Katolícke noviny*, February 10, 1946, no. 6, p. 3, and March 3, 1946, no. 9, p. 2.

45. *Katolícke noviny*, February 3, 1946, no. 5, p. 2, and March 24, 1946, no. 12, p. 3.

46. Vnuk, *Dokumenty*, 25–28.

47. Petranský, *Štát a katolícka cirkev*, 158.

48. See Petranský, *Štát a katolícka cirkev*, 151–60, for a detailed discussion of this issue.

49. Petranský, *Štát a katolícka cirkev*, 147.

50. *Slovenská národná rada, 1945*, vol. 1 (minutes of the meetings of the SNR plenum), meeting of July 25, 1945.

51. SNA, ÚP SNR, Carton 1, meeting of July 2, 1945.

52. Not all dormitories were taken over by the state at once, and of those that were, a number still had some success in the short term in retaining their confessional identity, if only de facto; see Petranský, *Štát a katolícka cirkev*, 151.

53. *Slovenská národná rada, 1945*, vol. 1, meeting of July 25, 1945.

54. As Germans in Slovakia were far less significant than Magyars, both numerically and symbolically, and because policy toward the Magyars was far more important, especially after the immediate postwar months, this discussion will concentrate on the Magyar minority.

55. The 1930 Czechoslovak census reported approximately 600,000 Magyars in Czechoslovakia, the overwhelming majority of which were in southern Slovakia; see Ludvík Němec, "Solution of the Minorities Problem," in Mamatey and Luža, *History*, 416; while most of these Magyars had resided in Czechoslovakia before the Second World War, a number, the so-called *anyasi*, had moved into the area after November 1938, when large portions of southern Slovakia, including the city of Košice, were awarded to Hungary in the Vienna Arbitration.

56. Šutaj, *Mad'arská menšina*, 57.

57. Vnuk, *Dokumenty*, 150.

58. Even predominately Slovak organizations could be affected by anti-Hungarian policies. For example, the Commission of the Interior reported that among the grounds justifying dissolution of the Association of Catholic Youth in Slovakia was the charge that it included members of minority nationalities and even allowed their languages to be used alongside Slovak in association business; see Vaško, *Neumlčená*, 92.

59. Šutaj, *Mad'arská menšina*, 93–95.

60. The archives and press of the time contain considerable evidence of local party bosses trying to co-opt Magyars, and mutual recriminations between Communists and Democrats over this; see, for example, *Pravda*, March 17, 1946, no. 64, p. 2, *Pravda*, June 15, 1946, no. 134, p. 2; *Nové prúdy*, March 17, 1946, no. 6, p. 165; SNA, ÚV KSS, Carton 789, meeting of June 16, 1945; SNA, ÚAV SNF, Carton 3, Folio 32.

61. Vnuk, *Dokumenty*, 15.

62. Šutaj, *Mad'arská menšina*, 55–56; Petranský, *Štát a katolícka cirkev*, 251.

63. *Katolícke noviny*, November 4, 1945, no. 23, p. 1. In their letter, the bishops noted that they had made a similar appeal during the war on behalf of their co-believers and other citizens whose personal, familial, and property freedoms were being violated, meaning Slovakia's Jews and Jewish converts to Christianity.

64. Šutaj, *Mad'arská menšina*, 56; Petranský, *Štát a katolícka cirkev*, 251–52; Vnuk, *Dokumenty*, 153.

65. Šutaj, *Mad'arská menšina*, 55–56; Petranský, *Štát a katolícka cirkev*, 251–52.

66. Petranský, *Štát a katolícka cirkev*, 251.

67. See Šutaj, *Mad'arská menšina*, 52–57, and Petranský, *Štát a katolícka cirkev*, 247–56.

68. Petranský mentions attempts by Slovaks to push the Slovak language at the expense of Magyar in sermons and songs; it was the Slovak Catholic Circle in Košice, for example, that unsuccessfully petitioned their bishop to severely restrict the use of Magyar in Catholic services in Košice; see Petranský, *Štát a katolícka cirkev*, 252–54.

69. Of course, the actual liturgy at this time was in Latin, so what was at issue was not the language of the liturgy, but that of the singing and preaching.

70. Šutaj, *Maďarská menšina*, 57
71. Petranský, *Štát a katolícka cirkev*, 253.
72. Ibid., 254.
73. Ibid., 253.
74. Šutaj, *Maďarská menšina*, 123; Vnuk, *Dokumenty*, 168–71.
75. Vnuk tells the story, with ample documentation, of the Hungarian Benedictines in the town of Komárno in southern Slovakia. They sought to maintain themselves by declaring independence of their Hungarian monastic superiors in Pannonhalma, Hungary, and placing themselves under the authority of Czech Benedictines. This step ultimately failed, largely due to the efforts of the pro-Communist Slovak priest Jozef Straka, who handled the matter for the state authorities, and by 1949 the Benedictines were removed from Komárno and their property taken over by the state; see Vnuk, *Dokumenty*, 172–78.
76. Vnuk, *Dokumenty*, 204–5; on June 25, 1945, the presidium of the SNR met and resolved, with respect to the question of allowing a Catholic periodical, that "if a group of progressive Catholic priests are found, they can submit a request for permission to issue a periodical and the Commission of the Interior will allow them a Catholic weekly." SNA, ÚP SNR, Carton 1, meeting of June 25, 1945.
77. Vnuk, *Dokumenty*, 27.
78. Čarnogurský, *Svedok*, 194, 239.
79. Vnuk, *Dokumenty*, 45.
80. Petranský, *Štát a katolícka cirkev*, 219–20.
81. *Pravda*, June 9, 1945, no. 88, p. 3.
82. *Nové slovo*, August 3, 1945, no. 10, pp. 6–7; "Na stráž!," meaning "On guard!," was a motto associated with the HSĽS during the war.
83. *Pravda*, June 9, 1945, no. 88, p. 3.
84. SNA, UP SNR, Carton 1, meeting of September 4, 1945.
85. Vnuk, *Dokumenty*, 26–27; see also SNA, ÚP SNR, Carton 3, meeting of January 8, 1946, for a complaint against the state authorities by apostolic administrator Bishop Pavol Jantausch for placing obstacles in the way of the church's spiritual ministry to prisoners.
86. Barnovský, *Na ceste*, 72.
87. Petranský, *Štát a katolícka cirkev*, 46–47.
88. SNA, ÚV KSS, Carton 789, meeting of March 13, 1945.
89. Čarnogurský discusses his meetings and ties with Husák in his memoirs; see Čarnogurský, *Svedok*, 135–37, 179; he also credits Husák and Novomeský's intervention for his release after a brief imprisonment in the summer of 1945; *Svedok*, 175–76.
90. Barnovský, *Na ceste*, 68.
91. Ibid., 67
92. Ibid., 83n.
93. SNA, Fond Demokratická Strana (hereafter referred to as DS), Carton 4, 19753/78, Folios 290, 297.
94. *Slovanský katolícky výbor.*

95. Vnuk, *Dokumenty*, 219.

96. SNA, ÚV KSS, Carton 789, meeting of July 13, 1945.

97. The Slovak branch of the Czechoslovak People's Party, also known as the Mičurovci after their leader Martin Mičura, was set up in Slovakia in the early 1920s after a rift between Czech Catholic leader Jan Šrámek and Hlinka. Though a tiny party, getting no more than a fraction of the Slovak vote, the Mičurovci were a gadfly that spent most of their energy attacking the HSĽS, to which the latter responded in kind. With respect to Straka's situation, membership in the Mičurovci gave him bona fide anti-HSĽS credentials.

98. Vnuk, *Dokumenty*, 220.

99. SNA, ÚV KSS, Carton 2157, Folder GT-245, Bundle 8, Folio 1.

100. Ibid.

101. SNA, ÚV KSS, Carton 789, meeting of July 13, 1945; the St. Vojtech Society was Slovakia's oldest and most prominent Catholic cultural institution and publishing house. It was founded in 1870 and located in Trnava.

102. SNA, ÚP SNR, Carton 1, meeting of June 25, 1945.

103. The Cyrilo-Methodian tradition is rooted in the belief that saints Cyril and Methodius, Greek missionaries to the Slavic peoples from the ninth century, were instrumental in bringing Christianity to Slovakia and Moravia, as well as to the Slavic peoples of the Balkans. This tradition was popular among Catholics and Slovak nationalists in Czechoslovakia.

104. SNA, ÚV KSS, Carton 789, meeting of June 13, 1945.

105. *Pravda*, November 11, 1945, no. 215, p. 4; see also *Pravda*, December 13, 1945, no. 241, p. 4.

106. *Pravda*, May 31, 1945, no. 81, p. 4.

107. *Nové slovo*, March 1, 1946, no. 8, pp. 1–2; along these lines, Čarnogurský recalls a conversation that he had with Novomeský in the latter weeks of the war in which Novomeský informed him that Stalin had ordered the Soviet occupation forces to have regard for the religious feelings of the population; Čarnogurský also claims that in his home region of Spiš, the Soviets requested the services of a Catholic priest for a liturgy in conjunction with the transfer of the remains of some dead Red Army soldiers; *Svedok*, 114–15.

108. *Pravda*, August 24, 1945, no. 150, p. l, and *Nové slovo*, December 7, 1945, no. 28, p. 5–6.

109. *Nové slovo*, December 7, 1945, no. 28, pp. 5–6.

110. Ibid., December 25, 1945, pp. 1–3.

111. *Pravda*, December 1, 1945, no. 232, p. l.

112. Ibid., December 2, 1945, no. 233, p. l.

113. Ibid., December 8, 1945, no. 238, p. 2.

114. Ibid., May 31, 1945, no. 81, p. 4; March 15, 1946, no. 62, p. 2; *Nové slovo*, March 1, 1946, no. 8, pp. 1–2.

115. *Nové slovo*, August 10, 1945, no. 11, pp. 3–4.

116. SNA, ÚV KSS, Carton 789, meeting of July 13, 1945.

117. Ibid., Carton 1, meeting of June 18, 1945; and ÚV KSS, Carton 789, meeting of June 13, 1945.

118. Ibid., Carton 789, meeting of June 13, 1945.

119. Ibid., meeting of July 14, 1945.

120. Ibid., meeting of July 13, 1945.

121. SNA, ÚP SNR, Carton 1, meeting of June 18, 1945.

122. Ibid., meeting of July 2, 1945.

123. SNA, ÚV KSS, Carton 789, meeting of July 13, 1945.

124. SNA, ÚV KSS, Carton 2160, Folder GT-268/3, Folio 1.

125. SNA, DS, Carton 99, Folder 403-99-8.

126. Ibid., Folder 403-99-9.

127. SNA, DS, Carton 1, Bundle 19.

128. *Čas*, June 19, 1945, no. 49, p. 1.

129. SNA, ÚP SNR, Carton 1, meeting of June 27, 1945; see also meeting of July 2, 1945.

130. Jozef Staško, "Katolíci a 'Aprílová dohoda,'" *Most* 23, nos. 1–2 (1976): 44.

131. Barnovský, *Na ceste*, 67; in an interview with historian Róbert Letz, Kempný recounted a conversation with Lettrich in which the latter expressed his hopes that Kempný would help thwart the KSS by attracting Catholics to the DS camp; see Letz, *Slovensko*, 30–31.

132. See Barnovský, *Na ceste*, 66, and Letz, *Slovensko*, 28.

133. Barnovský, *Na ceste*, 61n.

134. Letz, *Slovensko*, 48n.

135. SNA, ÚP SNR, Carton 1, meeting of June 25, 1945.

136. SNA, ÚV KSS, Carton 789, meeting of July 13, 1945.

137. SNA, ÚV KSS, Carton 1, meeting of KSS Secretariat of October 4, 1945.

138. *Ústredná katolícka kancelária.*

139. Letz, *Slovensko*, 32–33.

140. Barnovský, *Na ceste*, 69; the bishops allowed some exceptions to the ban, as the cases of Cvinček and Straka demonstrate.

141. SNA, ÚV KSS, Carton 789, meeting of June 13, 1945.

142. The one exception to the localized, uncoordinated nature of the Slovak underground was the STO (Slovenská Tajná Ochrana), composed of former members of the intelligence service of the Slovak state. It was paralyzed early on when its files were lost in May 1945; see Barnovský, *Na ceste*, 184–85.

143. Barnovský, *Na ceste*, 185–86.

144. Barnovský, *Na ceste*, 187; Letz, *Slovensko*, 136.

145. Petranský, *Štát a katolícka cirkev*, 237–39.

146. A leading young HSL'S radical in the 1930s, Ďurčanský held several ministerial posts in Slovakia's governments from October 1938 to July 1940, including the important positions of Minister of Foreign Affairs and Minister of the Interior. He was politically sidelined in summer 1940 for earning the disfavor of Nazi Germany and spent the remainder of the war as a law professor at the University in Bratislava. Fleeing Europe for

Argentina in May 1947, he was tried in absentia in spring 1947 and sentenced to death along with Jozef Tiso.

147. *Slovenský akčný výbor.*

148. Letz, *Slovensko*, 130–34.

149. Kolakovič published his memoirs, in conversation with the American writer Gretta Palmer, as *Through God's Underground; The Adventures of "Father George" among People under Soviet Rule as Told to Gretta Palmer* (London, 1953); see pages 140–41 for his account of the baptism of the Soviet security officers. It should be noted that Kolakovič's account of his exploits should be taken with a grain of salt, as his memoirs are highly unreliable.

150. While studying at the University of Louvain, Kolakovič had helped organize and minister to Belgian working-class Catholic youth, and had even been a worker himself for a time in Paris; see Vaško, *Neumlčená*, 96–97.

151. Regarding Kolakovič, see SNA, DS, Carton 1, Bundle 58; Barnovský, *Na ceste*, 69–72, 187; Letz, *Slovensko*, 100–102; František Mikloško, *Nebudete ich môcť rozvrátiť* (Bratislava: Archa, 1991), 15–36; Petranský, *Štát a katolícka cirkev*, 240–47; Vaško, *Neumlčená*, 95–103; and Anton Hlinka, *Sila slabých a slabosť silných* (Bratislava: Tatran, 1990), 57.

152. Prečan, "Úloha," 196; it is not clear whether the action began spontaneously or at the behest of the clergy, though some clergy clearly encouraged it and distributed crosses.

153. See *Katolícke noviny*, March 10, 1946, no. 10, p. 2.

154. SNA, ÚV KSS, Carton 2157, Folder GT-248, Bundle 6, Folio 1, and SNA, ÚV KSS, Carton 2159, Folder GT-255, Bundle 3, Folio 1.

155. Vnuk, *Dokumenty*, 225–26.

156. *Katolícke noviny*, February 10, 1946, no. 6, p. 3; a DS situation report of January 1946 from the region around Topoľčany refers to attacks against the wearing of crosses, which many people in the area were doing; see SNA, DS, Carton 4, Folio 277.

157. Cited in *Katolícke noviny*, March 10, 1946, no. 10, p. 2.

158. *Katolícke noviny*, February 3, 1946, no. 5, p. 1.

159. Petranský, *Štát a katolícka cirkev*, 267.

160. SNA, ÚV KSS, Carton 2156, Folder GT-237/1, Folios 1–4.

161. Slovakia gave support to Germany's invasion of Poland in September 1939.

162. SNA, ÚV KSS, Carton 2156, Folder GT-237/1, Folios 1–4.

163. Letz, *Slovensko*, 136–37 and 144–45.

164. The letter was signed by bishops Kmeťko, Čársky, Škrábik, Tomanóczy, Jantausch, and Nécsey. Absent from the signers were Vojtaššák and Buzalka.

165. SNA, ÚAV SNF, Carton 2, Folder 136/46.

166. Staško, "Katolíci," 49–50.

167. Barnovský, *Na ceste*, 76; Letz, *Slovensko*, 32; Ursíny confirms the disaffection among Catholics in the DS at this time in his memoir *Z môjho života*, 90.

168. *Kresťansko-republicánska strana.*

169. Staško, "Katolíci," 49.

170. Šrobár, long a close political ally of Beneš, was the Minister Plenipotentiary for the Administration of Slovakia from 1918 to 1920 and spent most of the interwar period teaching on the medical school faculty of Comenius University in Bratislava. He served as minister of finance in the immediate post–World War II period.

171. Letz, *Slovensko*, 32; Čarnogurský notes in his memoirs that he had already begun working for a Catholic party back in May 1945; see *Svedok*, 185.

172. Staško, "Katolíci," 127.

173. Barnovský, *Na ceste*, 73; Čarnogurský, *Svedok*, 48.

174. Barnovský, *Na ceste*, 73.

175. Ibid., 73–74; according to Barnovský, Široký and Friš supported the idea of a Catholic party; Husák, Novomeský, and Šmidke did not.

176. Letz, *Slovensko*, p. 33; see also footnote 52 of Letz, *Slovensko* for more evidence of Communist support for a Catholic party at this time.

177. Čarnogurský, *Svedok*, 186.

178. SNA, DS, Carton 4, Folio 262; see also Folio 277.

179. *Nové prúdy*, March 3, 1946, no. 5, p. 141; *Nové prúdy*, March 31, 1946, no. 7, pp. 173–74.

180. *Čas*, November 30, 1945, no. 183, p. 1; *Nové prúdy*, February 17, 1946, no. 4, pp. 119–20.

181. *Čas*, January 30, 1946, no. 25, p. 1; *Nové prúdy*, February 17, 1946, no. 4, p. 119–20.

182. *Čas*, March 1, 1946, no. 51, p. 1.

183. *Nové prúdy*, February 17, 1946, no. 4, pp. 119–20.

184. *Čas*, March 1, 1946, no. 51, p. 1; *Nové prúdy*, January 20, 1946, no. 2, p. 90.

185. *Nové prúdy*, February 17, 1946, no. 4, pp. 119–20.

186. Ibid.; NS is the Slovak abbreviation for *Narodné shromaždenie*, the Czechoslovak parliament.

187. SNA, DS, Carton 6, Folios 991–92.

188. SNA, DS, Carton 6, Folios 998–99.

189. SNA, DS, Carton 5, Folios 695–97.

190. DS situation reports from the region around Topoľčany referred to the wearing of crosses as "partly provocative" and urged the DS to support those who were wearing crosses in good faith and to discourage those who were wearing them for antistate reasons. One suggestion for accomplishing the latter was to point out that Czech Catholics had actually initiated the wearing of crosses, a disclosure that hopefully would sour some anti-Czech Slovak nationalists on the action; see SNA, DS, Carton 4, Folio 277 and SNA, DS, Carton 6, Folios 991–92.

191. *Pravda*, January 23, 1946, no. 10, p. 1.

192. Barnovský, *Na ceste*, 73.

193. Staško, "Katolíci," 129.

194. Ibid., 130; Letz, *Slovensko*, 34–35.

195. *Čas*, February 17, 1946, no. 41, p. 3.

196. Barnovský, *Na ceste*, 74–75.

197. SNA, ÚV KSS, Carton 789, meeting of March 13, 1946.

198. Staško, "Katolíci," 128.

199. SNA, ÚAV SNF, Carton 1, meeting of December 3, 1945.

200. Barnovský, *Na ceste*, 74.

201. SNA, ÚAV SNF, Carton 2, Folder 169/46.

202. SNA, ÚV KSS, Carton 2159, Folder GT-255, Bundle 2, Folio 19.

203. Barnovský, *Na ceste*, 77.

204. SNA, ÚV KSS, Carton 789, meeting of March 9, 1946.

205. Čarnogurský claims in his memoirs, though not convincingly, that the chief obstacle to the party's acceptance by the National Front was its refusal to make Šrobár its chairman; see *Svedok*, 198.

206. SNA, ÚAV SNF, Carton 2, Folder 169/46.

207. Štátny Oblastný Archiv, Bratislava (hereafter ŠOBA, Bratislava), Fond Národný Súd (hereafter NS), Hp 4/48a, testimony of Bugár, Folios 280–86.

208. For an account of the events leading up to the April Agreement, see Staško, "Katolíci," 132–33; ŠOBA, Bratislava, NS, Hp 4/48a, testimony of Bugár, Folios 280–86.

209. For the text of the April Agreement, see Staško, "Katolíci," 141–43.

Chapter 2: Bringing Home the Lion

1. Michal Barnovský, *Na ceste k monopolu moci: Mocenskopolitické zápasy na Slovensku v rokoch, 1945–1948* (Bratislava: Archa, 1993), 82.

2. Jozef Staško, "Katolíci a 'Aprílová dohoda'" *Most* 23, no. 1–2 (1976): 133.

3. Ibid., 133–34n.

4. *Čas*, April 11, 1946, no. 84, p. l.

5. Moyses, the Roman Catholic bishop of Banská Bystrica, and Kuzmány, the Lutheran superintendent from the same town, were instrumental in creating the Matica Slovenská in 1863 as Slovakia's preeminent cultural organization; Moyses served as that organization's chairman and Kuzmány as its deputy chairman; Elena Mannová, *A Concise History of Slovakia* (Bratislava: Historický ústav SAV, 2000), 199; Stanley J. Kirschbaum, *A History of Slovakia: The Struggle for Survival* (New York: St. Martin's Press, 1995), 135.

6. *Čas*, April 21, 1946, no. 92, p. l.

7. SNA, DS, K. 99, Folder 403-99-10.

8. SNA, DS, K. 99, Folder 403-99-10.

9. Petranský, *Štát a katolícka cirkev*, 103

10. Ibid., 106–7.

11. Information gathered by the KSS speaks of a number of cases of Catholic clergy appearing at DS rallies. Straka appeared at KSS rallies. Čarnogurský mentions priests celebrating Catholic mass for participants at KSS rallies in the heavily Catholic region of Orava; see Petranský, *Štát a katolícka cirkev*, 113, 115; Čarnogurský, *Svedok*, 162.

12. *Pravda*, April 12, 1946, no. 85, p. l.

13. One week after the Munich Agreement, the leaders of most of Slovakia's political parties met in Žilina, where they agreed on a program for autonomy for Slovakia devised largely by the HSĽS. A number of Agrarians, who later became Democrats, signed the agreement, including Ursíny and Polák. Though these Agrarians-turned-Democrats eventually abandoned the Populist wartime regime and participated in the Slovak National Uprising, the Communists found it useful to bring up the Žilina Agreement whenever Democrats pursued policies that the KSS found unpalatable; for a discussion of the Žilina Agreement, see Felak, *"At the Price of the Republic,"* 205–8.

14. The term "ludakization" comes from "Ľudák," Slovak for "Populist."

15. *Pravda*, April 21, 1946, no. 92, pp. 1–2.

16. SNA, DS, K. 99, Folder 403-99-10.

17. *Čas*, April 11, 1946, no. 84, p. l.

18. Ibid., April 13, 1946, no. 86, p. 1.

19. Ibid., April 11, 1946, no. 84, p. 1.

20. SNA, DS, K. 99, Folder 403-99-10.

21. SNA, ÚV KSS, Carton 2160, Folder GT-271/5, Folio 1.

22. Ibid., Folder GT-271/22, Folio 1.

23. SNA, ÚAV SNF 1945–1948, Carton 1, meeting of May 4–6, 1946.

24. Barnovský, *Na ceste*, 90.

25. SNA, ÚV KSS, Carton 2159, Folder GT-255, Bundle 2, Folio 2.

26. *Čas*, May 19, 1946, no. 113, p. 1.

27. Ibid., April 25, 1946, no. 94, p. 2.

28. SNA, DS, Carton 6, Folios 929-938; SNA, DS, Carton 99, Folder 403-99-10.

29. *Čas*, May 19, 1946, no. 113, p. 1.

30. Barnovský, *Na ceste*, 97.

31. SNA, DS, Carton 4, Folios 226–27.

32. For a detailed discussion of the Party of Freedom, see Ľubomír Lipták, *Politické strany na Slovensku, 1860–1989* (Bratislava: Archa, 1992), 271–75.

33. Petranský, *Štát a katolícka cirkev*, 117; both Communists and Democrats had good reason to object to the Party of Freedom's attempt to support parochial schools. For the Communists, this opposed a fundamental part of their program; for the Democrats, it represented an attempt by a rival to outflank them on an issue of concern to a crucial DS constituency.

34. SNA, DS, Carton 4, Folios 226–27, 258–59; SNA, DS, Carton 6, Folios 929–38; in an appeal to Catholics of May 18, 1945, the Party of Freedom's executive committee felt the need to deny any affinity with the Czechoslovak National Socialist Party; see Vaško, *Neumlčená*, 111–12.

35. Petranský, *Štát a katolícka cirkev*, 119.

36. SNA, DS, Carton 99, Folder 403-99-10.

37. *Pravda*, April 9, 1946, no. 82, p. 1.

38. Barnovský, *Na ceste*, 97.

39. *Čas*, May 12, 1946, no. 107, p. 2; *Pravda*, May 1, 1946, no. 99, p. 3; and *Nové prúdy*, May 5, 1946, no. 9, pp. 220–21; (see also *Čas*, April 17, 1946, no. 89, p. 3).

40. *Pravda*, May 1, 1946, no. 99, p. 3.

41. *Pravda*, April 12, 1946, no. 85, p. 1.

42. *Pravda*, May 5, 1946, no. 102, p. 7.

43. As reported in *Nové prúdy*, May 5, 1946, no. 9, pp. 220–21.

44. *Pravda*, May 23, 1946, no. 116, p. 1.

45. See footnote 84 on Tuka.

46. SNA, ÚV KSS, Carton 2150, Folder GT-210/1, Folio 8.

47. *Čas*, May 18, 1945, no. 112, p. 1.

48. Ibid., May 9, 1946, no. 105, pp. 1–2.

49. Ibid., May 19, 1946, no. 65, p. 1.

50. See *Čas*, May 19, 1946, no. 113, p. 1; May 9, 1946, no. 105, pp. 1–2; May 23, 1946, no. 116, p. 1. See also SNA, DS, Carton 2, Bundle 84, Folios 10–11.

51. *Čas*, May 11, 1946, no. 106, p. 3.

52. *Nové prúdy*, May 26, 1946, no. 10, pp. 242–44.

53. SNA, DS, Carton 2, Bundle 84, Folio 12.

54. *Čas*, May 14, 1946, no. 108, pp. 1–2; while the term "church" has been used throughout this book to refer to the Roman Catholic Church, in the context of the DS electoral appeal, "church" is taken to mean both any and all Christian churches.

55. *Nové prúdy*, May 26, 1946, no. 10, pp. 242–44.

56. *Čas*, May 24, 1946, no. 117, p. 2.

57. See SNA, DS, Carton 2, Bundle 142.

58. Ursíny, in his memoirs, alleges that there were cases of Communist provocateurs writing purportedly pro-DS slogans on walls meant to make the DS look like a revival of Tiso and the Populists; see *Z môjho života*, 94.

59. SNA, DS, Carton 2, Bundle 143, Folio 6.

60. SNA, UV KSS, K. 2150, Folder GT-208/2, Folio 1.

61. SNA, UV KSS, K. 2150, Folder GT-209/3, Folio 1; see Letz, *Slovensko*, 37–38 and SNA, DS, Carton 4, Folios 226–27 for more examples of intermittent election campaign violence.

62. *Katolícke noviny*, May 26, 1946, no. 21, p. 1.

63. One author in *Katolícke noviny* wrote that "empty ballots, for Catholics, mean not only an empty head but also an empty heart." *Katolícke noviny*, May 19, 1946, no. 20, p. 1; in its preelection issue, *Katolícke noviny* included excerpts from a speech by Pope Pius XII of March 1946, in which he reminded Catholics of their moral obligation to vote; *Katolícke noviny*, May 26, 1946, no. 21, p. 2.

64. See *Katolícke noviny*, May 12, 1946, no. 19, p. 2; *Katolícke noviny*, May 19, 1946, no. 20, p. 1; and *Katolícke noviny*, May 26, 1946, no. 21, pp. 1, 2.

65. Electoral data is taken from Barnovský, *Na ceste*, 97.

66. Letz, *Slovensko*, 39.

67. See Viera Hlavová, "Parlamentné vol'by na Slovensku v roku 1946," in *Prvé*

povojnové voľby v strednej a juhovýchodnej Europe, ed. Michal Barnovský and Edita Ivaničková (Bratislava, 1998), 83, for a list of those categories of Slovaks excluded from suffrage.

68. Barnovský, *Na ceste*, 103–4.

69. *Pravda*, May 28, 1946, no. 120, p. 1.

70. *Nové slovo*, June 7, 1946, no. 21, pp. 1–3.

71. A patriotic Slovak song from the nineteenth century that became closely associated with Slovak nationalism of the Populist variety.

72. *Nové slovo*, June 7, 1946, no. 21, p. 5; Guardists were members of the Hlinka Guard, a paramilitary organization founded in 1938 and led by radical Populists.

73. *Nové slovo*, June 7, 1946, no. 21, pp. 4, 7.

74. The Sixth Department, renamed the Seventh Department in 1947, had among its responsibilities the monitoring of the non-Communist parties in Slovakia; Letz, *Slovensko*, 55.

75. Barnovský, *Na ceste*, 103.

76. Milan Hodža was the leader of the Slovak branch of the Agrarian Party during the 1920s and 1930s. He was also significant on the statewide level, holding several ministerial posts during the interwar period, including prime minister from 1935 to 1938; for Tuka, see footnote 84.

77. Barnovský, *Na ceste*, 107.

78. SNA, ÚAV SNF, Carton 1, folios 53–58, 72–81.

79. Ibid., folios 72–81.

80. SNA, DS, Carton 6, Folios 940–43; Barnovský, *Na ceste*, 101–2, 106. According to an investigation by the Commission of Justice, it appears likely that Tiso in fact did sing "*Hej Slováci*" upon learning of the DS victory, though police reports that the entire prison was singing it appear to be inaccurate. See SNA, ÚV KSS, Carton 2156, Folder GT-236/5.

81. Barnovský, *Na ceste*, 101.

82. Ibid., 104.

83. SNA, ÚV KSS, Carton 2156, Folder GT-II-237/20, folios 1–3.

84. Vojtech Tuka and Alexander "Šaňo" Mach were two of the most important, and most pro-Nazi, leaders of the Slovak state. Tuka served as prime minister from October 1939 to September 1944 as well as foreign minister from July 1940, while Mach, among other things, served as interior minister.

85. SNA, ÚV KSS, Carton 789, meeting of July 15, 1946.

86. For a discussion of the Third Prague Agreement, see Rychlík, *Češi a Slováci, 1945–1992*, 47–50; Barnovský, *Na ceste*, 111–13, and Letz, *Slovensko*, 43–45.

87. As U.S. Ambassador to Czechoslovakia Laurence Steinhardt reported in May 1947: "For the Czech non-communist parties and their leaders, including Beneš, as a result of their experiences in 1938–1939 when Slovak aspirations contributed materially to the dissolution of the Czechoslovak State, feel with a deep intensity that Slovak autonomy, while acceptable in theory, must have definite limitations in practice. These leaders are therefore all too likely to side with the Communists on any issues to which

the latter are able to give a Czech versus Slovak or autonomy versus centralism complexion. As a result the Democrats are very frequently left to face the Communist onslaught alone; U.S. Department of State, Decimal Files, 860f00/5-2947, no. 2477.

88. Rychlík, *Češi a Slováci, 1945–1992*, 49.

89. SNA, ÚV KSS, Carton 2160, Folder GT-272/4, Folios 1–10.

90. SNA, ÚAV SNF, Carton 1, Folios 53–58.

91. Paul Ignotus, "The First Two Communist Takeovers of Hungary: 1919 and 1948," in *The Anatomy of Communist Takeovers*, ed. Thomas T. Hammond (New Haven, Conn.: Yale University Press, 1975), 394.

92. SNA, ÚAV SNF, Carton 1, Folios 53–58; SNA, ÚAV SNF, Carton 1, meeting of July 9, 1946, Folios 72–81.

93. SNA, DS, Carton 5, Folios 636–37.

94. Ibid.

95. Rychlík, *Češi a Slováci, 1945–1992*, 50–51.

96. Ursíny, in his memoirs, claims that the KSS got Ferjenčík appointed to the post while Ursíny, who suspected that Ferjenčík would be incapable of thwarting abuses by the police, was on vacation. Ursíny also notes that Ferjenčík's secretary remained pro-KSS, a holdover from the preceding commissioner, the Communist Viktory; *Z môjho života*, 98–99.

97. For a discussion of the distribution of seats in the Slovak national organs, see Barnovský, *Na ceste*, 115–17, and Rychlík, *Češi a Slováci, 1945–1992*, 51.

98. Barnovský, *Na ceste*, 104.

99. SNA, ÚV KSS, Carton 789, July 14, 1946.

100. Juraj Jánošík (1688–1713), the Slovak "Robin Hood," was a rebel and bandit renowned in Slovak lore for, among other things, stealing from rich Hungarians and giving aid to poor Slovaks in the Tatra Mountain regions. He was executed by the Hungarian authorities in Liptovský Svätý Mikuláš; see *Slovenský biografický slovník*, vol. 2 (Martin: Matica Slovenská, 1987).

101. SNA, UV KSS, Carton 2150, Folder GT-210/6, Folios 1–6.

102. *Nové slovo*, September 21, 1946, no. 36, pp. 9–10.

103. Ibid., October 19, 1946, no. 40, p. 4.

104. *Pravda*, July 25, 1946, no. 164, p. 3.

105. Ibid., July 30, 1946, no. 168, p. 3.

106. Ibid., November 3, 1946, no. 248, p. 5.

107. *Katolícke noviny*, December 8, 1946, no. 49, p. 5.

108. *Nové slovo*, June 14, 1946, no. 22, p. 15.

109. *Pravda*, July 30, 1946, no. 168, p. 3.

110. Ibid., July 2, 1946, no. 146, p. 3.

111. Ibid., November 3, 1946, no. 248, p. 5.

112. *Katolícke noviny*, July 28, 1946, no. 30, p. l.

113. Ibid., August 18, 1946, no. 33, p. 3.

114. Ibid., October 13, 1946, no. 41, p. 3.

115. Ibid., August 11, 1946, no. 32, p. 3.

116. SNA, ÚV KSS, Carton 1, meeting of KSS Secretariat of October 4, 1945.

117. *Katolícke noviny*, July 28, 1946, no. 30, p. 3; August 4, 1946, no. 31, p. 3.

118. Ibid., September 1, 1946, no. 35, p. 3.

119. Ibid., July 28, 1946, no. 30, p. 3.

120. See *Katolícke noviny*, July 21, 1946, no. 29, p. 1, and December 1, 1946, no. 48, p. 1.

121. *Katolícke noviny*, September 22, 1946, no. 38, p. l.

122. *Pravda*, September 22, 1946, no. 214, p. 3.

123. Vnuk, *Dokumenty*, Document II/5, pp. 29–32.

124. *Združenie katolíckej mládeže.*

125. Vnuk, *Dokumenty*, Document II/7, pp. 33–35.

126. Ibid., Document II/8, pp. 35–36.

127. Ibid., Document II/6, pp. 32–33.

128. Ibid., Document XI/C/6, p. 216.

129. *Nové slovo*, October 5, 1946, no. 38, p. 8.

130. *Katolícke noviny*, June 2, 1946, no. 22, p. 2.

131. SNA, DS, Carton 4, Folio 13.

132. Ibid., Folio 155.

133. Ibid., Carton 1, Bundle 2 ("Resolution of the Club of Democratic Academics").

134. *Katolícke noviny*, June 2, 1946, no. 22, p. 1.

135. Ibid., November 10, 1946, no. 45, p. 1.

136. Vnuk, *Dokumenty*, Document V/8, 102–3.

137. Ursíny admitted this in court in 1948. Bugár made the point during his own interrogation that the conflict between Catholics and Protestants in the DS was motivated not by religion, but because former Agrarians of the Lutheran confession were favoring their relatives and former party associates in handing out positions and favors (see Barnovský, *Na ceste*, 136–37). While testimony in Communist-run trials and interrogations should be used with caution, in this case the statements by Ursíny and Bugár corroborate the impressions gleaned from other types of sources.

138. Barnovský, *Na ceste*, 136.

139. SNA, DS, Carton 1, Bundle 40; SNA, DS, Carton 2, Bundle 91; and DS, Carton 2, Bundle 94, Folio 1.

140. Barnovský, *Na ceste*, 137; see also SNA, DS, Carton 2, Bundle 102, Folio 4–5.

141. *Nové slovo*, June 14, 1946, no. 22, p. 11.

142. See *Nové slovo*, June 28, 1946, no. 24, pp. 3–4; August 2, 1946, no. 29, p. 7; September 21, 1946, no. 36, pp. 9–10. See also *Pravda*, October 17, 1946, no. 235, p. 1.

143. *Pravda*, July 17, 1946, no. 157, p. 3.

144. See *Nové slovo*, October 12, 1946, no. 39, p. 8; October 26, 1946, no. 41, pp. 13–14; and November 16, 1946, no. 44, 8–9.

145. *Nové slovo*, November 16, 1946, no. 44, pp. 8–9.

146. *Čas*, July 26, 1946, no. 163, p. 3.

147. *Nové prúdy*, October 25, 1946, no. 21, pp. 465–66.

148. Ibid., November 24, 1946, no. 23, p. 518.

149. SNA, DS, Carton 3, Bundle 169, Folios 44–45.

150. Pavlík was the special representative of Commissioner Novomeský.

151. SNA, DS, Carton 3, Bundle 169, Folios 51–52.

152. Novomeský, it is worth noting, had for a Communist relatively good relations with Catholics. Though uncompromising in his support for nationalization of education, he was open to accommodating Catholic concerns to some extent in related issues, such as policies toward teachers who belonged to religious orders; see Čarnogurský, *Svedok*, 151.

153. See Vnuk, *Dokumenty*, Document IV/16, 77–78, for a detailing of these abuses.

154. Vnuk, *Dokumenty*, Document IV/16, 78n.

155. *Katolícka školská rada.*

156. Červinka, "Príspevok k histórii bojov," 42; *Nové slovo*, November 9, 1946, no. 43, pp. 1–2.

157. *Nové slovo*, November 9, 1946, no. 43, pp. 1–2; see also *Katolícke noviny*, December 15, 1946, no. 50, p. 3.

158. *Katolícke noviny*, December 15, 1946, no. 50. p. 3.

159. See *Katolícke noviny*, September 8, 1946, no. 36, pp. 1, 3; September 15, 1946, no. 37, pp. 1–2; September 6, 1946, no. 40, p. 1.

160. *Katolícke noviny*, September 8, 1946, no. 36, p. 3.

161. *Nové slovo*, November 9, 1946, no. 43, pp. 1–2.

162. See *Katolícke noviny*, October 27, 1946, no. 43, p. 4; November 10, 1946, no. 45, p. 3; and December 29, 1946, no. 62, p. 1, for coverage of the conflict over work on Sundays and holy days.

163. *Revolučné odborové hnutie.*

164. Šutaj, *Maďarská menšina*, 139, 196; according to the data presented by Šutaj, 55,487 Magyars were resettled to Hungary in accordance with an agreement between Czechoslovakia and Hungary, and an additional 34,000, approximately, were resettled outside the framework of the agreement.

165. For the text of the pertinent part of this memorandum, see Vnuk, *Dokumenty*, Document VIII A/2, 153–54.

166. Šutaj, *Maďarská menšina*, 125. The bishops' efforts in the end were not entirely without success. By October 1947, 90 Magyar priests, out of 305 at war's end, had received exemptions enabling them to remain in Slovakia; see Petranský, *Štát a katolícka cirkev*, 248n.

167. Šutaj, *Maďarská menšina*, 105.

168. Vnuk reproduces the text of three of these letters in *Dokumenty*, Documents VIII A/7, A/8 and A/9, 160–62.

169. The text of the appeal is presented in slightly different versions in Šutaj, *Maďarská menšina*, 189–90, and Vnuk, *Dokumenty*, Document VIII A/10, 162–65.

170. In one of the infrequent official replies to an episcopal protest concerning the minority question, Prime Minister Zdeněk Fierlinger wrote to Kmeťko on December 7, 1945, that abuses are unavoidable in such revolutionary days. See Petranský, *Štát a katolícka cirkev*, 251–52.

171. Šutaj, *Maďarská menšina*, 125; in autumn 1947, the bishops displayed the limits to this cooperation; on September 21, Hungary's Cardinal József Mindszenty had a proclamation read in Hungary's churches accusing Czechoslovakia of wanting to drive 700,000 Magyars out of their native lands in order to get hold of their property. The commissioner of information asked Slovakia's bishops to issue a response to Mindszenty's claims, but the bishops opted not to take a stand on the issue, reminding the commissioner that they had not been consulted in the past with respect to the transfers and had asked the government repeatedly, without success, to prevent abuses. See Šutaj, *Maďarská menšina*, 126.

Chapter 3: Dealing with the Past

1. Michal Barnovský, *Na ceste k monopolu moci: Mocenskopolitické zápasy na Slovensku v rokoch, 1945–1948* (Bratislava: Archa, 1993), 12.

2. Karel Kaplan, *Dva retribuční procesy: Komentované dokumenty, 1946–1947* (Prague: Ústav pro soudobé dějiny ČSAV, 1992), 16, and Document 14, pp. 132–33.

3. Ibid., Document 15, p. 134.

4. Ibid., Document 22, p. 155; in Fierlinger's account, Ritter recognized that Tiso had sanctioned horrible crimes committed in the last phases of the war, which his Slovak friends had confirmed for him.

5. The deputy prime minister, Communist Viliam Široký, called for a purge of the Bishops' Council at the government meeting of November 28, 1946; see Kaplan, *Dva retribuční procesy*, Document 22, p. 161.

6. SNA, ÚV KSS, Carton 789, meeting of September 20, 1946.

7. Ibid., meeting of December 2, 1946.

8. *Sedliacka banka.*

9. Kaplan, *Dva retribuční procesy*, 17; Čarnogurský, in his memoirs, alleges an oral promise by the DS to use its influence to see that people hostile to Tiso were not appointed to the body that would judge him; see Čarnogurský, *Svedok čias* (Bratislava: USPO, 1997), 198, 199, 241.

10. Kaplan, *Dva retribuční procesy*, 18.

11. SNA, ÚV KSS, Carton 2150, Folder GT-210/1, Folio 33–35.

12. SNA, DS, Carton 4, Folio 174.

13. Ibid., Folio 15.

14. František Vnuk, *Dokumenty o postavení katolíckej cirkvi na Slovensku v rokoch, 1945–1948* (Martin: Matica slovenská, 1998), 116–17.

15. Kaplan, *Dva retribuční procesy*, Document 23, p. 166.

16. Barnovský, *Na ceste*, 125–26.

17. Ibid., 126.

18. Kaplan, *Dva retribuční procesy*, Document 22, p. 155.

19. Ibid., 160.

20. Ibid., 19.

21. Barnovský, *Na ceste*, 125.

22. Ibid., 143n.
23. Vnuk, *Dokumenty*, Document VI/6, 116–17.
24. Kaplan, *Dva retribuční procesy*, Document 21, p. 153.
25. Ibid., Document 23, pp. 163–64.
26. The trial of five members of the Nazi controlled Czech wartime government was held in spring and summer of 1946. The verdicts announced on July 31 were lighter than expected, with none of the defendants receiving the death penalty and only one receiving life imprisonment. While the Communists pressed for harsh sentences, including death for some of the accused, the DS remained aloof from the trial as a purely Czech affair; see Bradley Abrams, "The Politics of Retribution: The Trial of Jozef Tiso," *East European Politics and Societies* 10, no. 2 (Spring 1996): 256–58 for a discussion of the trials of alleged Czech collaborators.
27. Kaplan, *Dva retribuční procesy*, Document 22, p. 161.
28. Vnuk, *Dokumenty*, Document VI/4, 112–14.
29. SNA, ÚP SP, Carton 16, Folder 337, letter of December 4, 1946, from Husák to Štefánik.
30. SNA, ÚV KSS, Carton 2156, Folder GT-237/1, meeting of November 30, 1946.
31. Vnuk, *Dokumenty*, Document VI/19, 130–31.
32. Barnovský, *Na ceste*, 124; see also SNA, ÚV KSS, Carton 2156, Folder GT-237/1, Folio 23.
33. Kaplan, *Dva retribuční procesy*, Document 19, pp. 144–51.
34. In fact, Daxner had earlier converted to Eastern Orthodoxy, but this did not stop him from being identified with the Lutheranism of his heritage. He was from a prominent Slovak Lutheran family.
35. Róbert Letz, *Slovensko v rokoch 1945–1948 na ceste ku komunistickej totalite* (Bratislava: Ústredie slovenskej kresťanskej inteligencie, 1994), 46.
36. *Nové slovo*, January 4, 1947, no. 1, pp. 1–3.
37. *Nové slovo*, February 8, 1947, no. 6, pp. 86–88; Husák alleged that Kempný and Staško attended a meeting of January 10, 1945, where Ďurčanský discussed such plans.
38. *Nové slovo*, March 8, 1947, no. 10, pp. 152–54.
39. Ibid., February 1, 1947, no. 5, pp. 76–77.
40. Ibid., March 1, 1947, no. 9, p. 134.
41. Ibid., March 15, 1947, no. 11, pp. 166–69.
42. Ibid., March 29, 1947, no. 13, p. 197.
43. *Čas*, January 18, 1947, no. 14, p. 1.
44. Ibid., February 4, 1947, no. 28, p. 2.
45. Ibid., March 5, 1947, no. 53, p. 3. The Communist media attacked Fraštacký's speech for implying that the support of Kmeťko and other Catholic bishops for an independent Slovakia during the war was no different than the expressed desires of several Communist activists in 1944 for an independent postwar Slovakia; see *Nové slovo*, March 15, 1947, no. 11, p. 164.
46. *Katolícke noviny*, March 2, 1947, no. 9, pp. 1, 3.

47. *Nové slovo*, March 15, 1947, no. 11, pp. 163–64.

48. *Katolícke noviny*, March 9, 1947, no. 10.

49. SNA, DS, Carton 3, Bundle 161, Folio 39–80.

50. Tiso's title in Slovak was *Vodca*, analogous to the German *Führer* used by Adolf Hitler or the Italian *Duce* used by Mussolini.

51. SNA, DS, Carton 4, Folio 173–74.

52. Ibid., Folio 50; SNA, DS, Carton 4, Folios 46–47.

53. Letz, *Slovensko*, 145.

54. For accounts of the demonstration in Piešt'any, see *Čas*, March 27, 1947, no. 72, p. 3; *Pravda*, March 24, 1947, no. 70a, p. 1; March 28, 1947, no. 74, p. 1; Letz, *Slovensko*, 145–46; Kaplan, *Dva retribuční procesy*, Document 19, pp. 199–203; and SNA, DS, Carton 3, Bundle 161, Folios 39–80 (KSS situation report on Slovakia from spring 1947).

55. A Commission of the Interior report alleged shouts of "Hang Beneš!" as well; Kaplan, *Dva retribuční procesy*, Document 19, p. 199.

56. For accounts of the demonstration in Nové Mesto nad Váhom, see Letz, *Slovensko*, 146–47; Kaplan, *Dva retribuční procesy*, Document 19, p. 199; Barnovský, *Na ceste*, 143n.

57. While women constituted the majority of participants in this as in all other demonstrations, it seems that the defacing of railroad cars was largely a male undertaking.

58. Letz, *Slovensko*, 226n.

59. For accounts of the Chynorany demonstrations, see SNA, DS, Carton 4, Folios 161–62 (report of district secretary of the DS in Topol'čany, March 1947); Letz, *Slovensko*, p. 147; Kaplan, *Dva retribuční procesy*, Document 19, p. 199; Letz notes that allegations that demonstrators at the railway station shouted "Away with Jews!" were later dismissed in court for lack of confirmation by witness testimony.

60. *Čas*, March 27, 1947, no. 72, p. 3; Letz, *Slovensko*, 147.

61. Letz, *Slovensko*, 146; SNA, UP SP, Carton 21, Folder 363, meeting of March 21, 1947.

62. SNA, DS, Carton 3, Bundle 161, Folios 39–80; Barnovský, *Na ceste*, 126; Kaplan, *Dva retribuční procesy*, Document 19, p. 201.

63. Barnovský, *Na ceste*, 126.

64. *Nové slovo*, April 5, 1947, no. 14, p. 212.

65. *Pravda*, March 22, 1947, no. 69, p. 1; see also SNA, DS, Carton 3, Bundle 161, Folios 39–80.

66. See *Nové slovo*, April 5, 1947, no. 14, p. 212; *Pravda*, March 22, 1947, no. 69, p. 3; *Pravda*, March 28, 1947, no. 74, p. 1.

67. *Nové slovo*, January 4, 1947, no. 1, p. 2.

68. *Čas*, March 27, 1947, no. 72, p. 1.

69. Ibid., p. 3; *Čas*, March 30, 1947, no. 75, p. 3.

70. *Čas*, March 27, 1947, no. 72, p. 3.

71. SNA, DS, Carton 4, Folios 161–62.

72. Letz notes that in November 1945 a Communist Party member and butcher organized a petition drive on Tiso's behalf in Bánovce; see Letz, *Slovensko*, 144.

73. For accounts of the demonstration, see *Pravda*, March 23, 1947, no. 70, pp. 1–2

74. *Katolícke noviny*, March 30, 1947, no. 13, p. 3.

75. *Pravda*, March 23, 1947, no. 70, pp. 1–2.

76. *Katolícke noviny*, March 30, 1947, no. 13, p. 3.

77. *Čas*, April 1, 1947, no. 76, p. 1.

78. *Pravda*, April 3, 1947, no. 79, pp. 1–2.

79. SNA, DS, Carton 3, Bundle 161, Folios 39–80.

80. SNA, Fond Národný súd (hereafter referred to as NS), 6/46, Carton 52, Folios 320, 325, 371, 551, and 552; see James Mace Ward, "'People Who Deserve It': Jozef Tiso and the Presidential Exemption," *Nationalities Papers* 30, no. 4 (December 2002): 571–601, which argues convincingly that Tiso helped spare far fewer Jews from deportation than his defenders would have us believe.

81. SNA, ÚP SNR, Carton 139, Folder 134, Folio 47.

82. SNA, DS, Carton 2, Bundle 99, Folios 1 and 2 (Rašla's notes of March 12, 1947).

83. Though Šujan and Rigan were in agreement at this meeting, Šujan later changed his mind; after the verdict and sentence on Tiso was announced, Rigan was the only prosecutor to put in a request for clemency.

84. Ján Ursíny, *Z môjho života* (Martin: Matica Slovenská, 2000), 113.

85. Kaplan, *Dva retribuční procesy*, Document 31, pp. 23, 205.

86. Anton Rašla and Ernest Žabkay, *Proces s dr. J. Tisom, Spomienky* (Bratislava: Tatrapress, 1990), 96–97.

87. Ursíny, *Z môjho života*, 113–14.

88. For coverage of the announcement of the verdict and punishment on Tiso, see *Čas*, April 17, 1947, no. 88, p. 1, and *Pravda*, April 17, 1947, no. 89, pp. 1–2.

89. *Čas*, April 17, 1947, no. 88, p. 1.

90. *Pravda*, April 17, 1947, no. 89, pp. 1–2.

91. Ibid., April 18, 1947, no. 90, p. 3.

92. Kaplan, *Dva retribuční procesy*, Document 37, p. 221.

93. Kaplan, *Dva retribuční procesy*, Document 34, pp. 211–14.

94. See Jelinek, *Parish Republic*, for the most extensive discussion of the differences between Tiso and the radicals; see also Jörg K. Hoensch, "The Slovak Republic, 1938–1939," in Mamatey and Luža, *History*, 271–95, and Ivan Kamenec, *Tragédia politika, kňaza a človeka (Dr. Jozef Tiso 1887–1947)* (Bratislava: Archa, 1998).

95. Mentioned in this respect were several moderates active during the wartime regime, namely Jozef Sivák, Martin Sokol, and Imrich Karvaš.

96. Kaplan, *Dva retribuční procesy*, Document 35, pp. 215–19.

97. Ibid., Document 36, p. 220.

98. The DS claimed the presidium had only ten minutes to look over the lengthy judgment; see *Čas*, April 23, 1947, no. 93, p. 1.

99. Ibid.

100. *Pravda*, April 18, 1947, no. 90, p. 1; the Slovak term *popľuvanie* could be rendered as "spitting on."

101. Ursíny, *Z môjho života*, 123–24.

102. SNA, ÚP SNR, Carton 139, Folder 134, Folios 49–58, SNR presidium meeting of April 16, 1947.

103. Kaplan, *Dva retribuční procesy*, Document 38, pp. 222–24.

104. Karel Kaplan, *Pět capitol o únoru* (Brno: Doplněk, 1997), 228.

105. Kaplan, *Dva retribuční procesy*, 25.

106. Prokop Drtina, *Československo můj osud*, vol. 2, bk. 2, p. 298.

107. For the minutes of the meeting, see Kaplan, *Dva retribuční procesy*, 225–54.

108. Ursíny, in his memoirs, recounts being asked by one member of the Partisan delegation: "Mr. Deputy Chairman, tell me, with whom do you want to go, with the Populist underground, or with us?" Another Partisan representative, however, spoke up for Ursíny as "one of the greatest Partisans" (see Ursíny, *Z môjho života*, 125).

109. The expression "*ani za cenu republiky*"—that is, "even at the price of the republic"—is a reference to a statement made by HSL'S leader Andrej Hlinka at a rally in Trenčín in 1932, where he asserted the degree to which his party would pursue Slovak interests; see Felak, *"At the Price of the Republic,"* 96.

110. "Politika je pánske huncútstvo" was an expression current among Slovaks, rooted in Slovakia's feudal past. It meant "Politics is the lords' mischief," expressing the peasant view that politics was the domain where the lords made their machinations apart from the influence of the common people.

111. Meeting at their synod in Turčianske Teplice, the Slovak Lutheran authorities sent a telegram to Beneš asking for clemency for Tiso; see Vaško, *Neumlčená*, 156.

112. Jan Měchýř, *Slovensko v Československu; Slovensko-české vztahy 1918–1991: Dokumenty, názory, komentáře* (Prague: Práce, 1991).

113. Kaplan, *Dva retribuční procesy*, 27.

114. Barnovský, *Na ceste*, 145n; Kaplan, *Dva retribuční procesy*, 28.

115. Kaplan, *Dva retribuční procesy*, 28; Letz, *Slovensko*, 48.

116. Ursíny, *Z môjho života*, 127.

117. Kaplan, *Dva retribuční procesy*, 29; the motive behind this attempt was to delay Tiso's execution and thus increase the chances that he would ultimately receive clemency.

118. Barnovský, *Na ceste*, 130.

119. For explanations of why the DS acted the way it did at the SNR presidium meeting of April 16, see Barnovský, *Na ceste*, 130; Letz, *Slovensko*, 47–48; Kaplan, *Dva retribuční procesy*, 24–26; Ursíny, *Z môjho života*, 123–24; *Čas*, April 23, 1947, no. 93, p. 1.

120. There are indications that the Communists feared an attempt by Beneš to isolate them in the government by granting Tiso clemency on humanitarian grounds; see Karel Kaplan, *Pět kapitol o únoru* (Brno: Doplněk, 1997), 228.

121. Polák sided with Gottwald and the Communists during the coup of February 1948; after the Communist takeover, Polák was Slovakia's Commissioner of Health and cofounder and one of the leading members of the new Party of Slovak Renewal (Strana Slovenskej Obrody), a pro-Communist offshoot from the DS, until his untimely death in 1951. In 1969, Czechoslovakia posthumously bestowed on him the Order of the Red Star; see *Slovenský biografický slovník*, vol. 4 (Martin: Matica Slovenská, 1990), 504.

122. Ursíny, *Z môjho života*, 124; Rašla also makes this point in his 1990 memoir on the Tiso trial, claiming that it was Polák's intent that the SNR presidium take no position on clemency, in order that the DS not be discredited as a defender of reaction; see Rašla and Žabkay, *Proces*, 50–51.

Chapter 4: Conspiracies

1. SNA, DS, Carton 3, Bundle 161, Folios 39–80; SNA, ÚP SP, Carton 22, Folder 369.

2. František Vnuk, *Dokumenty o postavení katolíckej cirkvi na Slovensku v rokoch, 1945–1948* (Martin: Matica Slovenská, 1998), Documents VI/7 and VI/8, pp. 118–19.

3. Ibid., Document VI/7, pp. 118–19.

4. Ibid. Such visitors, watched and photographed by police agents, continued to come to the cemetery for several weeks, especially over the Pentecost weekend in late May, when police observed several hundred people, mainly from the countryside, praying and singing religious songs at the purported Tiso gravesite; see Vnuk (*Dokumenty*, Documents VI/15 and VI/16), 128–29.

5. *Katolícke noviny*, April 27, 1947, no. 17, p. 3.

6. Ibid., May 4, 1947, no. 18, p. 1.

7. Though it is not clear from the context, Koza's reference to "orphans" could imply that Slovakia's Catholics were orphaned by Tiso's execution, by the loss of a state of their own, by the loss of a party of their own, and/or by the failure of the DS to satisfy their concerns. The sense of the article seems to imply that Koza meant above all that Slovak Catholics were under a regime not their own, living as stepchildren under a state that looked on them as enemies and denied them the right to defend their interests.

8. Michal Barnovský, *Na ceste k monopolu moci: Mocenskopolitické zápasy na Slovensku v rokoch, 1945–1948* (Bratislava: Archa, 1993), 139.

9. Ibid., 136–39, discusses the tensions within the DS.

10. Vnuk, *Dokumenty*, Document V/8, pp. 102–3.

11. Barnovský, *Na ceste*, 136–37.

12. Ibid., 137.

13. See *Čas*, April 30, 1947, no. 99, p. 1, for a refutation by Bugár of a number of rumors, including that Catholics were leaving the DS for the Party of Freedom.

14. Barnovský, *Na ceste*, 137–38.

15. *Čas*, April 23, 1947, no. 93, p.1.

16. SNA, DS, Carton 1, Bundle 38.

17. SNA, DS, Carton 3, Bundle 161, Folios 39–80.

18. That is, apparently, the responsibility for Tiso's execution.

19. SNA, ÚV KSS, Carton 2156, Folder GT-237/28, Folios 1–2.

20. On April 29, the Communist commissioners on Slovakia's Board of Commissioners issued a nearly identical proclamation; see SNA, ÚV KSS, Carton 2156, Folder GT-II-237-29.

21. *Pravda*, April 25, 1947, no. 96, p. 1.

22. Karel Kaplan, *Dva retribuční procesy: Komentované dokumenty, 1946–1947* (Prague: Ústav pro soudobé dějiny ČSAV, 1992), Document 43, pp. 262–67.

23. Some less pressing questions were also a part of the sparring between Communists and Democrats at this meeting. For instance, Ursíny argued with Gottwald and Široký over whether or not Tiso prayed right before his execution. This was an issue because *Čas* reported that he did, while the official report made no mention of any praying. One of *Čas*'s editors was now being investigated for his coverage of the trial.

24. Barnovský, *Na ceste*, 140.

25. Ibid.

26. This was a classic case of what would come to be called "salami tactics," an approach toward opposition employed by Communist parties across East Central Europe after World War II. The term was used in a 1952 speech by Hungarian Communist leader Mátyás Rákosi; see George Schöpflin, "Hungary," in Martin McCauley, ed., *Communist Power in Europe, 1944–1949* (London: Macmillan Press, 1977), 98.

27. *Pravda*, April 6, 1947, no. 80, p. 4; given that the article appeared on Easter, Straka's reference to Pharisees and money changers, some of the negative characters of the scriptural narrative of Christ's life and Passion, was meant to resonate with his Slovak readership. Jesus Christ regularly condemned the hypocrisy of the Pharisees in the harshest of terms, and he drove the money changers off the premises for disgracing God's temple.

28. *Pravda*, June 13, 1947, no. 134, p. 3.

29. SNA, ÚP SNR, Carton 139, Folder 134, Folios 49–58, SNR presidium meeting of April 16, 1947.

30. Mach was on friendly terms with the Communist Novomeský, who was his colleague in journalism. During the war, Mach remained in contact with Novomeský, intervening at Novomeský's behest for arrested Communists, and warning Novomeský of impending danger to him from the Nazis; see Rašla and Žabkay, *Proces*, 55–56; Yeshayahu Jelinek, *The Lust for Power: Nationalism, Slovakia, and the Communists 1918–1948* (Boulder, Colo.: East European Monographs, 1983), 53.

31. For accounts of the wartime Slovak state, which feature the factional conflict between Tiso and the group around Mach and Tuka, see Yeshayahu Jelinek, *The Parish Republic: Hlinka's Slovak People's Party, 1939–1945* (Boulder, Colo.: East European Monographs, 1976), and Jörg K. Hoensch, "The Slovak Republic, 1939–1945," in Mamatey and Luža, *History* (Princeton, N.J.: Princeton University Press, 1973), 271–95.

32. SNA, ÚP SNR, Carton 139, Folder 134, Folios 49–58, SNR presidium meeting of April 16, 1947.

33. Kaplan, *Dva retribuční procesy*, 31.

34. *Čas*, May 17, 1947, no. 112, pp. 1–2.

35. SNA, ÚP SNR, K. 139, Folder 134, Folio 34; it is worth noting that the SNR presidium did not answer this interpellation until January 21, 1948, with a statement that shed much doubt on the medical assessment of Mach; see Kaplan, *Dva retribuční procesy*, Document 47, p. 274.

36. The truth behind Mach's verdict remains hazy, although recently published memoirs allow us to sketch out its rough contours. Though there was widespread perception at the time that Mach's lighter sentence was due to the machinations of

Slovakia's Communists, in fact, other motivations seem to have been at work. Anton Rašla, one of the prosecutors, admits to arranging Mach's fraudulent bill of ill health, in collaboration with Daxner. Daxner may have wanted to repay Mach for favors Mach did him during the war, namely getting Daxner and his sister-in-law released from prison. Or he may have been moved by Mach's testimony and demeanor at the trial. In contrast to the unapologetic Tiso, Mach admitted his mistakes, accepted responsibility for his actions, and conveyed a sense of repentance that even Rašla regarded as sincere, if a bit too theatrical. Mach's testimony brought tears to the eyes of a number of those present, including one of the prosecutors and Daxner's wife. There is also the possibility that Daxner may have feared a greater likelihood of clemency for Tiso if he was convicted alongside Mach, who, though repentant, had more to be repentant for. For a discussion of Mach's trial and verdict, see Rašla and Žabkay, *Process*, 51–56, 102; Ursíny, *Z môjho, života* 128–29; Barnovský, *Na ceste*, 144n.

37. Kaplan, *Dva retribuční procesy*, Document 48, p. 275–83.

38. As a staunch Partisan, Polák was hostile to Mach and upset at the relatively lenient punishment he received. Lettrich (and probably Cvinček as well) were mainly upset with the contrast between Tiso's and Mach's sentence and the alleged chicaneries involved in bringing that about. At this meeting, Lettrich expressed his preference that Mach be sentenced to death, then granted clemency.

39. SNA, ÚP SNR, Carton 6, Folder 16, Folio 12, meeting of May 20, 1947.

40. SNA, ÚV KSS, Carton 2156, GT-236/1, Folios 1–6.

41. On May 26, Daxner issued a statement in response to the interpellation of May 19, in which he tried to document the case that Mach was indeed seriously ill on April 16, but well enough to appear in court by May 6, when he was a witness in a different case, and May 15, when he received his own verdict and sentence; see Kaplan, *Dva retribuční procesy*, Document 46, pp. 270–73, for a copy of Daxner's statement.

42. *Pravda*, May 23, 1947, no. 118, p. 1.

43. Kaplan, *Dva retribuční procesy*, Document 50, p. 287.

44. *Pravda*, May 25, 1947, no. 120, p. 3.

45. Ibid., May 28, 1947, no. 121, p. l.

46. Kaplan, *Dva retribuční procesy*, 31.

47. Ibid., 31–32.

48. Ursíny, *Z môjho života*, 130–31.

49. Kaplan, *Dva retribuční procesy*, Document 51, pp. 288–301.

50. Paragraph 13, article 2, of the retribution decree.

51. Paragraph 99, article 1, of the constitution of 1920.

52. See Kaplan, *Dva retribuční procesy*, pp. 300–301 for the text of the resolution.

53. Ibid., Document 52, pp. 302–3; it is unclear whether Lettrich wrote his letter on June 9, or later and antedated it. Some fuss was made about this question at the government meeting of June 17; Kaplan, *Dva retribuční procesy*, Document 53, pp. 304–15.

54. Kaplan notes that Lettrich's argumentation was correct, from the legal standpoint; Barnovský agrees. See Kaplan, *Dva retribuční procesy*, 32, and Barnovský, *Na ceste*, 135.

55. Kaplan, *Dva retribuční procesy*, pp. 304–15.

56. Karol Sidor was a leading HSLʼS activist of the 1930s, among other things the chief editor of the party's principal daily newspaper. His political career was cut short when Nazi German pressure forced him to resign the position of interior minister in the government of the Slovak Republic in April 1945. He spent the wartime years in Rome as Slovakia's representative at the Vatican, and remained in Italy after the war, where he was active in émigré circles favoring the restoration of Slovak sovereignty.

57. Kaplan, *Dva retribuční procesy*, Document 54, pp. 316–32.

58. Polák reported that he was no longer on speaking terms with Daxner, who, among other things, had hung up the telephone on him; see Kaplan, *Dva retribuční procesy*, 320.

59. For a discussion of the school law, see Červinka, "Príspevok," 19–65.

60. Červinka, "Príspevok," 54–55

61. *Katolícke noviny*, July 6, 1947, no. 27, p. 5.

62. Červinka, "Príspevok," 47.

63. *Nové slovo*, April 19, 1947, no. 16, pp. 249–50; *Pravda*, April 10, 1947, no. 83, p. 4; and *Pravda*, September 3, 1947, no. 201, p. 3.

64. *Nové slovo*, April 19, 1947, no. 16, pp. 249–50.

65. *Pravda*, April 10, 1947, no. 83, p. 4; *Nové slovo*, April 19, 1947, no. 16, pp. 249–50.

66. Ibid.

67. *Pravda*, May 22, 1947, no. 117, p. 1; *Pravda*, June 13, 1947, no. 134, p. 3.

68. *Katolícke noviny*, July 6, 1947, no. 27, p. 5.

69. Ibid., June 1, 1947, no. 22, p. 4; *Katolícke noviny*, June 8, 1947, no. 23, pp. 3–4.

70. The council in this respect was clearly appealing to the third of the freedoms pronounced by American president Franklin Delano Roosevelt in his annual message to Congress on January 6, 1941: "freedom of every person to worship God in his own way." With respect to the Atlantic Charter, there is virtually nothing in that joint declaration of August 14, 1941, by Roosevelt and Winston Churchill that seems applicable to the educational conflict in Slovakia.

71. See *Katolícke noviny*, July 15, 1947, no. 28, p. 1; *Katolícke noviny*, August 3, 1947, no. 31, pp. 1–2; and *Katolícke noviny*, August 17, 1947, no. 33, pp. 1–2.

72. *Katolícke noviny*, July 15, 1947, no. 28. p. l.

73. Ibid., August 17, 1947, no. 33, pp. 1–2.

74. At this time, parochial education was legal in the Czech lands. Its elimination in Slovakia was the result of a decision by the Slovak National Council made during the Slovak National Uprising; there were no parallel circumstances, or parallel decision, in the Czech lands.

75. Červinka, "Príspevok," pp. 33–61.

76. *Katolícke noviny*, May 25, 1947, no. 21, p. 2; *Pravda*, May 22, 1947, no. 117, p. 1.

77. *Nové prúdy*, August 3, 1947, no. 18, pp. 365–67.

78. *Nové prúdy*, September 14, 1947, no. 21, pp. 447–50.

79. Červinka, "Príspevok," 57

80. Ibid., 57–61; a report published in the journal *Školství a osvěta* in June 1947 included Ursíny as a member of the commission, though it appears that he did not take part.

81. For coverage of Gottwald's comments and commentary on them, see *Čas*, June 4, 1947, no. 126, p. 1; *Katolícke noviny*, June 15, 1947, no. 24, p. 5; and *Nové slovo*, June 7, 1947, no. 23, pp. 359–60.

82. Barnovský, *Na ceste*, pp. 140–42; *Pravda*, June 14, 1947, no. 135, pp. 1, 3; Karel Kaplan, *Nekrvavá revoluce* (Toronto: Sixty-Eight Publishers, 1985), 93–94.

83. Kaplan, *Nekrvavá revoluce* (Toronto, 1985), 394n.

84. Joseph Rothschild, *Return to Diversity: A Political History of East Central Europe since World War II*, 2nd ed. (Oxford: Oxford University Press, 1993), p. 100.

85. *Pravda*, June 14, 1947, no. 135, pp. 1, 3; Letz, *Slovensko*, 55; SNA, DS, Carton 4, Folder 19753/78, Folios 117–18.

86. Charles Gati, "From Liberation to Revolution," in *A History of Hungary*, ed. Peter F. Sugar (Bloomington: Indiana University Press, 1990), 371.

87. Letz, *Slovensko*, 54.

88. Karel Kaplan, *Pravda o Ceskoslovensku, 1945–1948* (Prague: Panorama, 1990), 187.

89. Barnovský, *Na ceste*, 140; Letz, *Slovensko*, 54.

90. Because the report mentions Tiso's execution, which occurred on April 18, but does not mention the exposure of the "antistate conspiracy," which occurred on September 16, it is safe to date it sometime between April and September 1947. Regarding Straka, his fingerprints seem to be all over the report. He was the KSS's top expert on the Catholic Church, and the document was clearly the work of someone who knew Slovakia's Catholic life from the inside, given its intimate acquaintance with those Catholics who could or could not be trusted. Even more telling, the report proposes a particular candidate for editor of *Katolícke noviny*, "if I myself am not accepted." Since Straka had long had ambitions of running *Katolícke noviny*, and the KSS wanted him on its board as their man, he was almost certainly the author of the report.

91. SNA, ÚV KSS, Carton 2158, Folder G-254II, Bundle 2, Folios 1–2.

92. *Ženská jednota*.

93. Pavel Gojdič was Greek Catholic bishop of Prešov since 1940; Vasil' Hopko was his assistant; Ambróz Lazík was the general vicar of the apostolic administrature and then apostolic administrator in the immediate postwar period; see *Slovenský biografický slovník* (Martin: Matica slovenská, 1987).

94. See *Pravda*, June 10, 1947, no. 131, p. 1; June 13, 1947, no. 134, p. 3; June 6, 1947, no. 137, p. 1; and *Nové slovo*, July 12, 1947, no. 28, pp. 437–39.

95. *Čas*, June 4, 1947, no. 126, p. 9.

96. Ibid., June 24, 1947, no. 142, pp. 1, 3.

97. *Nové prúdy*, June 22, 1947, no. 15, pp. 283–85.

98. Indeed, Communists did profess from time to time that they did not lump all former Populists and Hlinka Guardists together; see *Pravda*, July 16, 1947, no. 161, p. 3.

99. Letz, *Slovensko*, 55–56.

100. Barnovský, *Na ceste*, 193–94.

101. The Banderovci got their name from their leader, the anti-Communist Ukrainian Stefan Bandera.

102. *Čas*, August 23, 1947, p. 1.

103. *Sväz vojakov Slovenského národného povstania*, or *SVOJPOV*; Barnovský, *Na ceste*, 193–94.

104. Barnovský, *Na ceste*, 194.

105. *Katolícke noviny*, July 27, 1947, no. 30, pp. 1–2.

106. Jaroslav Pelikan, in *Mary Through the Centuries: Her Place in the History of Culture* (New Haven, Conn.: Yale University Press, 1996), 178, 183, notes the caution and prudence with which the Catholic Church has historically treated such apparitions.

107. Anton Hlinka, *Sila slabých a slabosť silných* (Trnava: Spolok Svätého Vojtecha, 1990), 25; Zúbek, "Katolícka cirkev," 160; Čarnogurský, *Svedok*, 257; see also Koza's article "Sú mariánske púte sabatážou vládneho programu" ("Are Pilgrimages to Marienka a Sabotaging of the Government Program"), *Katolícke noviny* 40 (October 6, 1946): 3.

108. The term "millionaires' tax," more rhetorical than real, was applied to a number of proposals aimed at increasing state revenues by extraordinary taxes on the propertied classes. One Communist proposal, for example, entailed taxing property worth in excess of 400,000 crowns, which at the time was the equivalent of US$8,000; Kaplan, *Short March*, 81.

109. *Nové slovo*, August 29, 1947, nos. 35–36, pp. 560–61.

110. *Pravda*, September 14, 1947, no. 211, p. 1.

111. SNA, ÚV KSS, Carton 789, meeting of June 22, 1946, and SNA, ÚV KSS, Carton 1, meeting of June 25, 1946.

112. Letz, *Slovensko*, 45.

113. Jozef Jablonický, *Podoby násilia* (Bratislava: Kalligram, 2000), 90.

114. SNA, ÚV KSS, Carton 789, meetings of September 20, November 11, and December 12, 1946.

115. SNA, ÚV KSS, Carton 789, meeting of December 12, 1946.

116. SNA, DS, Carton 3, Bundle 167, Folios 33–45.

117. *Partizán*, the organ of the Union of Slovak Partisans, an organization with close ties to the Sixth Department, published the letter in its December 8, 1946 issue, prompting Kempný to file a complaint in court.

118. For example, Ďurčanský opposed the April Agreement, while Kempný and Bugár were among its architects.

119. Jablonický, *Podoby*, 61.

120. Ibid., 62.

121. *Nové slovo*, January 11, 1947, no. 2, pp. 20–21; January 18, 1947, no. 3, pp. 39–42; February 8, 1947, no. 6, pp. 86–88.

122. Ibid., February 8, 1947, no. 6, pp. 86–88.

123. Jablonický, *Podoby*, 62–63; worthy of mention is Kempný's remark in the letter that the economic position he held in the Slovak state was "no more significant than the secretariat of the Union of Freight Carriers, or the editors-in-chief of [the journal]

Budovateľ," positions held by Husák and Novomeský, respectively, during the early years of the Slovak state.

124. SNA, DS, Carton 3, Bundle 169, Folio 39.

125. *Čas*, February 4, 1947, no. 28, p. 2.

126. *Nové slovo*, June 14, 1947, no. 24, pp. 378–80.

127. Ibid., June 28, 1947, no. 26, pp. 405–8.

128. Jablonický, *Podoby*, 95–96; *Nové slovo*, June 28, 1947, no. 26, pp. 405–8.

129. The veracity of Kempný's earlier denials that he had "met" with Ďurčanský hinges on what "met" meant—it is unlikely that Kempný had any personal, one-on-one meetings with Ďurčanský, nor attended meetings called by him. He was, however, present at some of the same meetings as Ďurčanský.

130. *Pravda*, May 22, 1947, no. 117, p. 1; in a speech in Parliament in July, KSS Central Committee member and parliamentary representative Karol Bacílek called for Staško's expulsion from both Parliament and the DS; see also *Pravda*, July 16, 1947, no. 161, p. 3.

131. Barnovský, *Na ceste*, 197; see also *Pravda*, June 14, 1947, no. 135, pp. 1, 3.

132. SNA, DS, Carton 3, Bundle 167, Folios 95–97; see also *Pravda*, September 27, 1947, pp. 1–2.

133. Jablonický, *Podoby*, 67.

134. Ibid., 67–68; the visitor was Rudolf Komandera, discussed below. Jablonický describes the three visits Komandera made to Kempný's summer cottage, twice showing up while Kempný was out of town and the third time given the cold shoulder by Kempný who would not let him past the gate.

135. *Nové slovo*, February 8, 1947, no. 6, pp. 86–88; June 28, 1947, no. 26, pp. 405–8; (see also *Nové slovo*, January 11, 1947, no. 2, p. 20; January 18, 1947, no. 3, p. 40).

136. Ibid., June 7, 1947, no. 23, pp. 364–65.

137. SNA, DS, Carton 1, extracts from a speech by Bugár given at a working conference of the DS in Zlaté Moravce on February 23, 1947, as reported by a confidant of the KSS; SNA, DS, Carton 3, Bundle 167, Folios 98–104.

138. SNA, DS, Carton 50, Folder 403-50-1, Folio 35.

139. Ibid., Carton 99, Folder 403-99-6.

140. Ibid., Carton 6, Folio 772; see also SNA, DS, Carton 2, Bundle 138, DS circular of September 27, 1947.

141. Kaplan, *Short March*, 87.

142. Giuliano Procacci, ed., *The Cominform: Minutes of the Three Conferences 1947/1948/1949* (Milan: Feltrinelli Editore, 1994), 285; lest his remark be seen as an attack on the rights of the Slovak nation, Slánský added that "a situation has now come about in which the Slovak people are unable to overcome with their own forces alone the emboldened forces of fascism and reaction," thus needing the help of "Czech progressive forces."

143. Letz, *Slovensko*, 56–57; *Pravda*, September 16, 1947, no. 212, p. 1.

144. Barnovský, *Na ceste*, 194.

145. SNA, ÚV KSS, Carton 789, meeting of September 15, 1947.

146. *Čas*, September 23, 1947, no. 217, p. 3; SNA, ÚAV SNF, 1945–1948, Carton 1, Folder 3, Folios 32–36, meeting of September 22, 1947.

147. *Čas*, September 24, 1947, no. 218, p. 2.

148. *Pravda*, September 24, 1947, no. 219, pp. 1–2.

149. SNA, ÚV KSS, Carton 789, meetings of September 29, 1947; October 11, 1947; and October 18, 1947.

150. SNA, ÚV KSS, Carton 2151, Folder GT-212/5; Communist leaflets also charged the DS with economic sabotage, profiteering, black marketeering, defense of German and Hungarian rural magnates from land reform and of millionaires from the "millionaires' tax."

151. *Čas*, September 17, 1947, no. 212, p. 1.

152. Ibid., September 18, 1947, no. 213, p. 1; September 19, 1947, no. 214, p. 1; September 25, 1947, no. 219, p. 1; September 28, 1947, no. 222, p. 1.

153. Ibid., October 5, 1947, no. 228, pp. 1, 3.

154. Ibid., September 19, 1947, no. 214, p. 1; for example, the bookseller Tvrdý, a member of the local KSS organization in Bytča.

155. See, for example, *Čas*, September 20, 1947, no. 215, p. 1, and September 21, 1947, no. 216, p. 1.

156. *Pravda*, September 19, 1947, no. 215, pp. 1–2.

157. Jablonický, *Podoby*, 104.

158. Barnovský, *Na ceste*, 197–98.

159. Ibid., 198; Jablonický, *Podoby*, 104.

160. Barnovský, *Na ceste*, 198.

161. Ibid., 198.

162. The Interior Ministry, wanting to get its hands on Kempný and Bugár, ordered police to secure the entrances of Pankrác prison and the court building in Prague, lest the men turn themselves in to the Ministry of Justice. Kempný and Bugár, meanwhile, had left Prague for Bratislava by train the day before, getting off in Břeclav in Moravia. They then went by car to Lamač, outside Bratislava, and, upon hearing that they had lost the vote in parliament, hurried to turn themselves in at the Palace of Justice in Bratislava, thus sparing themselves the experience of being in the custody of the security police; see Jablonický, *Podoby*, 108–10, for an account of this.

163. *Čas*, October 18, 1947, no. 239, pp. 1, 3.

164. *Pravda*, October 18, 1947, no. 240, pp. 1, 3.

165. Barnovský, *Na ceste*, 198.

166. For the most detailed discussion of the Obuch affair, see Jablonický, *Podoby*, 76–86; see also Barnovský, *Na ceste*, 195, 199–201, and Letz, *Slovensko*, 156–60; the discussion on the Obuch affair herein is based on these sources, unless otherwise indicated.

167. See SNA, DS, Carton 3, Bundle 150, Folio 2.

168. *Pravda*, October 4, 1947, no. 228, p. 1.

169. *Čas*, October 8, 1947, no. 230, p. 1.

170. Ursíny, *Z môjho života*, 137; Ursíny discusses the Obuch affair on pp. 134–37.

171. See, for example, Barnovský, *Na ceste*, 196–201; Jablonický, *Podoby*, 104; Letz, *Slovensko*, 108–28; see also SNA, DS, Carton 2, Bundle 170, Folios 57–63, for a letter sent by Michal Zibrín to Lettrich and Böhm of December 8, 1947, in which Zibrín outlines a number of abuses by Communists in the security and judicial apparati.

172. Barnovský, *Na ceste*, 196–97.

173. *Katolícke noviny*, September 21, 1947, no. 38, p. 2.

174. Ibid., September 28, 1947, no. 39, p. 1.

175. Ibid., October 26, 1947, no. 43, pp. 1, 3.

Chapter 5: Continuing Crisis

1. SNA, ÚV KSS, Carton 789, meetings of September 29, October 11, 18, 25, 1947.

2. See SNA, ÚV, KSS, Carton 789, meeting of October 11, 1947, for the enumeration of these goals.

3. SNA, ÚV, KSS, Carton 789, meetings of October 11 and October 18, 1947; the committee consisted of Husák, Bašťovanský, Friš, and František Zupka, all important Slovak Communists.

4. See SNA, ÚAV SNF, Carton 3, Folder 37, for the text of the declaration; see *Pravda*, November 1, 1947, no. 248, p. 1, for press coverage of the congress.

5. SNA, ÚP SNR, Carton 7, Folder 11, meeting of November 3, 1947; among those resigning, Husák included himself along with the board's other four Communists (Novomeský, Ján Púll, Jozef Šoltész, and Kazimír Bezek) as well as nonparty Commissioner of the Interior Ferjenčík, all of whom resigned on October 31. Regarding the seventh resignee, Husák claimed that Lettrich had informed him on October 16 that Democratic Commissioner of Food Filo had resigned, and that on October 17 Democratic Deputy Chairman of the Board Fraštacký told Husák of his own resignation, but revoked it on October 21. The DS denied that any Democrats had resigned.

6. *Sociálna demokracia na Slovensku*; founded in early 1946 under the name Party of Work (*Strana práce*), it again changed its name, to Czechoslovak Social Democratic Party in Slovakia (*Československá strana sociálnodemokratická na Slovensku*) in November 1947; see Ľubomír Lipták, *Politické strany na Slovensku, 1860–1989* (Bratislava: Archa, 1992), 275–80, for more on this party

7. *Čas*, November 4, 1947, no. 251, p. 1; the council was coordinating its activity with the KSS, and fulfilled its assigned role as tribune for the Congress and ultimatum-giver.

8. *Čas*, November 4, 1947, no. 251, pp. 1, 3; interestingly, as *Pravda* pointed out, Böhm alone among the Democratic commissioners did not sign the statement; see *Pravda*, November 5, 1947, no. 253, pp. 1–2.

9. For the text of the statement, see *Pravda*, November 4, 1947, no. 252, p. 3.

10. Michal Barnovský, *Na ceste k monopolu moci: Mocenskopolitické zápasy na Slovensku v rokoch, 1945–1948* (Bratislava: Archa, 1993), 213.

11. SNA, ÚV KSS, Carton 789, meeting of November 10, 1947; *Čas*, November 18, no. 263, pp. 1, 3. For a discussion of the Communist inspired Congress of Peasants held in Bratislava on November 14, where protestors attempted to enter the Commission of Agriculture building to "settle accounts" with Kvetko, and where there were calls for

"death to Lettrich," see Róbert Letz, *Slovensko v rokoch 1945–1948 na ceste ku komunistickej totalite* (Bratislava: Ústredie slovenskej kresťanskej inteligencie, 1994), 62.

12. SNA, ÚP SNR, Carton 7, Folder 12, November 10, 1947, Folios 3–8; Letz, *Slovensko*, 61; *Pravda*, November 6, 1947, no. 254, p. 1.

13. Barnovský, *Na ceste*, 213.

14. *Čas*, November 12, 1947, no. 258, p. 1.

15. For evidence of the Communist position on these issues, see the minutes of the meetings of the KSS's Central Committee of November 8, November 9, November 10, and November 14, 1947, in SNA, ÚV KSS, Carton 789; SNA, ÚV KSS, Carton 2151, Folder GT-211/3, Folios 1–3; and *Pravda*, November 12, 1947, no. 259, pp. 1–2; see also SNA, ÚP SNR, Carton 7, Folder 12, November 10, 1947, Folios 3–8; for the DS position, see coverage of the negotiations in *Čas*, November 12, 1947, no. 258, p. 1, November 18, 1947, no. 263, pp. 1, 3.

16. In a letter to Gottwald of November 10, Lettrich expressed an openness on the part of the DS to having the Party of Freedom take the Commissions of Food or Justice as part of a comprehensive compromise. Presumably, if the Party of Freedom got Food, the DS would hold on to Justice; see *Čas*, November 12, 1947, no. 258, p. 1.

17. *Čas*, November 18, 1947, no. 263, pp. 1, 3.

18. *Nové prúdy*, November 23, 1947, no. 26, p. 598.

19. *Nové slovo*, November 7, 1947, nos. 44–45, pp. 688–89.

20. *Pravda*, November 6, 1947, no. 254, p. 1; *Pravda*, November 9, 1947, no. 257, p. 1.

21. *Pravda*, November 12, 1947, no. 259, pp. 1–2.

22. Barnovský, *Na ceste*, 213, 216.

23. Letz, *Slovensko*, 62–63; Barnovský, *Na ceste*, 217.

24. Barnovský, *Na ceste*, 217.

25. SNA, ÚV KSS, Carton 2151, Folder GT-211/3, Folios 1–3; see also *Pravda*, November 9, 1947, no. 257, pp. 1–2.

26. Letz, *Slovensko*, 63.

27. Ibid., 63–64.

28. Barnovský, *Na ceste*, 221.

29. Ibid.

30. *Katolícke noviny*, November 2, 1947, pp. 1, 3.

31. Ibid., October 26, 1947, pp. 1, 3.

32. Ibid., November 2, 1947, p. 1.

33. Ibid., February 22, 1948, p. 1.

34. SNA, DS, Carton 4, Folio 197.

35. Ibid., Carton 3, Bundle 170, Folios 58–63.

36. Barnovský, *Na ceste*, 219.

37. Ibid., 218–19.

38. It should be noted that Ševčík apparently did intelligence work for the Soviet Union, both during and after the war; interestingly, the Slovak Communists only learned of this when Ševčík blabbed about it several times while drunk; see Barnovský, *Na ceste*, 219.

39. See Barnovský, *Na ceste*, 219–22, for the details of Pietor's intrigues.

40. Vilinskij was evidently reporting on Pietor to the security police and urging Communists to work with him on the grounds that he would do what they wanted. Nonetheless, Gottwald had other plans for dealing with the DS and did not take Pietor seriously; see Barnovský, 222.

41. Barnovský, *Na ceste*, 220–21.

42. Ibid., 221.

43. As Kaplan points out, Gottwald himself stated, "We prepared [for] February 1948 from 1945 on and particularly from 1947"; see Karel Kaplan, *The Short March: The Communist Takeover in Czechoslovakia, 1945–1948* (London: C. Hurst, 1987), 105

44. SNA, ÚV, KSS, Carton 789, meeting of February 13, 1948; ÚV KSS, Carton 2160, Folder GT-272/11, Folio 1.

45. Barnovský, *Na ceste*, 232.

46. SNA, ÚV KSS, Carton 789, meeting of January 9, 1948.

47. Barnovský, *Na ceste*, 232.

48. *Nové slovo*, January 10, 1948, no. 2, p. 24.

49. *Čas*, January 30, 1948, no. 24, p. 1; February 5, 1948, no. 29, p. 1

50. *Nové slovo*, February 7, 1948, no. 6, p. 83.

51. *Katolícke noviny*, February 22, 1948, no. 8, p. 1.

52. *Čas*, February 5, 1948, no. 29, p. 1.

53. SNA, ÚV KSS, Carton 789, meeting of January 9, 1948.

54. For information on Kyselý and his efforts to found a Catholic political party, see *Čas*, January 27, 1948, no. 21, p. 2; *Nové prúdy*, January 18, 1948, no. 2, pp. 17–19; and *Pravda*, January 27, 1948, no. 21, p. 3.

55. *Čas*, January 27, 1948, no. 21, p. 2.

56. *Pravda*, January 27, 1948, no. 21, p. 3; January 28, 1948, no. 22, pp. 1–2; see also *Čas*, January 27, 1948, no. 21, p. 2.

57. *Pravda*, January 27, 1948, no. 21, p. 3.

58. *Čas*, January 25, 1948, no. 20, pp. 1–2; January 27, 1948, no. 21, pp. 3–4; January 27, 1948, no. 21, p. 5.

59. For the text of Lettrich's speech, see *Čas*, January 27, 1948, no. 21, pp. 3–4.

60. See *Čas*, January 30, 1948, no. 24, p. 2, for the resolutions of the Cultural Commission of the DS Party Congress.

61. Barnovský, *Na ceste*, 234.

62. *Čas*, January 25, 1948, no. 20, pp. 1–2; January 27, 1948, no. 21, p. 2; January 27, 1948, no. 21, p. 5; both Ursíny's opening and closing speech mentioned the need for interconfessional harmony.

63. *Čas*, January 27, 1948, no. 21, pp. 1–2.

64. *Nové slovo*, January 24, 1948, no. 4, p. 56.

65. *Čas*, February 13, 1948, no. 36, p. 1; February 14, 1948, no. 37, p. 1.

66. Ibid., December 6, 1947, no. 279, p. 1.

67. *Katolícke noviny*, November 2, 1947, no. 44, pp. 1, 3.

68. *Nové slovo*, Christmas Day, 1947, nos. 51–52, pp. 809–10.

69. SNA, ÚV KSS, Carton 2157, Folder GT-248, Bundle 5.

70. *Čas*, February 4, 1948, no. 28, p. 1.

71. Ibid.

72. *Pravda*, February 19, 1948, no. 42, p. 3.

73. It should be noted that, while Catholics and Communists argued over how the modus vivendi should be interpreted, there was almost unanimous agreement among Slovaks that it was a good thing. On the twentieth anniversary of the agreement, in early February 1948, both the Democratic and the Communist press praised the modus vivendi for helping to consolidate Czechoslovakia both domestically and internationally. As Straka noted in *Pravda*, it gave Slovak clergy their own Theological Faculty in Bratislava, ending the need to train Slovak clergy in Vienna or Budapest; see *Nové slovo*, February 7, 1948, no. 6, 86–87; *Čas*, February 3, 1948, no. 27, pp. 1–2.

74. *Katolícke noviny*, November 2, 1947, no. 44, pp. 1, 3.

75. *Nové slovo*, January 24, 1948, no. 4, p. 57; *Čas*, January 30, 1948, no. 24, p. 1.

76. *Čas*, November 18, 1947, no. 263, pp. 1, 3; *Nové prúdy*, January 18, 1948, no. 2, pp. 17–19.

77. *Pravda*, November 19, 1947, no. 265, p. 1.

78. SNA, ÚP SNR, Carton 8, Folder 3, meeting of January 26, 1948.

79. *Čas*, January 10, 1948, no. 7, p. 1.

80. *Nové prúdy*, January 18, 1948, no. 2, pp. 17–19.

81. *Nové slovo*, January 31, 1948, no. 5, p. 69.

82. *Čas*, January 14, 1948, no. 10, p. 2.

83. *Nové prúdy*, November 9, 1948, no. 25, pp. 551–52.

84. *Nové prúdy*, January 18, 1948, no. 2, p. 27; January 25, 1948, nos. 3–4, pp. 36–38; and February 1, 1948, no. 5, pp. 57–58.

85. *Katolícke noviny*, November 23, 1947, no. 47, p. 1.

86. *Čas*, December 6, 1947, no. 279, p. 1.

87. *Nové slovo*, Christmas Day, 1947, nos. 51–52, pp. 801–2.

88. Kaplan, *Short March*, 105.

89. Ibid., 129.

90. Barnovský, *Na ceste*, 229–30.

91. Letz, *Slovensko*, 66.

92. *Ústredná rada odborov.*

93. Barnovský, *Na ceste*, 234.

94. Kaplan, *Short March*, 140.

95. Ibid., 145–46.

96. Ibid., 164–67, for a discussion of the government's meeting of February 13.

97. Ibid., 167–70.

98. *Pravda*, February 29, 1948, no. 50, pp. 5, 7.

99. Ibid., February 19, 1948, no. 42, p. 1; February 20, 1948, no. 43, p. 1.

100. Barnovský, *Na ceste*, 239.

101. Kaplan, *Short March*, 174.

102. Ibid., 171; *Čas*, February 22, 1948, no. 44, pp. 1–2; *Pravda*, February 29, 1948, no. 50, pp. 5, 7.

103. Letz, *Slovensko*, 67.

104. Kaplan, *Short March*, 175.

105. Ibid., 176.

106. *Čas*, February 22, 1948, no. 44, pp. 1–2.

107. See footnote 1 of the preface herein for a number of works on this period and issue.

108. Barnovský, *Na ceste*, 239.

109. The basic events which transpired in Prague and across Czechoslovakia in conjunction with the Communist takeover are well covered elsewhere, as noted in footnote 1 of the preface. The discussion therefore will focus chiefly on events in Slovakia, particularly to the extent they pertained to the DS and in particular the Catholic activists within it.

110. Barnovský, *Na ceste*, 240; SNA, DS, Carton 3, Bundle 166, Folios 6 and 7.

111. Ibid., 239.

112. Ibid., 239–40.

113. Letz, *Slovensko*, 69.

114. *Pravda*, February 23, 1948, no. 45a, p. 1.

115. Ibid., February 24, 1948, no. 46, p. 2.

116. SNA, DS Carton 3, Bundle 166, Folios 7 and 8.

117. Ibid., Folios 1–3.

118. Ibid., Folio 4.

119. See ibid., Folio 10, for a description of the removal of Commissioner Jozef Styk from his position as commissioner of agriculture by Husák and the police.

120. SNA, DS, Bundle 166, Folio 5.

121. Also indicted was Ursíny's brother-in-law and Democratic Commissioner of Finance Matej Josko.

122. Lichner at the time was an official in the Ministry of National Defense.

123. Barnovský, *Na ceste*, 244–45.

124. Ibid., 243–44.

125. Collaboration with the Communists in 1948 did not spare Ševčík from the purges; he was imprisoned from 1952 to 1960, and rehabilitated after his death in 1965; see *Slovenský biografický slovník*.

126. *Pravda*, February 28, 1948, no. 49, p. 1.

127. *Nové slovo*, March 13, 1948, no. 11, p. 162.

128. Letz, *Slovensko*, 70.

129. Barnovský, *Na ceste*, 246.

130. SNA, ÚV KSS, Carton 2151, Folder GT-214/2.

131. *Pravda*, February 29, 1948, no. 50, pp. 5, 7.

132. Ibid., February 27, 1948, no. 48, p. 3.

133. *Katolícke noviny*, March 7, 1948, no. 10, p. 1.

134. Peter Kenez, *Hungary from the Nazis to the Soviets: The Establishment of the Communist Regime in Hungary, 1944–1948* (Cambridge: Cambridge University Press, 2006), 176.

135. See Michael Phayer, *The Catholic Church and the Holocaust, 1930–1945* (Bloomington: Indiana University Press, 2000), 34–35, for examples of Catholic clergy who were implicated in Croatia's fascist Ustaša regime, and Kevin P. Spicer, *Resisting the Third Reich: The Catholic Clergy in Hitler's Berlin* (DeKalb: Northern Illinois University Press, 2004), 139–59, where Spicer discusses the pro-Nazi "brown priests."

SELECTED BIBLIOGRAPHY

Archive Collections

Slovenský Národný Archív, Bratislava (SNA)

Demokratická Strana (DS)

Národný Súd (NS)

Úrad Predsedníctva Slovenskej Národnej Rady (ÚP SNR)

Ústredný Akčný Výbor Slovenského Národného Frontu (ÚAV SNF)

Ústredný Výbor Komunistickej Strany Slovenska (ÚV KSS)

Štátny Oblastný Archív, Bratislava (ŠOBA, Bratislava)

Národný Súd (NS)

U.S. Department of State, Decimal Files

Records of the U.S. Department of State Relating to the Internal Affairs of Czechoslovakia, 1945–49

Articles and Books

Abrams, Bradley F. "The Politics of Retribution: The Trial of Jozef Tiso." *East European Politics and Societies* 10, no. 2 (Spring 1996): 255–92.

———. *The Struggle for the Soul of the Nation: Czech Culture and the Rise of Communism.* Harvard Cold War Studies Book Series. Lanham, Md.: Rowman and Littlefield, 2004.

Barnovský, Michal. *Na ceste k monopolu moci: Mocenskopolitické zápasy na Slovensku v rokoch, 1945–1948.* Bratislava: Archa, 1993.

———. *Od diktatúry k diktatúre.* Bratislava: Veda, 1995.

Barnovský, Michal, and Edita Ivaničková. *Prvé povojnové voľby v strednej a juhovýchodnej Európe.* Bratislava: Veda, 1998.

Beneš, Václav L. "Czechoslovak Democracy and Its Problems." In *A History of the Czechoslovak Republic, 1918–1948,* ed. Victor S. Mamatey and Radomír Luža, 39–98. Princeton, N.J.: Princeton University Press, 1973.

Čarnogurský, Pavol. *Svedok čias.* Bratislava: USPO, 1997.

Čavojský, Rudo. *Spomienky kresťanského odborára.* Bratislava: LÚČ, 1996.

Červinka, Jaroslav. "Príspevok k histórii bojov o jednotnú a štátnu školu v Československu v rokoch 1945–1948." In *Rozvoj spoločnosti a výchova,* ed. Ondrej Baláž, 19–65. Bratislava: Veda. 1977.

Conway, John S. "The Churches, the Slovak State and the Jews 1939–1945." *Slavonic and East European Review* 52, no. 126 (January 1974): 85–112.

Drtina, Prokop. *Československo můj osud.* Toronto: Sixty-Eight Publishers, 1982.

Ďurica, Milan S. *Dejiny Slovenska a Slovákov.* Bratislava: Slovenské pedagogické nakladateľstvo, 1995.

Felak, James Ramon. *"At the Price of the Republic": Hlinka's Slovak People's Party, 1929–1938.* Pittsburgh: University of Pittsburgh Press, 1994.

Gati, Charles. "From Liberation to Revolution, 1945–1956." In *A History of Hungary,* ed. Peter F. Sugar, Péter Hanák, and Tibor Frank, 368–83. Bloomington: Indiana University Press, 1990.

Held, Joseph, ed. *The Columbia History of Eastern Europe in the Twentieth Century.* New York: Columbia University Press, 1992.

Hlavová, Viera. "Parlamentné voľby na Slovensku v roku 1946." In *Prvé povojnové voľby v strednej a juhovýchodnej Európe,* ed. Michal Barnovský and Edita Ivaničková, 79–88. Bratislava: Veda, 1998.

Hlinka, Anton. *Sila slabých a slabosť silných.* Bratislava: Tatran, 1990.

Hoensch, Jörg K. "The Slovak Republic, 1939–1945." In *A History of the Czechoslovak Republic, 1918–1948,* ed. Victor S. Mamatey and Radomír Luža, 271–95. Princeton, N.J.: Princeton University Press, 1973.

Husák, Gustav. *Zápas o zajtrajšok.* Bratislava: Nakladateľstvo Obroda, 1948.

Ignotus, Paul. "The First Two Communist Takeovers of Hungary: 1919 and 1948." In *The Anatomy of Communist Takeovers,* ed. Thomas T. Hammond, 385–98. New Haven, Conn.: Yale University Press, 1975.

Jablonický, Jozef. *Podoby násilia.* Bratislava: Kalligram, 2000.

Janics, Kálman. *Czechoslovak Policy and the Hungarian Minority, 1945–1948* (War and Society in East Central Europe: The Effects of World War II, vol. 9). New York: Social Science Monographs, 1982.

———. *Roky bez domoviny: Maďarská menšina na Slovensku po druhej svetovej vojne, 1945–1948.* Budapest: Püski, 1994.

Jelinek, Yeshayahu. *The Lust for Power: Nationalism, Slovakia, and the Communists, 1918–1948.* Boulder, Colo.: East European Monographs, 1983.

———. *The Parish Republic: Hlinka's Slovak People's Party, 1939–1945.* Boulder, Colo.: East European Quarterly, 1976.

Johnson, Owen. *Slovakia, 1918–1938: Education and the Making of a Nation.* Boulder, Colo.: East European Monographs, 1985.

Kamenec, Ivan. *Slovenský stát (1939–1945).* Prague: Anomal, 1992.

———. *Tragédia politika, kňaza a človeka (Dr. Jozef Tiso, 1887–1947).* Bratislava: Archa, 1998.

Kamenec, Ivan, Vilém Prečan, and Stanislav Škorvánek, eds. *Vatikán a Slovenská Republika (1939–1945): Dokumenty.* Bratislava: Slovak Academic Press, 1992.

Kaplan, Karel. *Der kurze Marsch: Kommunistische Machtübernahme in der Tschechoslowakei, 1945–1948.* Munich: R. Oldenbourg Verlag, 1981.

———. *Die politischen Prozesse in der Tschechoslowakei, 1948–1954*. Munich: R. Oldenbourg Verlag, 1986.

———. *Dva retribuční procesy: Komentované dokumenty, 1946–1947*. Prague: Ústav pro soudobé dějiny ČSAV, 1992.

———. *Nekrvavá revoluce*. Toronto: Sixty-Eight Publishers, 1985.

———. *Pět capitol o únoru*. Brno: Doplněk, 1997.

———. *Poslední rok prezidenta: Edvard Beneš v roce 1948*. Prague: Ústav pro soudobé dějiny AV ČR, 1993.

———. *Pravda o Ceskoslovensku, 1945–1948*. Prague: Panorama, 1990.

———. *The Short March: The Communist Takeover in Czechoslovakia, 1945–1948*. London: C. Hurst, 1987.

———. *Stát a církev v Československu v letech, 1948–1953*. Brno: Ústav pro soudobé dějiny AV ČR, 1993.

Kenez, Peter. "The Hungarian Communist Party and the Catholic Church, 1945–1948." *Journal of Modern History* 75, no. 4 (December 2003): 864–89.

———. *Hungary from the Nazis to the Soviets: The Establishment of the Communist Regime in Hungary, 1944–1948*. Cambridge: Cambridge University Press, 2006.

Kirschbaum, Stanley J. *A History of Slovakia: The Struggle for Survival*. New York: St. Martin's Press, 1995.

Kmet', Norbert. *Postavenie cirkví na Slovensku, 1948–1951*. Bratislava: Veda, 2000.

Kolář, Petr. "Církev a stát v ČSR." *Střední Evropa: Revue pro středoevropskou kulturu a politiku* 12, no. 59 (April 1996): 67–83.

Korbel, Josef. *The Communist Subversion of Czechoslovakia, 1938–1948: The Failure of Coexistence*. Princeton, NJ: Princeton University Press, 1959.

———. *Twentieth-Century Czechoslovakia: The Meaning of Its History*. New York: Columbia University Press, 1977.

Kučera, Milan, and Zdeněk Pavlík. "Czech and Slovak Demography." In *The End of Czechoslovakia*, ed. Jiří Musil, 15–39. Budapest: Central European University Press, 1995.

Kusin, Vladimir V. "Czechoslovakia." In *Communist Power in Europe, 1944–1949*, ed. Martin McCauley, 73–94. London: MacMillan Press, 1977.

Letz, Róbert. "Biskup Michal Buzalka a politický život." In *Biskup Michal Buzalka; Zborník príspevkov z vedeckej konferencie pri príležitosti 40. výročia úmrtia Michala Buzalku, ktorá sa konala v Bratislave 7.decembra 2001*, 79–121. Bratislava: LÚČ, 2002.

———. *Slovensko v rokoch 1945–1948 na ceste ku komunistickej totalite*. Bratislava: Ústredie slovenskej kresťanskej inteligencie, 1994.

Lipták, Ľubomír. *Politické strany na Slovensku, 1860–1989*. Bratislava: Archa, 1992.

Luža Radomír. "Czechoslovakia between Democracy and Communism, 1945–1948." In *A History of the Czechoslovak Republic, 1918–1948*, ed. Victor S. Mamatey and Radomír Luža, 387–415. Princeton, N.J.: Princeton University Press, 1973.

Lukes, Igor. "The Czech Road to Communism." In *The Establishment of Communist Regimes in Eastern Europe, 1944–1949*, ed. Norman Naimark and Leonid Gibianskii, 243–65. Boulder, Colo.: Westview Press, 1997.

Machula, Jaromír. *Vatikán a Československo (1938–1948): Paměti*. Prague: Ústav pro soudobé dějiny AV ČR, 1998.

Mamatey, Victor S., and Radomír Luža, eds. *A History of the Czechoslovak Republic, 1918–1948*. Princeton, N.J.: Princeton University Press, 1973.

Mannová, Elena. *A Concise History of Slovakia*. Bratislava: Historický Ústav SAV, 2000.

Měchýř, Jan. *Slovensko v Československu: Slovensko-české vztahy 1918–1991: Dokumenty, názory, komentáře*. Prague: Práce, 1991.

Mikloško, František. *Nebudete ich môcť rozvrát'*. Bratislava: Archa, 1991.

Mináč, Vladimír, ed. *Slovenský biografický slovník: Od roku 833 do roku 1990*. Martin: Matica Slovenská, 1986–1994.

Myant, Martin R. *Socialism and Democracy in Czechoslovakia, 1945–1948*. Cambridge: Cambridge University Press, 1981.

Němec, Ludvík. "Solution of the Minorities Problem." In *A History of the Czechoslovak Republic, 1918–1948*, ed. Victor S. Mamatey and Radomír Luža, 416–27. Princeton, N.J.: Princeton University Press, 1973.

Palmer, Gretta. *Through God's Underground: The Adventures of "Father George" among People under Soviet Rule as Told to Gretta Palmer*. London: Hollis & Carter, 1953.

Pelikan, Jaroslav. *Mary through the Centuries: Her Place in the History of Culture*. New Haven, Conn.: Yale University Press, 1996.

Pešek, Jan, and Michal Barnovský. *Štátna moc a cirkvi na Slovensku, 1948–1953*. Bratislava: Veda, 1997.

Petranský, Ivan A. *Štát a katolícka cirkev na Slovensku, 1945–1946*. Nitra: Garmond, 2001.

Prečan, Vilém. "Úloha katolické hierarchie na Slovensku před Únorem 1948." In *Církve v našich dějinách*, ed. Jaroslav César, 179–231. Prague: Orbis, 1960.

Procacci, Giuliani, ed. *The Cominform: Minutes of the Three Conferences 1947/1948/1949*. Milan: Feltrinelli Editore, 1994.

Rašla, Anton, and Ernest Žabkay. *Proces s dr. J. Tisom, Spomienky*. Bratislava: Tatrapress, 1990.

Ratkaš, Peter, Jozef Butvin, Miroslav Kropilák, and Marta Varíková, eds. *Z prameňov našich dejín*. Bratislava: Slovenské Pedagogické Nakladatel'stvo, 1974.

Ripka, Hubert. *Czechoslovakia Enslaved: The Story of the Communist Coup d'état*. London: Gollancz, 1950.

Rothschild, Joseph. *East Central Europe between the Two World Wars*. Seattle: University of Washington Press, 1974.

———. *Return to Diversity: A Political History of East Central Europe since World War II*. 2nd ed. Oxford: Oxford University Press, 1993.

Rychlík, Jan. *Češi a Slováci ve 20. století. Česko-slovenské vztahy, 1945–1992*. Bratislava: Academic Elektronic Press, 1998.

Schmidt, Dana Adams. *Anatomy of a Satellite*. Boston: Little, Brown, 1952.

Schöpflin, George. "Hungary." In *Communist Power in Europe, 1944–1949*, ed. Martin McCauley, 95–110. London: MacMillan Press, 1977.

Slovenská národná rada, 1945. Vol. 1. Published Czechoslovak government papers.

Staško, Jozef. "Katolíci a 'Aprílová dohoda.'" *Most* 23, no. 1–2 (1976): 32–50, 126–43.

Šutaj, Štefan. *Maďarská menšina na Slovensku v rokoch, 1945–1948*. Bratislava: Veda, 1993.

Szabó, Csaba. *Die katholische Kirche Ungarns und der Staat in den Jahren, 1945–1965*. Munich: Verlag Ungarisches Institut, 2003.

Tigrid, Pavel. "The Prague Coup of 1948: The Elegant Takeover." In *The Anatomy of Communist Takeovers*, ed. Thomas T. Hammond, 399–432. New Haven, Conn.: Yale University Press, 1975.

Trapl, Miloš. *Political Catholicism and the Czechoslovak People's Party in Czechoslovakia, 1918–1938*. Boulder, Colo.: Social Science Monographs, 1995.

Ullman, Walter. "American and Vatican Reactions to the Tiso Trial." In *Bohemia: Jahrbuch des Collegium Carolinum* 18 (1977): 301–14.

Ursíny, Ján. *Z môjho života*. Martin: Matica Slovenská, 2000.

Vaško, Václav. "Církevněpolitické poměry v Československu 1945–1949." *Střední Evropa; Revue pro středoevropskou kulturu a politiku* 12, no. 59 (April 1996): 84–92.

———. *Neumlčená kronika katolické církve v Československu po druhé světové válce*. Vol. 1. Prague: Zvon, 1990.

Vnuk, František. *Dokumenty o postavení katolíckej cirkvi na Slovensku v rokoch, 1945–1948*. Martin: Matica Slovenská, 1998.

———. *Slovensko v rokoch, 1945–1948*. Vol. 1, *Volga sa vliala do Hrona*. Toronto: Zahraničná Matica Slovenská, 1994.

———. *Slovensko v rokoch, 1945–1948*. Vol. 2, *Vltava sa vliala do Váhu*. Toronto: Zahraničná Matica Slovenská, 1995.

Zinner, Paul E. *Communist Strategy and Tactics in Czechoslovakia, 1918–1948*. New York: Praeger, 1963.

Zúbek, Teodorik J. "Katolícka cirkev na Slovensku v rokoch, 1918–1948." In *Svedectvo jednej generácie*, ed. I. Kružliak and J. Okál, 131–64. Cambridge: Dobra Kniha, 1990.

INDEX